Growth of American Educational Thought and Practice

HARPER'S SERIES ON TEACHING

Under the Editorship of ERNEST E. BAYLES

Growth of American Educational Thought and Practice

ERNEST E. BAYLES *and* BRUCE L. HOOD

University of Kansas

Harper & Row, Publishers, New York

⁊⸎ *Contents*

v

11. *"Progressive Education"*

"Progressivism" Delineated. Early "Progressive" Schools. Analysis of Kilpatrick-Collings Thinking. Kilpatrick's "Project Method" and Instrumental Learning. McMurry's Consumer-Type "Projects" and the Absence of Instrumental Learning. From "Interests" to "Needs." Progressivism and Rousseau's Theory.

12. *Education as Progressive Reconstruction of Experience*

Authors as Critics as Well as Reporters. Dewey's Introduction of "Interaction." Idea of "Continuous Reconstruction of Experience." Education for Democracy—Reflective Teaching. The Build-a-New-Social-Order Movement. Teacher "Guidance" Without Indoctrination. Reflective Teaching. "Study the Tradition with a View to Its Progressive Refinement."

13. *Retrospect and Prospect*

2~ *Preface*

When there are as many fine textbooks in a given field as are available in the history of American education, it seems legitimate to ask why add another? If the reason is merely to get in on the competition, justification of the addition might well be questioned. The present authors, therefore, feel obligated to indicate why they feel this book is sufficiently different from others to make it useful.

History may be considered as a chronicle, "a record of *events* in the order of time." If so, as a subject for study it has to be learned memoriter and is not an acquisition that has broad application. It can serve for little more than eruditional ornamentation. If, on the other hand, the study of history enhances the *wisdom* of one who studies it, it has to deal with ideas, for it is possession of time-tested, dependable ideas and the ability to employ them when occasion demands that alone makes for sagacity. History as a record of the destiny of ideas, rather than a record of events per se, is what this book is designed to portray. Appreciation of the destiny of ideas is the legacy of history. What problems did mankind face? How were they handled? What was the outcome? What "lessons" should be drawn? This is the kind of history we hope to depict. It is seemingly the only way in which a study of the past will shed light upon the future.

Other books in the field commonly treat Puritan education as "education for salvation," and give something of the assumptions underlying it. But, after that, theory is dropped and events take over. Our innovation, we feel, is to portray the *thinking* through the subsequent stages of American educational growth to, and even beyond, mid-twentieth century. This is our justification for offering another book. We do not ignore events, but we do not enthrone them. Taking them as the *outcome* of thought and purpose, we record them with as much detail as seems necessary; that, however, does not require an exhaustive record, particularly when excellent ones of that kind are available elsewhere. We think of this book as furnishing the core of a course. At the ends of chapters we supply references to supplemental sources that are readily available and seem well-adapted for student use.

ERNEST E. BAYLES
BRUCE L. HOOD

Growth of American Educational Thought and Practice

In 1770 an unknown artist strikingly caught the essence of school and community in Salem, Massachusetts, with the whipping post significantly prominent. The
whipping post was probably town property and a constant in the life of every
school child.

1 ❧ *Education for Salvation*

From decade to decade as the years pass, indeed from century to century, comes the persistent plaint that we are being too easy on children; that steps need to be taken to regain the disciplinary values of the upbringing received in former times. "When I was young, I knew the feel of a well-applied razor strap or hickory switch, but nowadays youngsters never have to do anything they do not want to do. And it is the fault of the schools. School people have become so imbued with the roseate illusions regarding youth foisted upon them by 'Progressive Educationists' that discipline has become a lost art." Such is the general trend of the lament, at least in its mid-twentieth-century form.

The question of discipline is indeed an important one for education. Discipline implies personal responsibility, a quality that seems desirable in whatever aspect of life one may be inclined to examine. Is he a dependable person? This question is near the top of the list in virtually every serious inquiry one receives about people, whether for prospective employment or for almost any other purpose. Dependability is one of the marks of maturity; we think of an undependable person as one who simply has not grown up. Since education is supposedly promotive of the growing-up process, it should surely be promotive of a quality universally recognized as part of that process. Hence, education should be disciplinary.

But to what kind of education are we committed if we agree to such a claim?

For many of those who employ essentially the foregoing line of thought in support of the argument that schools are not now doing what they should, the
conviction is that we should cease being lenient. Schools should be places for
work rather than for play. We are turning out generations of softies; the moral
fiber of young people needs to be toughened, and this can be done only by requiring them to pursue "exact and exacting studies," by holding them to standards
that can be satisfied only by hard work. From this point of view it is the very
act of hard work on uncongenial tasks that turns the trick. There is no discipline in doing what one wants or likes to do. To do as one is told, particularly
when the point or the purpose of the doing is unknown—that, from a point of
view commonly employed, is the essence of discipline.

That discipline can, and doubtless should, mean something other than this
we readily admit. But this idea of the purpose and plan of schooling is widely
held, is responsible for a great deal of the criticism of present-day schoolroom
practices, and has a long and august history. Let us look into that history. Only
if school personnel are acquainted with our prenational as well as national experience with the foregoing idea of discipline can they deal discerningly and
effectively with those who entertain it.

When during 1620–1630 the Pilgrims set foot upon the "stern and rock-
bound coast" of what is now Massachusetts, they were firmly committed to an
outlook on life that we call Puritanism. Although known as Separatists because
of complete separation from the Church of England, they held, nevertheless, to
certain basic doctrines of the Church. Moreover, on these doctrines the Church
of England differed in no significant way from the Roman Catholic Church.
It will be remembered that when, in 1534, Henry VIII was made "Protector
and only Supreme Head of the Church and Clergy of England," there followed
no immediate changes from Catholicism either in dogma or in ritual.

Assumptions Regarding Man's "Original Nature"

The aspect of such a life outlook that is of concern to education is that which
refers to the assumed original or inborn (innate) nature of man. Stemming from
the biblical account of Adam's fall and subsequent ejection from the Garden
of Eden, came the doctrine of natural depravity. As stated in the *New England
Primer*, "In Adam's Fall we sinned all." And all children thereafter were
believed to be, as biblically expressed, "born in sin and iniquity and of this
earth earthy." What human nature, particularly that of children, is assumed

to be is fundamental to education, for that is a major part of the ideological foundation upon which a whole educational superstructure is built. And for the Puritans the doctrine of innate depravity was in no whit questioned.

Since assumptions regarding human nature are highly important for educational programs and since references to them will therefore be frequent as we proceed, special attention should be given them at this point. For every program (or theory) to be considered, we shall find it necessary to identify two key concepts—one having to do with the *good-bad* nature of man, the other with the *active-passive*.

Man in his pristine state, unaffected by surroundings or upbringing, may be assumed or considered as *good*, as *bad*, or as neither the one nor the other (*neutral*). If assumed naturally bad or depraved, much has to be done in order to "bring him 'round" or to "save him from himself." If assumed naturally good, he may be permitted to continue as he is, at least as long as some influence has not arisen to turn him to the bad. Finally, if neutral, then good influences seemingly ought to be brought to bear upon him, but they do not have to be as forceful as if he were originally bad and thus already embarked upon the "road to destruction."

There is a further set of assumptions, which might not be thought quite as crucial or important, but which is influential in emphasizing or de-emphasizing the good-bad set. This concerns the active-passive question. On the one hand, man may be considered as naturally a self-starter. He does not wait until something gives him a shove before he starts doing things but gets going "on his own." This is the "active" assumption. On the other hand, man may be considered as naturally a waiting phenomenon—having to be given a push or a pull in order to get him going, needing a *stimulus* before a *response* is evoked. He thus is taken as mechanically responsive rather than as spontaneously self-propelling. This is the "passive" assumption. From this point of view, human behavior is usually referred to as "response." As the reader is no doubt aware, this expression is common to or characteristic of one of the psychological theories widely espoused during the twentieth century—the connectionist or behaviorist theory. Finally, there is the midposition, one that is essentially active-reactive, in which both self and environment (nonself) are considered active constituents in the shaping of behavior. A term that has been commonly used in this connection is *interaction* (recently, to some extent, *transaction*). However, since this assumption does not play a significant role in educational theory before the twentieth century, we shall give it no further attention until much later in this book.

Thus, we see that, as we deal with each successive outlook on life and the way that outlook bears upon the educational enterprise, we need to be clear as to what assumptions are made regarding both the *good-bad* and the *active-passive* nature of man. How does he come into the world, and what, in consequence, must be done with him or to him to have him brought up or educated as he should be? These are key points in educational theory, and of such practical importance that, without first understanding them, it is almost impossible to get into the "run of the thought" of a given people at a given state of development or history, or to understand its ways and its institutions—even to the architecture of its buildings and the way they are equipped.

Puritanism: Education as Discipline and for Salvation

Returning now to Puritan education, what were the Puritan assumptions about human nature, the "original nature of man"? As we have seen in the doctrine of natural depravity—assumed by the Puritans as well as by their Anglican and Catholic predecessors—the *bad* side of the good-bad choice was taken. This is so much a part of common knowledge that it hardly seems to require discussion. Yet we should probably be remiss if we said nothing further about it.

Taking its rise in biblical texts such as, "For as in Adam all die, even so in Christ shall all be made alive" (1 Corinthians 15, 22), church doctrine has been built upon the tenet of efficacy of the Church to save children from the divine curse which Adam brought upon them. To save a child from this curse and make him acceptable to God, the sacrament or rite of baptism was (and is) performed. (There are, of course, certain denominations, notably Baptist, that are opposed to what is termed "infant baptism.") The conventional purpose or function of the rite is to seal an agreement whereby the Church contracts to save the child, should he die, from the damnation due to original sin. In return, the parents or Godparents promise to instruct the child in the ways of God and the Church until he reaches the "age of accountability," usually eight years or older, and is able and willing to take upon himself his religious obligations, thereby relieving parents or Godparents of their promises. The rite whereby this step is taken and acknowledged is known as "confirmation."

In consequence of this promise of religious instruction between baptism and confirmation, parental responsibility for religious instruction is established. Normally, the church has taken steps to see that schools are available for the purpose, hence religious or parochial[1] schools. It is this line of thought that is employed by the Catholic Church today (not followed by a majority of Protestants) to justify insistence that the principle of separation of church and state places schools under the jurisdiction of the church, not of the state.

Since the Puritans were a deeply religious people and considered salvation a primary purpose of life, salvation was their primary purpose of schooling. Moreover, due to the assumed innate depravity of children, their natures had to be broken, brought into subjection, given the right direction, and confirmed in that direction. Thus, education had first and foremost to be disciplinary in the sense of establishing discipleship, of making "followers." And, in line with the thought behind the later custom of characterizing early education as "the three R's," religion was in very fact "the first R." Hence, we arrive at what may be termed the basic characterization of Puritan education, *education as discipline.*

We can thus see a very clear and logical directive for Puritan schoolmasters (and except for the dame schools they were largely school*masters*) to be severe disciplinarians. With "natural" human nature vicious, whatever was deemed natural was also deemed bad and not to be tolerated. Since the desire to play seems to be a universal childhood trait, a natural one, to let children play is to countenance natural depravity, hence to do them a vast disservice. Play is something children should never be permitted to do if it can possibly be avoided. There is only one reasonable justification for it; to avoid a blowup by serving as a safety valve.

Before pursuing this point further, we need to bring to mind the second set of assumptions regarding original nature, the active-passive set. Although Puritan or other colonial educational and religious theory was not quite as explicit regarding active-passive assumptions as regarding good-bad, it seems that the logic of the thought line makes the matter quite clear. Obviously, the position assumed was the *active* one. Children were taken to be self-activating; forever active; "goin' places and doin' things." No normal child, if left completely alone, will long remain quiet. In fact, almost before one's back is turned, he starts doing something. This, coupled with his seemingly natural perversity, makes him a real problem. If we could only be assured that children when left to themselves would "stay put," child care would be a much simpler matter than it is. And, for all of us, habits (especially bad ones) seem to have a way of springing into action without provocation, causing us to do things about

---

[1] The word parochial is derived from "parish," a local church district. In common use, however, it is a general term applied to any church school, be it parish, diocese, or what.

which we may later become so chagrined as to remark, "I did that from force of habit; otherwise I would certainly not have done it."

Biblically, this human characteristic was often referred to as possession by an evil spirit or a demon. One of the sayings of Jesus, as reported by both Matthew and Luke, is much in point:

When the unclean spirit is gone out of a man, he (the spirit) walketh through dry places, seeking rest; and finding none, he saith, I will return unto my house, whence I came out. And when he cometh, he findeth it swept and garnished. Then goest he, and taketh to him seven other spirits more wicked than himself; and they enter in, and dwell there; and the last state of that man is worse than the first.[2]

The point of this saying seems to be that when an evil propensity is cast out of a person it must be replaced by a good one; otherwise, the evil one will sooner or later find its way back, probably with several others as bad or worse, and the person furnishing the habitation will be worse off than ever. In other words, (as time goes on) we actively and self-propulsively grow from bad to worse, unless something drastic is done to change the natural course of our ways.

Puritan theory had it, therefore, that man is not only originally and natively bad, but is actively so. Hence, *drastic* action is required, especially with children, to snatch them out of their actively bad, natural state and place them on the road to salvation. In permitting only enough play to avoid a blowup, the Puritans were employing what may be called the "safety-valve principle." Natural tendencies have a tremendous hold upon us; sometimes they require lifetimes to uproot. The play tendency seems to be of this kind and, until it is entirely uprooted, one has to strike somewhat of a compromise with it or pressure will increase to the exploding point. Thus, a Puritan schoolmaster or parent could justify a limited (though very limited) bit of play, simply to avoid catastrophe. But it must always be discouraged.

Consequent to the bad-active assumptions of the Puritans, the severity of schoolroom discipline was a logical necessity. And, although there doubtless were numerous exceptions, this indeed was the general rule. Schools were not pleasant places; the "Little *Red* Schoolhouse" had not yet arrived. The one-room structure was, typically, of unpainted logs, meagerly lighted, perhaps by window openings closed with greased paper, with rough planks for floors and benches, and probably heated by a capacious but highly inefficient fireplace that tended to scorch one side while the other was chilled by the drafts that

2 Luke 11, 24–26; also Matthew 12, 43–45.

entered through an ample supply of cracks and crannies. No blackboards and few if any wall decorations relieved the monotony of the dismal interior; nor was a musical instrument permitted—not even a tuning fork—for music and all that pertained thereto were thought of as devices used by Satan to lure children into evil ways. Much of the bleakness was, of course, a frontier necessity, but educational theory tended to confirm rather than to relieve it. And it was supported by curriculum (if it might be called such) and methodology equally bleak.

Content and Method

The subject matter for study was almost exclusively religious—the catechism, the Bible, the Psalter, and the Testament. For more than a century after its first printing about 1660 or possibly a little later, the *New England Primer* was the foremost text for primary schools, almost universally used. Beginning with "In Adam's fall, we sinned all," it provided in prose and verse all manner of moral and religious precepts, such as the first two from "An Alphabet of Lessons for Youth," in acrostic form:

> A wise son maketh a glad father, but a foolish son is the grief of
> his mother.
> Better is a little, with the fear of the Lord, than great treasure,
> and trouble therewith.

The alphabet was first learned through the *Hornbook*—a rectangular board with a handle, looking much like a wide paddle, on which was mounted a sheet of paper having the alphabet in lower and upper case, the vowels, a number of two-letter syllables, a benediction, and the Lord's Prayer. Over the printed sheet for protection was fastened a sheet of transparent "horn" (the plastic of that day), whence the name. The sheet of horn was a real necessity, since in some cases an entire school year may have been devoted to mastering the one page.

The methodology throughout was that of strict *re-ci.ation* of matters learned entirely by rote. This, too, was in strict accord with theory; for the point of view of the time was that of *innate ideas* and its concomitant of inherent and absolute connection between ideas and the words that denote them. A word and its meaning were taken to be so inextricably bound together that, if one were possessed, the other would willy-nilly be likewise possessed. This belief was reflected, for example, in the religious rite of christening, wherein the child not only received a name but also had the name chosen for him. The choosing—part of the ritual—was by first invoking divine guidance, then opening the Bible and placing a finger somewhere on the page. The word nearest the designated spot that could be construed as a name was the child's "own true name," not determined by chance but through direction by the hand of God. If, by some untoward circumstance, a wrong name should be given to a child—such as being christened Prudence when her "true" name was Joy—she (or he) would be permanently maimed. It was deemed highly important, therefore, that each child receive his own true name.

Many were the further ramifications of this principle, but one vital for schooling was its justification of rote memorization. If whichever was first learned—a word or its meaning—was of no consequence otherwise, then a schoolmaster (since *he* was not being disciplined) was obviously justified in taking the easier way; require memorization of the right words and thus insure right meanings (in the form of right actions). Hence, the catechism, selected Bible verses ("golden texts"), and the words of the minister in his sermon of the previous Sunday, all were to be learned by rote. And such learning was taken to be the kind needed by children to rescue their innately depraved souls from the curse brought upon them by the sin of Adam—*education for salvation*. To say the right words at the right time was as efficacious as making "the sign of the cross." And, on this matter, the Calvinistic Puritans of New England were, in their own way, as firmly committed as was the Catholic Church against which they had made their protestation. The devil was a potent force in colonial New England. He had to be circumvented, regardless of cost.

From the foregoing, it is understandable that children would not be happy with school. But it was not intended that they should be. If what is natural is bad and if play is (as seems obvious) one of the most natural propensities of childhood, then play is bad, as would be any other natural pursuit of children—anything they might find enjoyable. Traditionally, then, pupils were pitted against teacher, and vice versa, as a matter of basic principle. The hickory switch, the whipping post, the prism-shaped block on which to kneel, the heavy book to be held at arm's length, these were characteristic devices for physical punishment to be administered by the teacher; as the dunce stool and cap were for mental punishment. Devices employed, in turn, by pupils were thrashings administered either singly or collectively by any boys who were big enough, studied and systematic embarrassments attempted by girls, especially the older ones (if they were admitted at all), periodically "barring out" the teacher, shooting beans and paperwads, and employing any underhandedly disruptive devices that ingenuity could contrive. The epithetical nature of "teacher's pet" who "never had a lickin' yet" bears full witness to how deeply ingrained was the feud, and perhaps how honorific the tradition.

Universal Literacy

The disciplinary aspect of Puritan schooling was not its only one. On education *for salvation* and *as discipline,* as noted, Catholic and Protestant were agreed. But Luther's protestation bore fruits not only in altered church doctrine but also in modified school policy; and both grew out of the same principle.

When Luther first protested what he considered the improprieties of John Tetzel, separation from the Church (Catholic) was probably furthest from his thoughts. In fact, if he had thought of it at all, he might reasonably have expected advancement; certainly not separation. He was calling Rome's attention to a serious fault, which he expected would be rectified once it was clearly understood. He was already a respected, as well as respectful, member of the hierarchy. Confronted, however, with the opposition that arose and called upon to justify his action, he questioned the very nature of papal authority by arguing that, since popes were chosen and installed by the acts of men, they held office on human rather than divine authority. Instead of speaking only to and through the pope, God would speak to any and every man and, in fact, did so by way of the Bible. Hence, ultimately, every man is his own priest—the doctrine of the *universal priesthood of man.* He is not divinely required to receive God's word through the hierarchy.

With regard to what else was included in the Ninety-five Theses (1517), we need not here be concerned because we are dealing with education, not theology. But, if every man were to be his own priest and God's word were available to him through the Bible, he must know, of course, how to read. Moreover, the Bible should be available in the vernacular of the people, since this was much simpler than having everyone learn to read Latin, Greek, or Hebrew—the only languages in which the Bible was then available. Therefore, Luther went to work at once and in 1519 produced a German translation. A translation in French appeared in 1520 and a New Testament in English in 1525. The King James version was first published in 1611. Fortunately, movable-type printing had been invented about a century before, hence wide dissemination of the new vernacular Bible was at once possible. Also, Luther quickly appealed to his friends among the German princes for establishment of schools wherein reading would be taught, so that at least a start was made toward literacy on the part of all.

The New England Pattern

In England, Puritanism came early in the Reformation; from this fact came the Pilgrim-Separatist voyages via Holland to the Plymouth landing of 1620. Ten years later, in 1630, Boston Colony was established and this is the date that we select to mark the beginning of American education.

The question may arise as to why we do not recognize the founding of St. Augustine, Florida, about 1565, as this beginning. Actually, by shortly after 1600 the rudiments of an elementary, secondary, and even higher educational system were in existence under the auspices of Spanish Franciscans. But by midcentury it had greatly declined and no significant influence on American education in general has come of it. Also, the date of the Jamestown colony, 1607, or of the Plymouth colony, 1620, might better be taken. But, since neither Jamestown nor Plymouth took immediate steps to set up schools, they are not given credit for educational beginnings. Spanish influence has left its mark on the Southwest, including southern California, but this is only regional and does not represent the general pattern of education even there.

It is from the English settlement at Boston that the educational pattern of what is now the United States of America can be continuously traced; hence, the choice of 1630 as a starting date. In 1635, a Latin grammar school was set up and in 1636 Harvard College was founded; amazing accomplishments when one considers that it was the settlers themselves who were responsible and it was done in a new land within the time span of six short years while even bare existence itself was at stake. Conviction of the educational need, albeit with the shortcomings we now recognize, was enormous and seemingly should elicit from us who have profited therefrom the profound respect of a grateful people. Ours is an English heritage, though not exclusively so, a fact well typified in American educational growth.

Developments in Boston were, however, not confined to Boston alone, but involved the Massachusetts Bay Colony as a whole. In 1634 and 1638, laws were enacted which established the principle that all property might be taxed for common town-and-colony benefits, among which schools were to be included. But in 1642 and 1647 were enacted two laws that stand second to none in significance for American education.

After first trying voluntary home instruction, apprenticeship, and perhaps an occasional dame school and finding the voluntary principle unsatisfactory, the colonists passed the law of 1642 requiring town officials to see that all parents and guardians took care of teaching their children to read. Thus, for the first time in the English-speaking world did a civic legislative body establish what we now recognize as a compulsory educational requirement. Fines might be imposed for failure to comply. But, since this law did not require schools of any kind, enforcement was almost impossible for many were the parents and guardians (of apprentices) who could not possibly expend either time or money to teach their children to read, even if they themselves knew how—and many did not.

It soon became evident, therefore, that another law was necessary and this was the Old Deluder Satan Law of 1647, called such because of the opening words of the preamble. The law follows:

It being one of the chief projects of that old deluder Satan to keep men from the knowledge of the Scriptures, as in former times by keeping them in an unknown tongue, that so in these latter times by persuading from the use of tongues, so at least the true sense and meaning of the original might be clouded by false gloss of saint-seeming deceivers, that learning may not be buried in the grave of our fathers in the church and commonwealth, the Lord assisting our endeavors:

It is therefore ordered, That every township in this jurisdiction, after the Lord hath increased them to the number of fifty householders, shall then henceforth appoint one within their town to teach such children as shall resort to him to write and read, whose wages shall be paid either by the parents or masters of such children, or by the inhabitants in general, by way of supply, as the major part of those that order the prudentials of the town shall appoint: *Provided,* Those that send their children be not oppressed by paying much more than they can have them taught for in other towns; and

It is further ordered, That where any town shall increase to the number of one hundred families or householders; they shall set up a grammar school, the master thereof being able to instruct youth, so far as they may be fitted, for the university: *Provided,* That if any town neglect the performance hereof above one year, that every such town shall pay five pounds to the next school until they shall perform this order.[3]

As can be seen, this law did not itself require establishment of tax-supported schools, nor even civic control. It merely stipulated that a school be available and that, if reasonable private expenditures were not sufficient, community support should be provided to make up the deficiency. But in these two laws,

[3] Frederick Eby, *The Development of Modern Education: In Theory, Organization, and Practice,* 2nd ed. © 1952. Prentice-Hall, Inc., Englewood Cliffs, N.J., pp. 237–238.

for the first time in the English-speaking world (as well as much beyond that) is established the principle of compulsory education for all children, basically supported by public taxation, and under public control—the essential tenets of the American public educational system of today. Once established in Massachusetts, other New England colonies followed suit and this then became the New England pattern.

It should not be assumed that compliance was universal or that all children in New England soon became literate. The law of 1647 applied only to towns of 50 families (householders) or more, the fines were very mild indeed, and compliance, though widespread, was not universal. But it was Luther's principle—the universal priesthood of man—at work. And it was Puritan New England that set a pattern for public education which, though far from universally adopted, has spread to all parts of today's world.

At this point, a short recapitulation may be desirable. Following traditional Catholic doctrine and in full accord therewith, the Puritans of New England embraced the bad-active assumptions regarding original human nature, together with the logical implication of education *for salvation* and *as discipline* and the austerity if not severity of schoolroom practice that these implications entailed. With the doctrine of absolute connection between words and their meanings, rote memorization followed as a matter of course and *re-citation* (recitation) was fully justified. But Luther's principle of the universal priesthood of man introduced a second aspect which became a major feature in Puritan school policy, *universal literacy.* Although after Luther Catholic educational policy followed suit, on that score the latter was not the originator. Before Luther, Catholic schooling promoted literacy only for the hierachy and for such of the aristocracy as chose to take advantage of it. Then, thirdly, because many of those responsible for the upbringing of children could not or would not voluntarily assume the responsibility for helping them become literate, the civic authority was, by the laws of 1642 and 1647, empowered and commissioned to require "schooling" for all children, and the groundwork was laid for what by mid-nineteenth century became in the United States a full-scale, public educational program. Hence, for this third step, the New England Puritans were the pioneers.

The Middle-Colony Pattern

We turn now to two other educational patterns that existed in English colonial America—that of the middle and that of the southern colonies. The middle-colony pattern is typified by Pennsylvania—Penn's Woodlands.

William Penn, a Quaker, receiving a crown grant of lands in satisfaction of a royal debt owed to his father, took steps to develop these lands by sales to colonizers. This, of course, was also done in Massachusetts (perhaps with more grants than sales) but with one great difference. Whereas, as anyone who has studied American history knows, the Massachusetts Bay Colony (typical of New England in general) was essentially a theocracy and tolerant of only the Puritan faith of Governor John Winthrop and Pastor John Cotton, the government of Pennsylvania was distinctly secular and, true to Penn's Quaker faith, thoroughly tolerant of religions other than his own. Hence, Pennsylvania was settled by groups having a variety of religious faiths—Quakers, Lutherans, Moravians, Mennonites, German-Reformed, Presbyterians, Baptists, Catholics, etc. These were scattered throughout the colony, living side by side without religious dissension.

Schooling, however, was greatly affected by this difference between religiously intolerant Massachusetts and religiously tolerant Pennsylvania. In both colonies it was a case of education for salvation, and each demonomination or sect considered its own faith as the one and only one that represented true salvation, hence the one into which its children were to be inducted. Religion was the first "R," reading the second, and "'ritin'" a somewhat poor third. In early colonial times "'rithmetic" came in a poor fourth. A prospective teacher was first to be certified in the faith; second, he had to be able to read; and third, he was expected to be able to write but that was taken rather as a matter of course and not given a particularly careful check.[4] As to "ciphering," if the prospect knew even a modicum about it, that was a windfall, not expected but gladly accepted.

In Pennsylvania, the obvious course regarding religious instruction was taken; each denomination was permitted to set up its own school and to inculcate its own faith. Schooling was, therefore, a nonpublic concern; it was in the hands of "church" rather than of "state,"[5] and church or "parochial" schools were the rule. This parochial school pattern was characteristic of the middle colonies. And it was—seemingly paradoxical on first thought but really quite logical—a case of a *religiously tolerant* commonwealth (state) fostering a *religiously nontolerant* school pattern. To catch the logic of this turn, it may be necessary for you to reread this paragraph. But to catch it is important for understanding American education even today, because between 10 and 15 percent of all

---

[4] As to spelling, perusal of almost any document of the time will show the great leeway permitted to and practiced by even the most erudite. "Creativity" in spelling was then indeed an art, and there were few inhibitions.

[5] One result, important for a democratic people but not quite pertinent to the matter under discussion here, was the nonconcern of the state for promotion of universal literacy or of education in general; therefore the educational effort was not so widespread as in New England.

elementary and secondary school children are today in attendance at parochial schools.

In Massachusetts, on the other hand, since no religious heresy was permitted,[6] there was (in principle at least) no religious difference between church and state. Those in charge of state matters (secular or civic) held religious beliefs in agreement with those in charge of the church. Being a theocracy, if any differences should arise, the church would dispose of them forthwith because the church was dominant. Actually, probably many persons held membership in both governing bodies—they were both elders and selectmen. In consequence, there could be division of duties and responsibilities between the two bodies and, by what may well be termed a historical accident, the care of schooling was placed in the hands of the civic board—the selectmen—and was permitted there to remain.

However, as time went on and education became more and more secular (religion dropping out and 'rithmetic taking a place as the third "R"), education remained under civic auspices. Finally, with the arrival of national independence and the constitutional separation of church and state, the schools had long been under state control and continued to be so. But this meant a *religiously tolerant* school pattern. Hence, by a mere accident of history, a *religiously intolerant* commonwealth (state) gave rise to a *religiously tolerant* school pattern. The predominant educational pattern of the United States today—the public educational pattern under which 85–90 percent of all elementary and secondary school children are enrolled—thus derived its public or civic character from the violently intolerant parochial schools of the New England colonies.

The Southern Pattern

In the southern colonies there was a third educational pattern. With the tobacco-cotton economy, large plantations worked by slaves, and an owning class derived largely from the upper levels of British society, the dominant religion was Anglican or Church of England. This meant that religion did not wield the power over personal thought and aspiration that it did in New England. Bible reading by all was, therefore, not a matter of public concern, and the owning class was quite able to care for the education of its own children—by private tutors (often Negro slaves or indentured servants), parish priests, or endowed tuition schools. For these reasons, the educational program of the South is characterized as laissez faire; "let it take care of itself."

[6] Recall the cases of Roger Williams and Anne Hutchinson.

This, however, is not quite the entire story. There was the practice of apprenticeship, which we shall discuss a bit later. This was a practice whereby poor children, especially orphans, were enabled to learn a trade. A degree of philanthropic goodwill was involved, but in those days there were many tasks around home and shop that could be performed by children, so they were a real economic asset; they were "worth their keep."

On the other hand, there was a distinctly philanthropic force at work, especially in the South but through the middle colonies as well and perhaps overflowing a bit into New England. An occasional plantation owner might use a shanty and assign an indentured servant or even a literate slave to teach a bit of reading and writing, possibly to a few carefully chosen slave children (a literate slave tended to be worth more than a nonliterate one) and maybe to a few poor whites who were about. Being out in the field, it would be called a "field school," and, held possibly on certain Sundays when the children might not be doing field work, it might be called a "Sunday school." The Sunday school movement, however, did not get started in this country until after 1775. It was patterned after the work of Robert Raikes in England, and not until after 1815–1825 was it taken up by the churches and made into a school for religious instruction alone. But, running through the whole colonial period and stemming especially from the South, there was this philanthropic attitude at work. Even though it was mild and scattered, it can be counted as a factor.

Moreover, beginning about 1700 two philanthropic societies were established in England which for more than a century were active in setting up schools, both in the three R's and the grammar schools—the Society for the Promotion of Christian Knowledge (SPCK) and the Society for the Propagation of the Gospel in Foreign Parts (SPG). The SPG was the more important of the two, and its work was essentially that of the various foreign missionary societies in the churches of the twentieth century. These Societies were supported by private subscriptions, even by occasional crown grants. Schools were established in various parts of the South and in some of the larger communities of the middle colonies; even a few in New England.

Thus, in the southern colonies was an educational pattern that has been characterized as *laissez faire-philanthropic*. Moreover, since the philanthropic aspect was directed toward providing schooling for children of parents who could not themselves afford it, it was thought of as providing schools for paupers—hence, the *pauper school* principle.

As a result of the foregoing regional differences, we had therefore three distinctly different educational patterns in the American colonies: (1) the public-school pattern of New England; (2) the parochial-school pattern of the middle colonies; (3) the laissez-faire attitude of the South, supplemented by the phil-anthropic, pauper-school principle. Hence, although in the North the public-school principle was from the beginning taken as a matter of course, in the South any and all schools that were not strictly private were looked upon as pauper schools and therefore not to be patronized by parents who could possibly afford anything else. Not until the Great Educational Awakening of 1825–1860 did the public-school idea take full hold in the United States, and then only very laggardly in the South.

Elementary, Secondary, and Higher Schools

Before terminating our study of colonial education, a short sketch should perhaps be given of the various types of school represented in the colonies. On the primary or elementary level were the dame schools, the New England town schools, the parochial schools, private writing-schools, scattered SPG schools, apprenticeship, and the variety just described in the South.

The dame schools, an old English institution, were for very young children who were primarily being cared for while parents were otherwise occupied—an old version of today's baby-sitting. A housewife (usually a widow who had a living to earn) would care for a group of neighborhood children in her home, occupying them with learning to read and possibly to write. For this she would be paid by the parents a small fee for each child. The very nature of the arrange-ment would tend to preclude it for older children, of probably eight years or older.

The New England town schools were in a regular school house and, except for some cases in summers, in charge of a regularly appointed schoolmaster (a male), one who was duly certified on religious grounds and also on reading and writing. Ability in "cyphering" and "numerology" would also be sought, but was not always obtainable or required. These men were, on the whole, quite able and respected persons, sometimes even with a college education. Occasionally, the master would preach on Sundays, or he might be the preacher himself, or a farmer who kept a school during winter months, or some other person who worked at two or more callings. In some cases, particularly in middle-colony parochial schools, they were indentured servants working out their passage fee for the ocean voyage from England. In certain cases during summer months when the school "master" might be doing farm or carpenter work, women were temporarily employed to do the instructing. And, since the parochial schools of the middle colonies were essentially of this kind, what is said above applies equally to them as also to the SPG schools on the elementary level.

As to writing, it was often taught as quite an art, with many elaborate flourishes which required much drill. In such cases, a "scrivener" would often set up a school for that purpose alone—a private studio—and might go from place to place as business would warrant; hence, the name, *traveling scrivener*.

Finally, the practice of apprenticeship was well established in all the colonies. It was, in a way, a public institution, for public officials were in many places commissioned by law to see that poor or orphaned children who might otherwise become public charges would be taught a trade so as to be self-supporting. A legal contract would be executed before the proper authority whereby the child would be apprenticed to a workman or a tradesman as guardian for a stipulated number of years. During the apprenticeship the guardian had full authority over the child, the latter to do whatever was required of him in the form of tasks or services. In return, the guardian contracted to teach him his skill or trade and, as was practically always required, to see that he became literate. This, of course, was a variation of the pauper-school principle previously noted.

On the secondary level was the one school—the Latin grammar school—present in all the colonies but more numerous in the northern and middle ones. This had been long existent in England, was exactly copied in America, and was strictly college preparatory. Boys who were destined for college had to learn Latin and Greek, so as to be able to pass the college-entrance examinations requiring both ability at translation and at composition. A grammar-school master, therefore, had himself to be a college graduate. Hence, he was a well-trained and very highly respected member of a community. In fact, his training was the same as that of the minister and in prestige perhaps only the colonial governors were higher. One whose name comes down to us today was Ezekiel Cheever (1614–1680), who conducted grammar schools in New Haven, Ipswich, Charlestown, and finally Boston. His *Latin Accidence: an Elementary Grammar of the Latin Language* was for a century the most widely used introductory Latin textbook in New England. Cotton Mather and Michael Wigglesworth were among his illustrious pupils.

The curricula of those grammar schools were almost exclusively Latin and Greek—"classical." There was, of course, much Bible reading, together with required reports on Sunday sermons. Actually, the ages of pupils were considerably below those in today's secondary schools; students often entered at 10 years and even younger and left for college at 13 or 14. College students of the time probably averaged 15–16 years of age. Requirements for entrance into a grammar school were little more than ability to read and write, and graduation meant only capacity in Latin and Greek with little or no attention to the use of English. Though what is said above is more strictly applicable to New England grammar schools than to those of the middle colonies, even in the latter the "classical" studies were predominant.

The early colonial colleges (Harvard, 1636; William and Mary, 1693; Yale, 1701) were designed almost solely as preparatory for the ministry—today comparable schools are called theological seminaries—except that they were not sectarian in the extremely narrow sense. In fact, although 50 percent or more of their graduates went into the ministry, many became doctors and lawyers after serving what might be called a postgraduate apprenticeship, the college training having an undeniable general disciplinary value. Not until well into the eighteenth century, however, did they become secularized to the point of justifying the name, liberal-arts colleges. By the time of the American Revolution, nine colleges had been established in the colonies,[7] and all had become "liberalized" enough to have contributed many of the leaders of the Revolution. As to curricula, the change from the earlier to the later colonial pattern has been described as follows:

The curricula of the newer institutions became much broader than in the older institutions. French was added, and also German. In addition to the ancient languages and the philosophic branches, psychology, logic, ethics, and metaphysics were offered. More attention was devoted to mathematical branches: algebra, geometry, and trigonometry. History became a new interest, and also the sciences, geography, and astronomy. Several institutions added, also, such practical lines as surveying, navigation, husbandry, commerce, and government.[8]

How Different Now?

What, now, can we say of the help that this look at American colonial education may have furnished as we contemplate the problems facing American education today? In light of the recurrent claim of too much thrill and too little drill, we have examined the Puritan theory—in line with Catholic theory and even more emphasized by Calvinistic Protestantism—of education *for salvation* and *as discipline*. It was indeed disciplinary to the point of severity, even at times bordering on sadism. Perhaps it would not be out of order to ask, of those

[7] In addition to the three named above, they were as follows: Princeton, 1746; Pennsylvania, 1753; Columbia, 1754; Brown, 1764; Rutgers, 1766; Dartmouth, 1769.
[8] Eby, *op. cit.*, pp. 403–404.

who see too much softness in today's schools, whether that is the kind of discipline they have in mind. If they do not want a return to the barrenness of curricula and methods of that time, just what modifications do they contemplate?

These and many other related questions are what the innovators in American educational theory have been wrestling with for three centuries. Perhaps an educationally justifiable comment on today's schools is not that they have departed too much from "time-honored" practice, but rather that *they have not departed enough.*

Just what are the fundamentals of education anyway? Are they the same today as in the seventeenth century? Take the three R's, for example. Even as late as 1800, we were a genuinely rural people—only 3 percent urban, as the Census Bureau defines the term. When youngsters grew up then, they were side by side with adults; working with them (as economic assets), playing with them, hearing them talk, genuinely sensing their inmost thoughts and feelings. Under such conditions, one of the most important educational objectives of any and all times—a matured outlook on life—is more or less automatically handled by the normal process of growing up. About all that school needs to do is care for a few of the skills not so promoted, the three R's being the main ones.

Today, however, when as a nation we are practically 75 percent urban and even more than that if we include those living under urbanlike conditions, youngsters are not continually living, thinking, and feeling with oldsters as they were one and one-half centuries ago. Hence, grown-up outlooks do not have nearly the avenues of automatic ingress to the consciousness of youngsters that they once had, and the program of formal (or school) education has to be adjusted accordingly. What used to suffice as "the fundamentals" no longer does so. Science, higher mathematics, social studies, art and aesthetics, even philosophy, have now become as fundamental as are the three R's. Moreover, our whole idea of what constitutes "the good life" has greatly changed and the educational program must reflect this change.

As to method, the process of drill—in the sense of memorization by rote and of recitation (re-citation) of what we now recognize as barren words (devoid of meaning)—is now recognized as wholly inappropriate as a way to develop an adult outlook on life, especially one that stands in need of the progressive construction and reconstruction that is so sorely needed today. With the tremendous speed-up of change experienced in the past half-century alone, we can hardly fail to realize that youngsters of today have to be trained—today—to participate in making the decisions and solving the problems of tomorrow. *Drill* on the answers of yesterday, or even on those of today, is patently out of line with the methodological needs of the educative process today.

Therefore, as we complete our review of the pattern of educational thought worked out by our colonial ancestors, we find much in which we can even today take pride. They were the innovators of their time, laying the foundation for a system of universal public education that today is viewed by the rest of the world as a pattern to be adopted as rapidly as possible. As our study progresses, we shall perhaps become progressively more and more cognizant of what this statement means and why it can legitimately be made. During our entire colonial period, even though with thoughts and aspirations such as these, we looked to Britain and western Europe (the homelands) for patterns that were transplanted almost bodily and without alteration to the new soil. But, by the end of the period and with our own advent as a sovereign nation, we began to realize that we must build an educational system of our own, one truly American or New World, and to the building of that new system we shall now turn our attention.

Suggested Readings

Bailyn, Bernard, *Education in the Forming of American Society*. New York: Vintage Books, 1960; particularly the list of references.

Bainton, Roland H., *Here I Stand: A Life of Martin Luther*. New York: Mentor Books, 1955.

Bode, Boyd H., *How We Learn*. Boston: Heath, 1940, Chaps. 2, 3, 7.

Butts, R. F., and Cremin, L. A., *A History of Education in American Culture*. New York: Holt, Rinehart and Winston, 1953, Chaps. 1–4.

Callahan, Raymond E., *An Introduction to Education in American Society*. New York: Knopf, 1960, Chap. 6.

Cubberley, Ellwood P., *Public Education in the United States*. Boston: Houghton Mifflin, 1934, Chaps. 2, 3.

Curti, Merle, *The Social Ideas of American Educators*. Paterson, N.J.: Littlefield, Adams, 1961, Chap. 1.

Eby, Frederick, *The Development of Modern Education: In Theory, Organization, and Practice*, 2nd ed. © 1952. Prentice-Hall, Inc., Englewood Cliffs, N.J.

Edwards, Newton, and Richey, Herman G., *The School in the American Social Order*, 2nd ed. Boston: Houghton Mifflin, 1963, Chaps. 1–5.

Ford, Paul (ed.), *The New England Primer*. New York: Dodd, Mead, 1899.

Fosdick, Harry E., *Great Voices of the Reformation*. New York: Modern Library, 1952.

Good, H. G., *A History of American Education*. New York: Macmillan, 1962, Chaps. 1, 2.

Gross, C. H., and Chandler, C. C., *The History of American Education Through Readings*. Boston: Heath, 1964, Part I, The Colonial Period, pp. 3–56.

Kolesnik, Walter B., *Mental Discipline in Modern Education.* Madison: University of Wisconsin Press, 1962.

Meyer, Adolphe E., *An Educational History of the American People.* New York: McGraw-Hill, 1957, Chaps. 1–6.

Savelle, Max, *The Colonial Origins of American Thought.* Princeton: Van Nostrand, 1964.

LXXI.
Subdititiæ Comæ Concinnator.
Der Perruquier. Parucken Macher.

Crinibus, Comis lotis & coctis	Wann die Haare 1 gewaschen und gesotten/ werden Gestricke gemacht / 2	Coma, f. 1. Crinis, m. 3. das Haar.
Capillaria texuntur,		
Comæque innectuntur,	und die Haare mit eingeflochten, 3	
Calamistro crispantur,	mit einem warmen Eisen gekräuselt, 4	Calamistrum, n. 2. Krauß-Eisen.
Basi capillamenti suffiguntur, & pectuntur;	auf dem Perruquen-Stock angehefftet 5 und gekämmet; 6	Basis Capillamenti, Perruquen-Stock.
Capillamenta, Comas adscititias, adoptivas, inspergit (pulverat) adscititiorum capillamentorum textor	Die Perruquen pudert der Perruquen-Macher 7	Capillamentum, n. 2. Comæ adscititiæ, adoptivæ, Perruquen.
pulvere Cyprio, pulvere odorario, odorato pulvisculo.	mit wolriechender Puder.	Pulvis Cyprius. Pulvis odorarius. Pulvisculus, & Pulvisculum odoratum, Haar-Puder.

Qui

A page from Comenius' Orbis Sensualium Pictus, the first children's textbook to utilize illustrations, planned by Comenius to implement his theory that education should progress from the familiar to the less familiar. The book is small in trim and about 950 pages thick with excellent woodcuts.

2 ❧ COMENIUS, the Pioneer

Colonial America during the seventeenth century was hard at work building a homeland in the New World. It had little time, perhaps little inclination, to play with ideas either new or old. But in this century two Old World thinkers, one European and one British, were forging an outlook on life that in the following century was to make a great difference to the course of American educational thought and practice. These two were John Amos Comenius, the European, and John Locke, the Briton.

A user of this book may ask why we devote an entire chapter to Comenius; for it was Locke rather than Comenius whose writings seemingly exerted the direct and immediate influence on the educational (as well as political) thinking of Franklin and Jefferson. And, though Locke's work was about a half-century later than that of Comenius, Locke may not actually have been acutely aware of, or significantly influenced by, the latter's thought. Moreover, the general bearing of the writings of the two men was in some ways the same, so the direction of American educational reform might be accounted for quite satisfactorily without even mentioning Comenius.

However, there were aspects in the thinking of Comenius that were hardly, if at all, recognized—certainly not emphasized—by Locke, and these aspects have during the past 100 years come to be recognized as of great educational importance. Hence, to become acquainted with the thinking of this seventeenth-century educator would seem highly desirable. He may well be characterized as a man ahead of his time and as one who, though harboring self-contradictions, did in very fact foreshadow the future. As we shall see, he seemingly anticipated not only Locke, but Rousseau and Pestalozzi as well. And since chronologically he preceded Locke, we shall deal with him first.

His Life

John Amos Comenius was born on March 28, 1592, in Nivnitz, in Moravia, now part of Czechoslovakia, and died in Amsterdam on October 15, 1671. His family name was Komensky, which he later latinized to Comenius. His father, a fairly prosperous miller, was a member of the Moravian Brethren, founded in mid-fifteenth century as an outgrowth of the evangelical movement of John Hus, and generally known now in the United States as the United Brethren. Comenius early decided to become a minister in the church and was elected a bishop in 1632, but he was equally, if not more, interested in educational reform. In fact, even before and during college he seemingly was thinking about improvement of teaching methods. Throughout his adult life, he was a prolific writer, both on religion and on education, but his major works (*Janua, Pansophia, The Great Didactic*) were mostly written between 1628 and 1642, while he was living at Lissa, in Poland. After 1636, he became head (Rector) of the Gymnasium at Lissa, so had ample opportunity to try his ideas in classrooms.

During his lifetime, Comenius was principally known for his school textbooks, of which the *Janua* was most popular. This book was essentially a reader for beginning students in Latin.

The material with which he started was about 8000 of the most common Latin words, which he arranged so as to form 1000 sentences. At the beginning of the book these were short and simple to suit the stumbling efforts of the beginner, gradually becoming complex and involving more difficult constructions towards the end. Each word was used in its root-signification, and with the exception of particles like *et, sed, quia,* etc., only occurred once in the whole work. In the formation of the sentences care was taken to bring out the differences that existed between the vernacular, Czech in the first instance, and Latin, while no grammatical construction of importance was omitted.

The scientific side of the work was accentuated by its division into one hundred sections or chapters, each dealing with some one class of phenomena in nature, art, or society, such as fire, diseases, trade, arithmetic, learned conversation and angels.[1]

The first edition of the *Janua* was published at Lissa in 1631. It quickly became extremely popular; so much so that by around 1650 it had been translated into twelve European languages and four Asian. Possibly within a year after its original publication, an English version appeared, which made such an impression that it led to an invitation—and in 1641 a visit—to London.

Actually, the invitation was related to Comenius' *pansophic* (all-knowledge) idea—which had to do with college rather than with elementary or secondary school—and contemplated a prolonged stay on his part. The thought was to set up an institution of higher learning very different from the "English-type college" as represented by Oxford and Cambridge, which were devoted mainly to training for the higher levels of British civil service, both foreign and domestic. *Pansophia* was to acquaint students with the whole of human knowledge, to promote scholarliness of a high order regardless of what would be done with it. However, a revolt by the Irish took the King's attention away from matters educational and crown grants were not forthcoming. Hence, the plan came to naught and Comenius returned to Sweden, where he had already been for a year or so, and spent several years helping to remodel Swedish elementary and secondary education, particularly working on the preparation of textbooks.

Although today it is Comenius' general treatises on education—particularly *The Great Didactic*—that are considered important, in his own time and even into the late nineteenth century they received little serious notice. In fact, *The Great Didactic* remained in manuscript until, after discovery in 1841, it was published in Prague in 1849. Keatinge says,[2]

Had Rousseau been put through a course of Comenian method, his *Emile* might have lost in paradox and in piquancy, but the educationist would have gained, where the lover of polite literature lost. In *How Gertrude Teaches her Children*, Pestalozzi, from a different point of view, enunciates principles that have much in common with those of the *School of Infancy*, and, had Pestalozzi been led to study the *Great Didactic*, he would probably have confined himself to the development, on the subjective side, of the objective principles embodied

[1] M. W. Keatinge, *The Great Didactic of John Amos Comenius*, 2 vols. London: A. & C. Black, 1921, Part I, Introduction, p. 21.
[2] *Ibid.*, pp. 100–101.

in that treatise. Subsequent writers were wittier than Comenius, none possessed, in combination, his sympathy with children, his power of analysis, and his breadth of mind.

Didactica Magna—The Great Didactic

The educational ideas of Comenius are essentially encompassed in *The Great Didactic*. Although an important strain in his thinking stemmed from the realistic philosophy of Francis Bacon—that truth comes to the mind by way of the sense organs—Comenius was fundamentally idealistic in the Christian tradition as is witnessed by the headings of the opening chapters of the *Didactic*:

1. Man is the highest . . . of things created.
2. The ultimate end of man is beyond this life.
3. This life is but a preparation for eternity.
4. There are three stages in the preparation for eternity: to know oneself (and with oneself all things); to rule oneself; and to direct oneself to God.

The fourth chapter expresses these three stages as follows:

From this it follows that man is naturally required to be: (1) acquainted with all things; (2) endowed with power over all things and over himself; (3) to refer himself and all things to God, the source of all.

Now, if we wish to express these three things by three well-known words, these will be:

1. Erudition.
2. Virtue or seemly morals.
3. Religion or piety.

Under Erudition we comprehend the knowledge of all things, arts, and tongues; under Virtue, not only external decorum, but the whole disposition of our movements, internal and external; while by Religion we understand that inner veneration by which the mind of man attaches and binds itself to the supreme Godhead.[3]

At the end of the chapter, he says that "we advance towards our ultimate end in proportion as we pursue Learning, Virtue, and Piety in this world. These three are the main issues of our life; all else are side channels, hindrances, or ornamentations."[4]

[3] Keatinge, *op. cit.*, Part II, pp. 37–38.
[4] *Ibid.*, p. 39.

Then comes the crucial fifth chapter of the book—"The seeds of these three (Learning, Virtue, and Piety) are naturally implanted in us"—one that merits close study for it carries the key to Comenius' whole pattern of educational thought.

The chapter opens with the following:

1. By the word *nature* we mean, not the corruption which has laid hold of all men since the Fall (on which account we are naturally called the children of wrath, unable of ourselves to have any good thoughts), but our first and original condition, to which, as to a starting-point, we must be recalled. It was in this sense that Ludovicus Vives said, "What else is a Christian but a man restored to his own nature, and, as it were, brought back to the starting-point from which the devil has thrown him?" (Lib. i. *De Concordia et Discordia*). In this sense, too, must we take the words of Seneca, "This is wisdom, to return to nature and to the position from which universal error (that is to say, the error of the human race, originated by the first men) has driven us," and again, "Man is not good but becomes so, as, mindful of his origin, he strives toward equality with God. No man who is viciously inclined ventures the ascent towards the place whence he descended" (Epist. 93).[5]

Here Comenius is stating his assumption regarding the "original nature of man," neatly avoiding the assumption of innate depravity, yet remaining biblical. Thus, he could remain true to his church yet deny the whole system of *education as discipline,* which we have seen as basic to American colonial schools and schooling. For is it not the true logic of the story of the Garden of Eden that Adam and Eve were innately good; that depravity came afterwards, due to the Fall that was the work of Satan? Hence, with a single stroke of his pen, Comenius rid himself of the weight of tradition, serving as it did to force schools into the mold of prisons wherein schoolmasters were duty bound to see that children should never be permitted to enjoy themselves. (It makes no difference what you teach a boy, as long as he doesn't like it.)[6]

Several pages follow in which is developed the idea that man's mind itself encompasses all possible knowledge, at first in embryonic form and afterwards as much developed as time and circumstances may allow.

Philosophers have called man a Microcosm of Epitome of the Universe, since he inwardly comprehends all the elements that are spread far and wide through the Macrocosm, or world at large; a statement the truth of which is shown

---

[5] *Ibid.,* p. 40.

[6] Agnes E. Benedict, *Progress to Freedom: The Story of American Education.* New York: Putnam, 1942, Part I, pp. 3–52.

elsewhere. *The mind, therefore, of a man who enters this world is very justly compared to a seed or to a kernel in which the plant or tree really does exist, although its image cannot actually be seen.* This is evident; since the seed, if placed in the ground, puts forth roots beneath it and shoots above it, and these, later on, by their innate force, spread into branches and leaves, are covered with foliage, and adorned with flowers and fruit. *It is not necessary, therefore, that anything be brought to a man from without, but only that that which he possesses rolled up within himself be unfolded and disclosed, and that stress be laid on each separate element.* Thus Pythagoras used to say that it was so natural for a man to be possessed of all knowledge, that a boy of seven years old, if prudently questioned on all the problems of philosophy, ought to be able to give a correct answer to each interrogation; since the light of Reason is a sufficient standard and measure of all things.[7]

In this excerpt we find Comenius introducing the principle of "unfoldment"; what is *enfolded* ("rolled up within") may *unfold*. On the next page is said, "The examples of those who are self-taught show us most plainly that man, under the guidance of nature, can penetrate to a knowledge of all things. Many have made greater progress under their own tuition, or . . . with oaks and beeches for their teachers, than others have done under the irksome instruction of tutors."[8] Thus, we find Comenius anticipating Rousseau in the latter's doctrine of *education as unfoldment* and the principle of *negative education* (*q.v.*). This is a logical consequence of the shift from the assumption of human nature as innately *bad* (depraved) to that of human nature as not only innately *good*, but *active* (spontaneous, self-starting, tutors not needed) as well. Hence, at this stage of the chapter, Comenius definitely expresses the *good-active* assumption regarding man's innate nature.

However, such an assumption is immediately tempered. The last sentence of the paragraph quoted from page 42 is, "Still it is true that, since the Fall, Reason has become obscure and involved, and does not know how to set itself free; while those who ought to have done so have rather entangled it the more."[9]

And later we find,

Thus Cicero says, "The seeds of virtue are sown in our dispositions, and, if they were allowed to develope [sic], nature herself would lead us to the life of the blest." *This goes too far!* "Now, however, from the time we are brought

[7] Keatinge, *op. cit.*, Part II, p. 42. Italics ours.
[8] *Ibid.*, p. 43.
[9] *Ibid.*, p. 42.

forth to the light of day, we continually move in all wickedness, so that we almost seem to suck in faults with our nurse's milk" (Tuscul. iii.).[10]

It seems quite clear, therefore, that Comenius merely skirted the idea of *active* (self-activating) goodness. Not even in theory did he "take it whole," though he came close. So, at about midchapter, we find the following:

The things to which our minds may be likened teach the same lesson. For the earth (with which the Scriptures often compare our heart) receives seeds of every description. One and the same garden can be sown with herbs, with flowers, and with aromatic plants of every kind, if only the gardener lack not prudence and industry. And the greater the variety, the pleasanter the sight to the eyes, the sweeter the attraction to the nose, and the more potent the refreshment to the heart. *Aristotle compared the mind of man to a blank tablet on which nothing was written, but on which all things could be engraved.* And, just as a writer can write or a painter paint whatever he wishes on a bare tablet, if he be not ignorant of his art, thus it is easy for one who is not ignorant of the art of teaching to depict all things on the human mind. If the result be not successful, it is more than certain that this is not the fault of the tablet (unless it have some inherent defect), but arises from ignorance on the part of the writer or painter. There is, however, this difference that on the tablet the writing is limited by space, while, in the case of the mind, you may continually go on writing and engraving without finding any boundary, because, as has already been shown, the mind is without limit.[11]

And the next paragraph continues,

Again, the comparison of our brain, the workshop of thought, to wax which either receives the impress of a seal, or furnishes the material for small images, is an apt one. For just as wax, taking every form, allows itself to be modelled and remodelled in any desired way, so the brain, receiving the images of all things, takes into itself whatever is contained in the whole universe. This comparison throws a remarkable light on the true nature of thought and of knowledge. Whatever makes an impression on my organ of sight, hearing, smell, taste, or touch, stands to me in the relation of a seal by which the image of the object is impressed upon my brain.[12]

In the two preceding paragraphs, it is evident that the concept of *mind* as *dormant seeds* is not to be employed. Now, *mind* is taken to be the *soil* (earth)

[10] *Ibid.*, p. 46. Italics ours.
[11] *Ibid.*, p. 44. Italics ours.
[12] *Ibid.*, pp. 44–45.

that *receives* the seeds. Moreover, the "gardener" (the environment, focused in the person of the tutor?) is to choose the seeds to be sown and, presumably, to tend the garden properly. This, we see, is a fundamental shift. Innate human nature (the soil) does not already carry within it the enfolded pattern of virtue. These patterns are implanted by the gardener (the tutor).

Then follows the significant sentence, "Aristotle compared the mind of man to a blank tablet on which nothing was written, but on which all things could be engraved." (See above.) Here, in so many words, is the idea of *tabula rasa* or shaven tablet, imputed by many writers to John Locke but explicitly adopted by Comenius and rightfully credited by him to Aristotle.

What assumptions regarding innate human nature are implied by *tabula rasa?* The expression is Latin and referred originally to a wax tablet from which previous inscriptions have been shaven, hence is blank. Such a tablet, therefore, has no inherent character of its own—its character will be determined by what is impressed upon it. Thus, a mind comparable to a shaven tablet is devoid of innate goodness or badness—it is innately *neutral.* Moreover, a tablet does not write upon itself—the writing comes, not from within, but from without. The tablet itself is *passive;* not active. Hence, the *tabula rasa* concept means that mind is innately *neutral-passive.* That Comenius intended to imply this is attested a few paragraphs later when he says, "Finally, the eye (or a mirror) resembles the mind in many ways. If you hold anything before it, of whatever shape or color, it will soon display a similar image in itself."[13]

The concept of *tabula rasa* is also known as *sense impressionism.* It is that all knowledge enters originally through the senses; none is originally resident in the mind in the form of *innate ideas.* The doctrine of innate ideas means an "active" mind, a self-activator, out of which may by proper questioning or other handling be drawn (*ex-ducere,* to draw out, to educate) all that can or need ever be known.

In light of all of the foregoing quotations from the fifth chapter of *The Great Didactic,* it is evident that Comenius was at one and the same time employing two mutually exclusive sets of assumptions: the *good-active* and the *neutral-passive,* the former early in the chapter and the latter midway through. This is what is ordinarily called a self-contradiction or an inconsistency. To employ a self-contradiction or an inconsistency is a violation of logic—a *logical* impossibility—for to be logical is to be consistent. But it is *psychologically* possible, and indeed very likely. All of us need to watch ourselves closely if we wish to avoid it. For it is easy, by the use of different words on different occasions, to fail to realize that what we say and/or do at one time may run exactly counter to (thereby serving to undo) what we say and/or do at another.

[13] *Ibid.,* p. 46.

Perhaps Comenius did vaguely sense the inconsistency in chapter 5 because in closing the chapter he returns to the overarching goodness of God and how recognition by us of that goodness would effect better people and a better world. There is this, but nothing more.

Chapter 6 returns to the theme that "the seeds of knowledge, of virtue, and of piety are, as we have seen, naturally implanted in us; but the actual knowledge, virtue, and piety are not so given," and goes on to affirm that education is necessary to actuate them. Chapter 7 credits the period of childhood and youth as the *only* time wherein mankind can learn what he needs to learn, and chapter 8 expands upon the title, "The young must be educated in common, and for this schools are necessary." Thus does Comenius develop his stand in behalf of universal schooling for all children and in schools to which all go together— boys and girls, rich and poor, of high and of low estate. Chapters 9 and 10 continue this line of thought.

Then Comenius turns to school reform. Chapter 13 bears the title, "The basis of school reform must be exact order in all things." Chapter 14, "The exact order of instruction must be borrowed from nature, and must be of such kind that no obstacle can hinder it," opens with this paragraph:

Let us then commence to seek out, in God's name, the principles on which, as on an immovable rock, the method of teaching and of learning can be grounded. If we wish to find a remedy for the defects of nature, it is in nature herself that we must look for it, since it is certain that art can do nothing unless it imitate nature.[14]

The imitation of nature then becomes the theme on which are based Comenius' teaching principles: nine in chapter 16, ten in chapter 17, ten in chapter 18, and eight in chapter 19. But a lot of picking and choosing is done as to what "natural" principles are to be employed, as well as highly personal interpretations of what those principles may be; therefore, the teaching principles that are given seem suspiciously to be much more Comenius than "nature." This is not to say, however, that adoption of the principles would not have represented a great improvement over the disciplinarian and barrenly memoriter practices of the day. Indeed, American teachers of today would do well to heed many of them, for they bear a modernity that is little short of amazing when it is recalled that they were formulated more than three centuries ago. For example, the nine principles given in chapter 16 are as follows:

1. Nature observes a suitable time.
2. Nature prepares the material, before she gives it form.

[14] *Ibid.*, p. 98.

3. Nature chooses a fit subject to act upon, or first submits one to a suitable treatment in order to make it fit.
4. Nature is not confused in its operations, but in its forward progress advances distinctly from one point to another.
5. In all the operations of nature development is from within.
6. Nature, in its formative processes, begins with the universal and ends with the particular.
7. Nature makes no leaps, but proceeds step by step.
8. If nature commence anything, it does not leave off until the operation is completed.
9. Nature carefully avoids obstacles and things likely to cause hurt.[15]

Comenius has a very interesting way of treating each principle. It is first stated and an example given. Then follows the "Imitation" which is an example of how human beings, in various occupations other than teaching, follow the principle of "nature." Then comes the "Deviation," a delineation of how existent schoolroom practices violated the principle. Finally is given the "Rectification," in which Comenius specifies what should be done in the schools in order to carry out the principle. Following is the full discussion of the first principle:

Nature observes a suitable time. For example: a bird that wishes to multiply its species, does not set about it in winter, when everything is stiff with cold, nor in summer, when everything is parched and withered by the heat; nor yet in autumn, when the vital force of all creatures declines with the sun's declining rays, and a new winter with hostile mien is approaching; but in spring, when the sun brings back life and strength to all. Again, the process consists of several steps. While it is yet cold the bird conceives the eggs and warms them inside its body, where they are protected from the cold; the air grows warmer it lays them in its nest, but does not hatch them out until the warm season comes, that the tender chicks may grow accustomed to light and warmth by degrees.

Imitation. In the same way the gardener takes care to do nothing out of season. He does not, therefore, plant in the winter (because the sap is then in the roots, preparing to mount and nourish the plant later on); nor in summer (when the sap is already dispersed through the branches); nor in autumn (when the sap is retiring to the roots once more); but in spring, when the moisture is beginning to rise from the roots and the upper part of the plant begins to shoot. Later on, too, it is of great importance to the little tree that the right time be chosen for the various operations that are needful, such as manuring, pruning, and cutting. Even the tree itself has its proper time for putting forth shoots and blossoms, for growing, and for coming to maturity.

In the same manner the careful builder must choose the right time for cutting timber, burning bricks, laying foundations, building, and plastering walls, etc.

[15] *Ibid.*, pp. 112–126.

Deviation. In direct opposition to this principle, a twofold error is committed in schools.

1. The right time for mental exercise is not chosen.

2. The exercises are not properly divided, so that all advance may be made through the several stages needful, without any omission. As long as the boy is still a child he cannot be taught, because the roots of his understanding are still too deep below the surface. As soon as he becomes old, it is too late to teach him, because the intellect and the memory are then failing. In middle age it is difficult, because the forces of the intellect are dissipated over a variety of objects and are not easily concentrated. The season of youth, therefore, must be chosen. Then life and mind are fresh and gathering strength; then everything is vigorous and strikes root deeply.

Rectification. We conclude, therefore, that

1. The education of men should be commenced in the springtime of life, that is to say, in boyhood (for boyhood is the equivalent of spring, youth of summer, manhood of autumn, and old age of winter).

2. The morning hours are the most suitable for study (for here again the morning is the equivalent of spring, midday of summer, the evening of autumn, and the night of winter).

3. All the subjects that are to be learned should be arranged so as to suit the age of the students, that nothing which is beyond their comprehension be given them to learn.[16]

Thus, we see that Comenius' "principles" are based on what he takes the *good-active* assumption to be. Nature is *good* and must be followed. This is almost, though not quite, what he recommends in the first part of chapter 5; not quite, because there he momentarily extols the doctrine of letting Nature take her course, the teacher merely serving to protect the child from "unnatural" influences (including those of misguided adults). With his "principles," Comenius takes the position that we must *follow* nature, but that, in order to do so, we must know what the natural order is and take steps to establish that order. This is by no means a "hands-off" policy, such as the policy of "negative education" that we shall later find as the full commitment of the *theory* promulgated by Rousseau (see our Chapter 5). It is, therefore, a considerable weakening of the "active" part of the *good-active* assumption but without a clearly formulated substitute. This we shall again find when we come to study Pestalozzi, supposedly a follower of Rousseau (see our Chapter 6) yet one who felt constrained to avoid the excesses of "negative education." The *neutral-passive* side of Comenius we shall note when we deal with *Orbis Pictus*.

It is hardly the domain of the present treatise to present Comenius' principles

[16] *Ibid.,* pp. 112–114.

in toto, desirable as that might be. The reader is recommended to go to the publication on which the present report is based to get them in full detail. Our own feeling, when we read *The Great Didactic,* is one of wonder that mankind is so unbelievably slow at taking advantage of the recommendations of fertile minds; minds that are focused upon current malpractice and looking toward its rectification.

Here we are today, three centuries and more since the *Didactic* was written, with perhaps a majority of teachers doing what Comenius decried and a host of lay critics castigating those who have made only minor innovations along the lines indicated by him. Note the modernity of the following paragraph, picked almost at random and given here in full, without alteration:

Knowledge is unsuitable when it is uncongenial to the mind of this or that scholar. For there is as great a difference between the minds of men as exists between the various kinds of plants, of trees, or of animals; one must be treated in one way, and another in another, and the same method cannot be applied to all alike. It is true that there are men of great mental power who can compass every subject; but there are also many who find the greatest difficulty in mastering the rudiments of some things. Some display great ability for abstract science, but have as little aptitude for practical studies as an ass has for playing on the lyre. Others can learn everything but music, while others again are unable to master mathematics, poetry, or logic. What should be done in these cases? If we attempt to counteract a natural disinclination we are fighting against nature, and such effort is useless. For there will be either no result or one totally incommensurate with the energy expended. The teacher is the servant and not the lord of nature; his mission is to cultivate and not to transform, and therefore he should never attempt to force a scholar to study any subject if he see that it is uncongenial to his natural disposition; since it is more than probable that what is lacking in one direction will be compensated for in another. If one branch be cut off a tree, the others become stronger, because more vitality flows into them; and if none of the scholars be forced to study any subject against his will, we shall find no cases in which disgust is produced and the intelligence is blunted. Each one will develope in the direction of his natural inclinations (in accordance with the Divine will), and will serve God and man in his station in life, whatever that may be.[17]

After the "principles," Comenius goes to specific recommendations for the various fields—the sciences, the arts, the languages, morals, and piety. Chapter 22, on the languages (foreign), is of particular note because therein he outlines

[17] *Ibid.,* pp. 181–182.

the nature, place, and function of each of his four Latin textbooks: *Vestibulum,
Janua, Palatium,* and *Thesaurus.* In keeping with his time, Comenius thought
Latin to be the most useful of foreign languages and the first to be learned;
perhaps, in fact, it was, at least much more so than now. For then there was not
yet the literature in the European and English vernaculars, such as we have
today. As Comenius himself wrote, "For the reading of serious books Latin
is advisable, as it is the common language of the learned,"[18] so it was considered
a curriculum essential because it was useful, not because it was "disciplinary."
Likewise, the vocabulary was not to be "stuffed with uncommon words and
with matter quite unsuited to a boy's comprehension." "Obsolete and unusual
words" were to be avoided; "subtler investigation into the causes and connecting
links, the similarities and dissimilarities, the analogies and anomalies that exist
in things and in words, is the business of the philosopher, and does but delay
the philologist."[19] Thus, all languages are to be learned "by practice, combined
with rules of a very simple nature that only refer to points of difference with the
language already known, and by exercises that refer to some familiar subject."[20]
Language study should follow the following stages:

The first		babbling infancy		indistinctly
The second		ripening boyhood		correctly
The third	age is	maturer youth	in which we learn to speak	elegantly
The fourth		vigorous manhood		forcibly[21]

Chapter 27 gives a brief sketch of the four divisions of the schools that
Comenius considered suitable:

1. For infancy	The	The mother's knee.
2. For childhood	school	The Vernacular school.
3. For boyhood	should	The Latin school or gymnasium.
4. For youth	be	The University and travel.[22]

[18] *Ibid.,* p. 203.
[19] *Ibid.,* p. 206.
[20] *Ibid.,* p. 207.
[21] *Ibid.,* p. 207.
[22] *Ibid.,* p. 256.

The next four chapters are devoted to descriptions of these four divisions. The last of these (chapter 31, "Of the University") should receive our attention because in it is presented Comenius' idea of *Pansophia*. He says,

> Our ideal scheme is as follows:
> 1. The curriculum should be really universal, and provision should be made for the study of every branch of human knowledge.
> 2. The methods adopted should be easy and thorough, that all may receive a sound education.
> 3. Positions of honour should be given only to those who have completed their University course with success, and have shown themselves fit to be entrusted with the management of affairs.[23]

All children were to attend the vernacular school and these schools were to be "public." Although not specifically stated, not all would be expected perhaps to attend the Latin school, since the training was to be for grammarians, dialecticians, rhetoricians, mathematicians, musicians, astronomers, physicists, geographers, chronologers, historians, moralists and theologians.

> When this course is finished, the youths, even if they have not a perfect knowledge of all these subjects (indeed at their age perfection is impossible since experience is necessary to complete the theoretical knowledge that they have acquired, and the sea of learning cannot be exhausted in six years), should, at any rate, have laid a solid foundation for any more advanced instruction that they may receive in the future.[24]

But attendance at the university was to be confined to Latin-school graduates who would satisfactorily pass a public entrance-examination administered by the university faculty. Also, "Care should be taken to admit to the University only those who are diligent and of good moral character."[25] Here the curriculum should be presumably the whole of extant knowledge (much more achievable, of course, then than now). Thus, scholarliness—not discipline—was to be the aim. A glimpse as to at least an aspect of teaching method is given by the following:

> As regards academic exercises, I imagine that public debates, on the model of a Gellian society, should be of great assistance. Whenever a professor delivers lectures on any subject, works which treat of that subject and these the best that exist, should be given to the students for their private reading. Then the morning

23 *Ibid.*, p. 281.
24 *Ibid.*, pp. 274–275.
25 *Ibid.*, p. 282.

lecture of the professor should serve as the subject for an afternoon debate, in which the whole class may join. One student may ask a question about some point that he does not understand, and may point out that in the author which he has been studying he has found an opinion, backed by reasonable arguments and opposed to that of the professor. Any other student may then rise (some forms of order being observed), and may answer the question raised; while others may then decide if the point has been properly argued. Finally *the professor, as president,* may terminate the discussion. In this way, the private reading of each student will be of use to the whole class, and the subject will be so impressed on their minds that they will make real progress in the theory and practice of the sciences.[26]

Note, in this excerpt on method, how the professor is to serve both as a re-source person and as a presiding officer; he is not to be taken as a final authority whose very words are "sacred" that cannot be questioned. This, in conjunction with many other aspects of Comenius' far-flung educational program such as universal attendance at the *public* vernacular school, is indicative of the highly democratic character of his proposals. In comparison, John Locke, who came a half-century later and spoke for a Britain that for the most part was in the forefront of growth toward democracy, presented an aristocratic, class-levels system of education, and a college that was not a university in either the Comenian or the modern sense, but was an institution to train English gentle-men to behave like gentlemen.

What might have happened to English and possibly American education had it been inspired by Comenius rather than rationalized by Locke? This is an intriguing speculation, one given passing attention by Alexander Meiklejohn, as follows:

In the year 1641–1642, when John Locke was a boy of nine or ten, Comenius, then a man of fifty, was in London. He had come, it is said, by invitation of the Long Parliament, to put into effect plans for a great new institution of learning. He had already won wide fame in Europe because of his theories of knowledge and of teaching. He had written new textbooks, devised new schools, made new and significant suggestions for the organization of the intellectual life of a people. And the English Parliament, at the suggestion of a group of persons who were interested in the New Learning, was seriously considering the granting of funds, the assignment of buildings for the institution which Comenius was to set up and carry on. It was a time when English interest in the advancement of learn-ing was rising to the point of decisive action. Apparently the same impulse

[26] *Ibid.*, pp. 283–284. Italics ours.

which, eighteen years later, led to the founding of the Royal Society, was already gathering force. Comenius found enthusiastic and powerful support awaiting him in London. For a time the outlook was favorable. But in the end nothing was done. Parliament had other more pressing business to attend to. It was harassed by cares more immediate and urgent. It did not act negatively. It simply failed to act. And so Comenius the Czech, after eleven months of waiting for England to do something went back to the Continent, a sadly disappointed man.

It is interesting to speculate on what might have happened in England, in Western Europe, in the United States, in the British Dominions, in the modern industrial world, if the Parliament had acted favorably. The failure to act was, I think, one of the momentous decisions of modern history. What it meant was that John Locke, rather than John Amos Comenius, became the spokesman, the interpreter, the guide, in words at least, of the course of English and American teaching. The boy of nine, when his time came, took the place which was nearly given to the man of fifty. The *Thoughts Concerning Education* received the hearing which might have been won by the *Great Didactic*. And the tragedy lies in the fact that, in spite of common elements of attitude and idea, the principles of these two men were leading in radically different directions. Between them there was opening up the Great Divide in social and educational theory. And as one sees the outcome of England's characteristic prudence, one cannot help lamenting that Comenius was disappointed. I do not know how much he might have accomplished. I do wish he might have had his chance.[27]

This ends our presentation of *The Great Didactic*, one of the great classics of western education if not of world education. Though its writing was probably completed by 1632, it was never published during Comenius' lifetime. As noted previously, it remained in manuscript until its rediscovery in 1841 and its publication in Prague in 1849. The first English translation is the one by Keatinge (1896), from which the quotations in this chapter have been taken.

Orbis Pictus (The World in Pictures)

There is one additional aspect of Comenius' work that must not be ignored, though it may be a bit out of line with the *Didactic* and was not part of it. In fact, it was not written until 1651–20 years after completion of the *Didactic*—and was published in 1658. This is the book *Orbis Pictus* (The World in

[27] Alexander Meiklejohn, *Education Between Two Worlds,* 3rd ed. New York: Harper & Row, 1942, pp. 13–14.

Pictures), perhaps Comenius' most widely known school textbook with the possible exception of the *Janua,* and credited by many as providing the inspiration if not the pattern for our famed *New England Primer* (*q.v.,* p. 7).

Orbis Pictus was a Latin primer, much like the *Janua* but designed probably with somewhat younger children in mind—shorter, simpler, and profusely illustrated with engravings. This is a school book that quite strictly and clearly follows the assumption of *tabula rasa,* introduced by Comenius near the midpoint of the fifth chapter of the *Didactic* (see p. 29). In fact, in this regard it quite clearly departs from the *Janua.* In the latter, Comenius rather distinctly fails to follow his oft-repeated precept of "nothing in the intellect that has not first existed in the senses," using words only, without first relating them to sensations, preferably of actual objects, or with pictures if the objects are not easily obtainable.

In *Orbis Pictus,* for each topic there is first a picture with each object numbered. In the left-hand column of the text, commonly below the picture, is a set of sentences about the picture, using the pupil's native language. To the right are corresponding sentences in Latin, thereby (theoretically) getting direct experience with objects (or their pictures) first, then with the words symbolizing those objects and the way these words are used in sentences. Thus, we have the beginning, at least for modern times, of the movement toward "experience curricula," a movement that has made much headway in American twentieth-century educational practice.

His Contribution

In the educational aspects of the life work of John Amos Comenius we seemingly come to an effectual turning point in educational theory. Taken singly and in isolation from one another, perhaps no proposal was original with him. But, as a total pattern, it does seem that for him we can claim uniqueness, and certainly can put him down as a pioneer of the first order. He labored incessantly in the face of obstacles that would have overwhelmed most. His writings dealing with education alone, to say nothing of those religious and political, were unbelievably voluminous as well as of generally very high quality; and they emphasized the practical as well as the theoretical. But it was his school textbooks (the practical) that impressed the people of his time as well as those of immediately succeeding generations. His treatises on theory—*The Great Didactic* and *Pansophia*—were not taken seriously by his contemporaries and were overlooked by, or unknown to, his successors. "A man before his time" is an old expression but it is indeed applicable to Comenius.

However, honor was his during his lifetime, for his *Janua* and his *Orbis Pictus* were known in many nations and used in many tongues. And now his remains lie honored *in his native land,* though they are in a crypt at Naarden, a town in the heartland of the Netherlands, where he spent his later years. For the few square feet of land occupied by the crypt have been ceded by Holland to Comenius' native Czechoslovakia. Hence, after almost a lifetime of labor in exile from his homeland, his remains now rest in peace and honor, at home.

Suggested Readings

Benedict, Agnes E., *Progress to Freedom: The Story of American Education.* New York: Putnam, 1942.

Clauser, Jerome K., *The Pansophist: Comenius.* In Nash, Paul, Kazamias, Andreas M., Perkinson, Henry J., *The Educated Man: Studies in the History of Educational Thought.* New York: Wiley, 1965, Chap. 7, pp. 164–188.

Comenius, John Amos, *Orbis Pictus,* translated by Charles Hoole. Syracuse: C. W. Bardeen, 1887.

Cubberley, Ellwood P., *The History of Education.* Boston: Houghton Mifflin, 1920, pp. 408–416.

Eby, Frederick, *The Development of Modern Education: In Theory, Organization, and Practice,* 2nd ed. Englewood Cliffs, N.J.: Prentice-Hall, 1952, Chap. 7.

Eby, Frederick, and Arrowood, Charles F., *The Development of Modern Education.* Englewood Cliffs, N.J.: Prentice-Hall, 1934, Chaps. 7, 15, 19.

Keatinge, M. W., *The Great Didactic of John Amos Comenius,* 2 vols. London: A. & C. Black, 1921.

Laurie, S. S., *John Amos Comenius.* Syracuse: C. W. Bardeen, 1892.

Monroe, W. S., *Comenius and the Beginnings of Educational Reform.* New York: Scribner, 1900.

Parker, Samuel C., *A Textbook in the History of Modern Elementary Education.* Boston: Ginn, 1912, pp. 135–150.

Price, Kingsley, *Education and Philosophical Thought.* Englewood Cliffs, N.J.: Allyn and Bacon, 1962, Chap. 5.

Ulich, Robert, *History of Educational Thought.* New York: American Book, 1950, pp. 188–199.

A portrait of John Locke painted by Sir Godfrey Kneller. It hangs in Christ Church Library. Locke is said to have been one of the most learned men of his age. His view that knowledge is derived from sensation and experience of the mind furnishes the basis of the modern concept of empiricism. (Courtesy of The Governing Body of Christ Church, Oxford, England)

3 ➳ *JOHN LOCKE:*

Education as Habit Formation

The English philosopher John Locke was born at Wrington, Somerset, on August 29, 1632, and died at Oates, Essex, on October 28, 1704. He received the bachelor's degree at Oxford in 1656 and the master's degree in 1658. He later studied medicine, but never became a practicing physician. His major interests were philosophy and politics and in these two fields he made major contributions. No study of either philosophic or political theory can be considered even reasonably complete without inclusion of his *Essay Concerning Human Understanding*[1] for the former and *Of Civil Government*[2] for the latter.

Locke's place in philosophy rests largely on his leadership in the British "sensationist" movement—*Nihil in mensa sed primus in sensu;* nothing in the mind except first in the senses. We hasten, for the record, to add that, if we

1 From the book *An Essay Concerning Human Understanding* by John Locke. Abridged and edited by Raymond Wilburn. Everyman's Library. Reprinted by permission of E. P. Dutton & Co., Inc., New York. (Original Foreword dated May 24, 1689.) The excerpts and page numbers given in this chapter, however, are from the original, unabridged (Routledge) edition.

2 John Locke, *Of Civil Government.* London: Dent; also New York: Dutton, Everyman's Library Edition, 1924.

were to present an exhaustive study of Locke *as Locke,* we should quickly find him no strict sensationist. In fact, a great criticism of Locke even among his contemporaries and his immediate successors was that he did not "stay put"; that his first assumptions were sensationist, but that he quickly added further assumptions essentially denying the first ones. Hence, his followers or his interpreters who did not clearly see the self-contradiction either made very confused presentations or took one side or the other. Interpreters divided into opposing camps because one group took the one Locke and the other the other. Moreover, Locke's place in political theory—his doctrine of "unalienable rights" which is part of our Declaration of Independence—depends on a point of view that Locke could not possibly have received by way of his senses (i.e., by observation).

Essay Concerning Human Understanding

Locke begins his *Essay Concerning Human Understanding* by denying that there are any "innate principles in the mind." This he does in the heavy, ponderous style he adopts when writing "a discourse designed for public view"; quite different from the style in his *Thoughts Concerning Education,* which is, in his own words, "such as a man writes carelessly to his friends, when he seeks truth, not ornament, and studies only to be in the right and to be understood."[3] To start us on Locke's thinking and to show his style as well, the opening section of Book I, chapter 2, in which Locke begins his "research," follows in toto:

The way shown how we come by any knowledge, sufficient to prove it is not innate.—It is an established opinion among some men, that there are in the understanding certain innate principles; some primary notions, κοιναὶ ἔννοιαι, characters, as it were, stamped upon the mind of man, which the soul receives in its very first being, and brings into the world with it. It would be sufficient to convince unprejudiced readers of the falseness of this supposition, if I should only show (as I hope I shall in the following parts of this discourse) how men, barely by the use of their natural faculties, may attain to all the knowledge they have, without the help of any innate impressions, and may arrive at certainty without any such original notions or principles. For I imagine, anyone will easily grant, that it would be impertinent to suppose the ideas of colours innate in a creature to whom God hath given sight, and a power to receive them by

[3] John Locke, "Some Thoughts Concerning Education," in John W. Adamson (ed.), *The Educational Writings of John Locke.* New York: Longmans, 1912, p. 36.

the eyes from external objects: and no less unreasonable would it be to attribute several truths to the impressions of nature and innate characters, when we may observe in ourselves faculties fit to attain an easy and certain knowledge of them as if they were originally imprinted on the mind.

But because a man is not permitted without censure to follow his own thoughts in the search of truth, when they lead him ever so little out of the common road, I shall set down the reasons that made me doubt of the truth of that opinion as an excuse for my mistake, if I be in one; which I leave to be considered by those who, with me, dispose themselves to embrace truth wherever they find it.[4]

The chapter continues under section headings such as the following:

2. General assent the great argument (p. 12).
3. Universal consent proves nothing innate (p. 12).
4. "What is, is"; and, "It is impossible for the same thing to be, and not to be," not universally assented to (p. 13).
5. Not on the mind naturally imprinted, because not known to children, idiots, &c. (p. 13).
6. That men know them when they come to the use of reason, answered (p. 14).
7. Doubtful expressions, that have scarce any signification, go for clear reasons to those who, being prepossessed, take not the pains to examine even what they themselves say (p. 14).
8. If reason discovered them, that would not prove them innate (p. 14).
9. It is false that reason discovers them (p. 15).
11. Those who will take the pains to reflect with a little attention on the operations of the understanding, will find that this ready assent of the mind to some truths, depends not either on native inscription, or the use of reason; but on a faculty of the mind quite distinct from both of them, as we shall see hereafter (p. 16).
12. The coming to the use of reason, not the time we come to know these maxims (p. 16).
13. By this they are not distinguished from other knowable truths (p. 16).
14. If coming to the use of reason were the time of their discovery, it would not prove them innate (p. 17).
16. A child knows not that three and four are equal to seven till he comes to be able to count to seven, and has got the name and idea of equality; and then, upon explaining those words, he presently assents to, or rather perceives the truth of that proposition (p. 18).

[4] *An Essay Concerning Human Understanding, op. cit.,* p. 12.

17. Assenting as soon as proposed and understood, proves them not innate (p. 19).
21. These maxims not being known sometimes till proposed, proves them not innate (p. 21).
22. Implicitly known before proposing; signifies that the mind is capable of understanding them, or else signifies nothing (p. 21).
23. The argument of assenting on first hearing, is upon a false supposition of no precedent teaching (p. 22).

The next two chapters, concluding Book I, continue in the same vein, the following section headings giving a running sketch of the line of thought:

No moral principles so clear and so generally received as the fore-mentioned speculative maxims (p. 26).
Faith and justice not owned as principles by all men (p. 27).
Objection. "Though men deny them in their practice, yet they admit them in their thoughts," answered (p. 27).
Moral rules need a proof; ergo, not innate (p. 28).
Virtue generally approved, not because innate, but because profitable (p. 29).
Conscience no proof of any innate moral rule (p. 30).
Instances of enormities practised without remorse (p. 30).
Men have contrary practical principles (p. 31).
Whole nations reject several moral rules (p. 32).
Those who maintain innate practical principles, tell us not what they are (p. 34).
Contrary principles in the world (p. 39).
Principles not innate, unless their ideas be innate (p. 42).
Ideas, especially those belonging to principles, not born with children (p. 42).
Identity, an idea not innate (p. 43).
Whole and part, not innate ideas (p. 43).
Idea of worship not innate (p. 44).
Idea of God not innate (p. 44).
Ideas of God various in different men (p. 48).
If the idea of God be not innate, no other can be supposed innate (p. 50).

Thus, by way of an extensive and closely knit argument, even though it may not be considered finally and incontrovertibly proven, Locke established the proposition that human minds at birth are not stocked with a fund of innate ideas—neither good ones nor bad. Hence (we can add), if ideas lead to actions and actions to character, it follows that human nature is to be assumed as innately *neither* good nor bad, but *neutral*.

The next question is, therefore, "How men commonly come by their principles."⁵ This is the question to which Locke comes in the first chapter of Book II. The chapter starts with this paragraph:

Idea is the object of thinking. Every man being conscious to himself, that he thinks, and that which his mind is applied about, whilst thinking, being the ideas that are there, it is past doubt that men have in their mind several ideas, such as are those expressed by the words, "whiteness, hardness, sweetness, thinking, motion, man, elephant, army, drunkenness," and others. It is in the first place then to be inquired, How he comes by them? I know it is a received doctrine, that men have native ideas and original characters stamped upon their minds in their very first being. This opinion I have at large examined already; and, I suppose, what I have said in the foregoing book will be much more easily admitted, when I have shown whence the understanding may get all the ideas it has, and by what ways and degrees they may come into the mind; for which I shall appeal to every one's own observation and experience.⁶

His answer immediately follows:

All ideas come from sensation or reflection. Let us then suppose the mind to be, as we say, white paper, void of all characters, without any ideas; how comes it to be furnished? Whence comes it by that vast store, which the busy and boundless fancy of man has painted on it with an almost endless variety? Whence has it all the materials or reason and knowledge? To this I answer, in one word, From experience: in that all our knowledge is founded, and from that it ultimately derives itself. Our observation, employed either about external sensible objects, or about the internal operations of our minds, perceived and reflected on by ourselves, is that which supplies our understandings with all the materials of thinking. These two are the fountains of knowledge, from whence all the ideas we have, or can naturally have, do spring.⁷

Again, at the close of this chapter, Locke sums up his argument in the following paragraph:

In the reception of simple ideas, the understanding is for the most part passive. In this part the understanding is merely passive; and whether or no it will have these beginnings and, as it were, materials of knowledge, is not in its own power. For the objects of our senses do many of them obtrude their particular ideas upon our minds, whether we will or no; and the operations of our minds will not let us be without at least some obscure notions of them. No

⁵ *Ibid.,* p. 39.
⁶ *Ibid.,* p. 59. Italics in original.
⁷ *Ibid.,* p. 59. Italics in original.

man can be wholly ignorant of what he does when he thinks. These simple ideas, when offered to the mind, the understanding can no more refuse to have, nor alter when they are imprinted, nor blot them out and make new ones itself, than a mirror can refuse, alter or obliterate the images or ideas, which the objects set before it do therein produce. As the bodies that surround us do diversely affect our organs, the mind is forced to receive the impressions, and cannot avoid the perception of those ideas that are annexed to them.[8]

Thus, we see Locke taking the position that the *first beginnings* of *all* ideas in any and all minds are in sensations received through the sense organs. This is the doctrine of "sensationism," widely designated as *tabula rasa* (often characterized by Locke as "white paper" rather than "shaven tablet"). This means a *passive* mind, as both the opening and the closing sentences of the last quotation show. These result in what he categorizes as "simple ideas," and, further, as "ideas got by sensation" (p. 69). Hence, *simple ideas of sensation* are obtained solely by a mind passively receiving the light rays, sound waves, and other environmental phenomena that come to it and impinge upon our various kinds of receiving mechanisms, to which we today refer as "sensory end-organs." These set up "sensations" or nerve impulses that in turn are conveyed to "the mind" and register there as "ideas of sensation."

At this point, to keep the record straight, we pause to note that Locke immediately introduces another set of "simple ideas," "ideas of reflection."

The original of all our knowledge. In time the mind comes to reflect on its own operations about the ideas got by sensation, and thereby stores itself with a new set of ideas, which I call "ideas of reflection." These are the impressions that are made on our senses by outward objects, that are extrinsical to the mind; and its own operations, proceeding from powers intrinsical and proper to itself, which, when reflected on by itself, become also objects of its contemplation, are as I have said, the original of all knowledge. Thus the first capacity of human intellect is, that the mind is fitted to receive the impressions made on it, either through the senses by outward objects, or by its own operations when it reflects on them. This is the first step a man makes towards the discovery of anything, and the ground-work whereon to build all those notions which ever he shall have naturally in this world. All those sublime thoughts which tower above the clouds, and reach as high as heaven itself, take their rise and footing here: in all that great extent wherein the mind wanders in those remote speculations it may seem to be elevated with, it stirs not one jot beyond those ideas which sense or reflection have offered for its contemplation.[9]

[8] *Ibid.,* p. 70. Italics in original.
[9] *Ibid.,* pp. 69–70. Italics in original.

Thus, the mind is first stocked with "simple ideas" and these coalesce into whatever "complex ideas" a mind may become capable of achieving. The point is reiterated again and again, as at the beginning of chapter 12, "Of Complex Ideas":

Made by the mind out of simple ones. We have hitherto considered those ideas, in the reception whereof the mind is only passive, which are those simple ones received from sensation and reflection before mentioned, whereof the mind cannot make one to itself, nor have any idea which does not wholly consist of them. But as the mind is wholly passive in the reception of all its simple ideas, so it exerts several acts of its own, whereby out of its simple ideas, as the materials and foundations of the rest, the other are framed.[10]

Thus, we find a highly confusing point: that a mind can be wholly passive, yet be reflective, i.e., obtain "simple ideas of reflection." This, as we have previously noted, was a big problem more or less glossed over by Locke but unsolved by him. For a reflective mind is an *active* one, and to be both active and *reactive* (i.e., passive) at the same time is a phenomenon that seemingly taxes to the breaking point the concept of *tabula rasa*. The difficulty was implicit in Aristotle's defection (such as it was) from Plato. We have seen the rumblings of the problem in Comenius. We shall run into it repeatedly as we come to Rousseau, to Pestalozzi, and to Herbart. Only when we come to Dewey do we find the problem squarely met and handled in a seemingly satisfactory manner— his basic innovation, the principle of *inter*action, which we will discuss in Chapter 12. During the intervening centuries, it has been a continuing cause of recurrent attempts at solving the problem of teaching method and of recurrent failures to work out a satisfactory solution.

Some Thoughts Concerning Education

We find it hard to break away from Locke's line of thought as developed in the *Essay,* but our purpose in this book will not be served by pursuing it further. Locke's contribution to American education, in its attempts to break the hold of the Puritanic principle of *education as discipline* with its enthronement of the method of *re-citation,* lay in the degree to which he more or less strictly adhered to the principle of *tabula rasa.* And, to follow this, we must go to *Some Thoughts Concerning Education,* to which we shall hereafter refer as

[10] *Ibid.,* p. 108. Italics in original.

Thoughts; a book which Leibniz, a critical contemporary of Locke, considered to be "a more important book than the *Essay on Human Understanding.*"[11]

The *Thoughts* were originally a series of letters written by Locke to a friend, Mr. Edward Clarke of Chipley. Later these letters were revised for publication and appeared in 1692 or 1693. The style is easy and readable, much different from that of the *Essay*. It represents Locke's advice to an English gentleman—a man of means—as to the way he should bring up his son. Though dismissed by many writers as not a significant document, the present writers find in the *Thoughts* the "true" Locke, telling simply and clearly what he considers the education of a gentleman's son should be and, in so doing, clearly depicting the essential framework of an educational program that may be characterized as *education as habit formation* and *for use*.

With a *tabula rasa* mind, ideas have to come "from experience" (*Thoughts*, p. 59), i.e., from our "sensations." (Recall now Comenius' *Orbis Pictus*.) Hence, sensations come first; these lead to ideas; ideas in turn lead to actions; actions repeated often enough give rise to habits; and the sum total of our habits represents what we call "character." Thus, the order is

Sensations ⟶ ideas ⟶ actions ⟶ habits ⟶ character

And once ideas are formed, and *not until* they are formed, we give names to them. Not till we *get* an idea are we to give it a name; ideas *must* come first. Words are merely arbitrarily assigned symbols, which are to be used to designate (but not stand in the place of) ideas. Moreover, *habits* are the outcome of the educative process; hence *education as habit formation*.

The opening sentence of the *Thoughts* is, "A sound mind in a sound body, is a short, but full description of a happy state in this world."[12] Then Locke goes into a discussion of the importance of health and gives a set of ideas about health education that, though having a degree of justification in light of present-day knowledge, can only be looked upon now with a certain amount of amusement.

First, he says that "most children's constitutions are either spoil'd, or at least harm'd, by *cockering* and *tenderness*."[13] He goes on,

The first thing to be taken care of, is, that children be not too *warmly clad or cover'd*, winter or summer. The face when we are born, is no less tender than

---

[11] John Locke, *Some Thoughts Concerning Education, with Introduction and Notes by The Rev. R. H. Quick, M.A.,* 2nd ed. Cambridge: The University Press, 1889, Preface to the second edition, p. xiv.

[12] *Ibid.,* p. 1.

[13] *Ibid.,* p. 2. Italics in original.

any other part of the body. 'Tis use alone hardens it, and makes it more able to endure the cold. And therefore the *Scythian* philosopher gave a very significant answer to the *Athenian*, who wonder'd how he could go naked in frost and snow. *How*, said the *Scythian, can you endure your face expos'd to the sharp winter air? My face is us'd to it*, said the *Athenian. Think me all face*, reply'd the *Scythian.* Our bodies will endure any thing, that from the beginning they are accustom'd to.[14]

Then he continues,

I will also advise his *feet to be wash'd* every day in cold water, and to have his *shoes* so thin, that they might leak and *let in water* whenever he comes near it. Here, I fear, I shall have the mistress and maids too against me. One will think it too filthy, and the other perhaps too much pains, to make clean his stockings. But yet truth will have it, that his health is much more worth than all such considerations, and ten times as much more. And he that considers how mischievous and mortal a thing taking *wet in the feet* is, to those who have been bred nicely, will wish he had, with the poor people's children, gone *bare-foot*, who, by that means, come to be so reconcil'd by custom to wet in their feet, that they take no more cold or harm by it, than if they were wet in their hands. And what is it, I pray, that makes this great difference between the hands and the feet in others, but only custom? I doubt not, but if a man from his cradle had been always us'd to go bare-foot, whilst his hands were constantly wrapt up in warm mittins, and cover'd with *hand-shoes*, as the *Dutch* call *gloves;* I doubt not, I say, but such a custom would make taking wet in his hands as dangerous to him, as now taking wet in their feet is to a great many others.[15]

And on page 8 he speaks out against "strait-lacing" and "hard-bodices" much as we shall later find Rousseau speaking against "swaddling clothes." "Let nature have scope to fashion the body as she thinks best."[16]

As to diet, it is to be in general a natural one, but we cannot refrain from including the following excerpt merely for its entertainment value:

Fruit makes one of the most difficult chapters in the government of health, especially that of children. Our first parents ventur'd *Paradise* for it; and 'tis no wonder our children cannot stand the temptation, tho' it cost them their health. The regulation of this cannot come under any one general rule; for I am by no means of their mind, who would keep children almost wholly from *fruit*, as a thing totally unwholesome for them: by which strict way, they make them but the more ravenous after it, and to eat good or bad, ripe or unripe, all that

[14] *Ibid.*, pp. 2–3. Italics in original.
[15] *Ibid.*, p. 4. Italics in original.
[16] *Ibid.*, p. 8.

they can get, whenever they come at it. *Melons, peaches,* most *plums,* and all sorts of *grapes* in *England* I think children should be *wholly kept from,* as having a very tempting taste, in a very unwholesome juice; so that if it were possible, they should never so much as see them, or know there were any such thing. But *strawberries, cherries, gooseberries,* or *currans,* when thorough ripe, I think may be very safely allow'd them, and that with a pretty liberal hand, if they be eaten with these cautions: 1. Not after meals, as we usually do when the stomach is already full of other food: But I think they should be eaten rather before or between meals and children should have them for their breakfast. 2. Bread eaten with them. 3. Perfectly ripe. If they are thus eaten, I imagine them rather conducing than hurtful to our health. *Summer-fruits,* being suited to the hot season and fainting under it; and therefore I should not be altogether so strict in this point, as some are to their children; who being kept so very short, instead of a moderate quantity of well-chosen *fruit,* which being allow'd them would content them, whenever they can get loose, or bribe a servant to supply them, satisfy their longing with any trash they can get, and eat to a surfeit.[17]

Coming to the heart of Locke's program, he decries the teaching of "rules" or "laws," but maintains that the tutor (or "governor") should "beget habits" instead. By rules or laws, Locke is referring to verbal statements or aphorisms; by habits, he means the actions themselves, not the words.

Let therefore your *rules* to your son be as few as possible, and rather fewer than more than seem absolutely necessary. For if you burden him with many *rules,* one of these two things must necessarily follow; that either he must be very often punish'd, which will be of ill consequence, by making punishment too frequent and familiar; or else you must let the transgressions of some of your rules go unpunish'd, whereby they will of course grow contemptible, and your authority become cheap to him. Make but few *laws,* but see they be well observ'd when once made. Few years require but few laws, and as his age increases, when one rule is by practice well establish'd, you may add another.

But pray remember, children are *not* to be *taught by rules* which will be always slipping out of their memories. What you think necessary for them to do, settle in them by an indispensable practice, as often as the occasion returns; and if it be possible, make occasions. This will beget *habits* in them, which being once establish'd, operate of themselves easily and naturally, without the assistance of the memory. But here let me give two cautions. 1. The one is, that you keep them to the practice of what you would have grow into a habit in them, by kind words, and gentle admonitions, rather as minding them of what they forget, than

---

[17] *Ibid.,* pp. 13–14. Italics in original.

by harsh rebukes and chiding, as if they were wilfully guilty. 2. Another thing you are to take care of, is, not to endeavour to settle too many *habits* at once, lest by variety you confound them, and so perfect none. When custom has made any one thing easy and natural to 'em, and they practise it without reflection, you may then go on to another.[18]

Note the one-at-a-time principle of working to establish habits. This is part of the "atomistic" nature of *sensationism,* in which it is assumed that character (or a total personality) is merely a *summation* of habituated acts or actions (behavioral "atoms"). In other words, "the whole is equal to the sum of its parts."

Locke immediately continues,

This method of teaching children by a repeated *practice,* and the same action done over and over again, under the eye and direction of the tutor, 'till they have got the habit of doing it well, and not by relying on *Rules* trusted to their memories, has so many advantages, which way soever we consider it, that I cannot but wonder (if ill customs could be wonder'd at in any thing) how it could possibly be so much neglected.[19]

Note here the principle that habit formation is a matter of *strict repetition;* in other words, it is a matter of "drill" in the time-honored sense of the term—doing something over and over until it springs into action automatically and dependably.

Thus, the "true function of the tutor" is stated as follows:

The great work of a *governor,* is to fashion the carriage and form the mind; to settle in his pupil good habits and the principles of virtue and wisdom; to give him by little and little a view of mankind, and work him into a love and imitation of what is excellent and praise-worthy; and, in the prosecution of it, to give him vigour, activity, and industry.[20]

What habits shall be taught? Only those that are "good and useful"; hence, the principle of *education for use,* a vital aspect of Locke's program of *education as habit formation.* On page 113, he says that "all the plays and diversions of children should be directed towards good and useful habits, or else they will introduce ill ones," and on page 176 we find that those in charge of the young "will do well to remember, in all the parts of education, that most time and

[18] *Ibid.,* p. 39. Italics in original.
[19] *Ibid.,* p. 39. Italics in original.
[20] *Ibid.,* p. 75. Italics in original.

application is to be bestowed on that which is like to be of greatest consequence and frequentest use in the ordinary course and occurrences of that life the young man is designed for."

All this adds up to the four ends of education required for the upbringing of a gentleman as seen by Locke: *virtue, wisdom, breeding,* and *learning.*[21] Moreover, this is also the order of merit or importance. He says, "I place virtue as the first and most necessary of these endowments" (p. 115) and devotes several pages to showing that "the foundations of virtue" are laid "in a true notion of a God" and "by accustoming him [the child] to pray to Him."[22]

By *wisdom,* he means "a man's managing his business ably and with foresight in this world" (p. 119). By *breeding* he means, as he says, "not to think meanly of ourselves, and not to think meanly of others" (p. 120; italics in the original), and he expands for several pages on the characteristics of good breeding and also those of bad breeding.

Finally, when he comes to "learning," he has this to say:

You will wonder, perhaps, that I put *learning* last, especially if I tell you I think it the least part. This may seem strange in the mouth of a bookish man; and this making usually the chief, if not only bustle and stir about children, this being almost that alone which is thought on, when people talk of education, makes it the greater paradox. When I consider, what ado is made about a little *Latin* and *Greek,* how many years are spent in it, and what a noise and business it makes to no purpose, I can hardly forbear thinking that the parents of children still live in fear of the school-master's rod, which they look on as the only instrument of education; as a language or two to be its whole business.[23]

Evidently, by "learning" Locke means what we commonly call "erudition," i.e., knowledge of matters commonly thought to be proper. And uppermost in his mind seemed to be the knowledge of a foreign language or two.

Thus, we see that Locke's idea of the subject matter of education was quite different from that of Comenius, who used knowledge and wisdom as interchangeable terms and placed them in the precedential order of knowledge (or wisdom), virtue, piety. In fact, Locke's order is exactly the reverse.

Moreover, though not explicitly emphasized in *Thoughts* but implicit therein and explicit elsewhere, Locke's idea was continually and persistently that each child was to be educated (or trained?) for *his* place in life, and not for some other. The *Thoughts* were on the education of a gentleman's son, preferably

21 *Ibid.,* p. 115.
22 *Ibid.,* p. 118.
23 *Ibid.,* p. 128. Italics in original.

to be handled by a private tutor. At one point, more or less offhand, Locke makes a sharp contrast on the class-level basis:

Latin I look upon as absolutely necessary to a gentleman; and indeed custom, which prevails over every thing, has made it so much a part of education, that even those children are whipp'd to it, and made spend many hours of their precious time uneasily in *Latin,* who after they are once gone from school, are never to have more to do with it as long as they live. Can there be any thing more ridiculous than that a father should waste his own money and his son's time in setting him to learn the *Roman language,* when at the same time he designs him for a trade, wherein he having no use of *Latin,* fails not to forget that little which he brought from school, and which 'tis ten to one he abhors for the ill usage it procured him? Could it be believed, unless we had every where amongst us examples, of it, that a child should be forced to learn the rudiments of a language which he is never to use in the course of life that he is designed to, and neglect all the while the writing a good hand and casting accounts, which are of great advantage in all conditions of life, and to most trades indispensably necessary? But though these qualifications, requisite to trade and commerce and the business of the world, are seldom or never to be had at grammar-schools, yet thither not only gentlemen send their younger sons, intended for trades, but even tradesmen and farmers fail not to send their children, though they have neither intention nor ability to make them scholars.[24]

Close reading of the preceding excerpt discloses not only the class distinction, but also Locke's principle of *education for use.* The latter is especially emphasized in his treatment of foreign language teaching and in the place he gives to play. As to foreign language,

As soon as he can speak *English,* 'tis time for him to learn some other language. This no body doubts of, when *French* is propos'd. And the reason is, because people are accustomed to the right way of teaching that language, which is by talking it into children in constant conversation, and not by grammatical rules. The *Latin* tongue would easily be taught the same way, if his tutor, being constantly with him, would talk nothing else to him, and make him answer still in the same language.[25]

On the next page we find,

But how necessary soever *Latin* be to some, and is thought to be to others to whom it is of no manner of use and service; yet the ordinary way of learning

[24] *Ibid.,* pp. 138–139. Italics in original.
[25] *Ibid.,* pp. 137–138. Italics in original.

it in a grammar-school is that which having had thoughts about I cannot be forward to encourage. The reasons against it are so evident and cogent, that they have prevailed with some intelligent persons to quit the ordinary road, not without success, though the method made use of was not exactly what I imagine the easiest, and in short is this. To trouble the child with no *grammar* at all, but to have *Latin*, as *English* has been, without the perplexity of rules, talked into him; for if you will consider it, *Latin* is no more unknown to a child, when he comes into the world, than *English*; And yet he learns *English* without master, rule, or grammar and so might the *Latin* too, as *Tully* did, if he had some body always to talk to him in this language. And when we so often see a *French* woman teach an *English* girl to speak and read *French* perfectly in a year or two, without any rule of grammar, or any thing else but prattling to her, I cannot but wonder how gentlemen have overseen this way for their sons, and thought them more dull or incapable than their daughters.[26]

On pages 145–156, Locke deals with Latin extensively, reiterating more than once the advantages of the conversational method, of having the language "talked into" the youngster. But grammar is not forgotten. Although "grammar is not necessary . . . for the ordinary . . . communication of thoughts in common life" or even for "persons of quality of the softer sex,"

Others there are, the greatest part of whose business in this world is to be done with their tongues and with their pens; and to these it is convenient, if not necessary, that they should speak properly and correctly, whereby they may let their thoughts into other men's minds the more easily, and with the greater impression. Upon this account it is, that any sort of speaking, so as will make him be understood, is not thought enough for a gentleman. He ought to study grammar amongst the other helps of speaking well, but it must be the grammar of his own tongue, of the language he uses, that he may understand his own country speech nicely, and speak it properly, without shocking the ears of those it is addressed to, with solecisms and offensive irregularities. And to this purpose grammar is necessary; but it is the grammar only of their own proper tongues, and to those only who would take pains in cultivating their language, and in perfecting their stiles.[27]

Grammar also should be learned by those who would *teach* the language (pp. 147–148). And *when* should it be taught? ". . . when it is thought time to put anyone upon the care of polishing his tongue, and of speaking better than the illiterate, then it is time for him to be instructed in the rules of grammar,

---

[26] *Ibid.*, p. 139. Italics in original.
[27] *Ibid.*, 146–147.

and not before."[28] Is it not rather a commentary on the reluctance of humanity to make changes that only today are foreign-language teachers beginning to inaugurate language laboratories in which the conversational method is employed—more than two and one half centuries after Locke?

The place Locke gives to play in education is highly important because it is a key point in educational theory. If, as with the Puritans, human nature is taken to be innately *bad,* then play (being natural) is also bad and must be avoided if at all possible. If, however, as with Locke, nature is taken to be *neutral,* then play (being natural) is also neutral—in and of itself neither good nor bad—and can, therefore, be permitted if good use is made of it. Moreover, since it may involve running about or physical exercise, it may also be conducive to health and for that reason be desirable. Moreover, it will certainly improve attitudes toward school work.

Locke went to considerable lengths to show how he would have play used.

I have always had a fancy that *learning* might be made a play and recreation to children; and that they might be brought to desire to be taught, if it were proposed to them as a thing of honour, credit, delight, and recreation, or as a reward for doing something else; and if they were never chid or corrected for the neglect of it.[29]

Further, on the same page, he says,

There may be dice and play-things, with the letters on them to teach children the *alphabet* by playing; and twenty other ways may be found, suitable to their particular tempers, to make this kind of *learning a sport* to them.

Thus children may be cozen'd into a knowledge of the letters; be *taught to read,* without perceiving it to be any thing but a sport, and play themselves into that which others are whipp'd for.[30]

And on the next page he goes into detail:

I have therefore thought, that if *play-things* were fitted to this purpose, as they are usually to none, contrivances might be made *to teach children to read,* whilst they thought they were only playing. For example, what if an *ivory-ball* were made like that of the royal-oak lottery, with thirty two sides, or one rather

28 *Ibid.,* p. 148.
29 *Ibid.,* pp. 129–130.
30 *Ibid.,* p. 130. Italics in original.

of twenty four or twenty five sides; and upon several of those sides pasted on an A, upon several others B, on others C, and on others D? I would have you begin with but these four letters, or perhaps only two at first; and when he is perfect in them, then add another; and so on till each side having one letter, there be on it the whole alphabet. This I would have others play with before him, it being as good a sort of play to lay a stake who shall first throw an A or B, as who upon dice shall throw six or seven. This being a play amongst you, tempt him not to it, lest you make it business; for I would not have him understand 'tis any thing but a play of older people, and I doubt not but he will take to it of himself. And that he may have the more reason to think it is a play, that he is sometimes in favour admitted to, when the play is done the ball should be laid up safe out of his reach, that so it may not, by his having it in his keeping at any time, grow stale to him.

To keep up his eagerness to it, let him think it a game belonging to those above him: and when, by this means, he knows the letters, by changing them into syllables, he may *learn to read*, without knowing how he did so, and never have any chiding or trouble about it, nor fall out with books because of the hard usage and vexation they have caus'd him. Children, if you observe them, take abundance of pains to learn several games, which, if they should be enjoined them, they would abhor as a task and business. I know a person of great quality, (more yet to be honoured for his learning and virtue than for his rank and high place) who by pasting on the six vowels (for in our language Y is one) on the six sides of a die, and the remaining eighteen consonants on the sides of three other dice, has made this a play for his children, that he shall win who, at one cast, throws most words on these four dice; whereby his eldest son, yet in coats, has play'd himself *into spelling*, with great eagerness, and without once having been chid for it or forced to it.[31]

It is interesting to contemplate what the Massachusetts Bay Colony Puritans would have thought of Locke's recommendations on curriculum content, had they read them. That *dice* should even be thought of! Blasphemy! Here is an example of what our *theories* cause us to do. Ideas indeed have a way of pre-ceding, and causing, actions. Ideas are *very* practical; and *very* real. This is why, in this book, we are paying much attention to the *ideas* at work in men's minds. To know how our forebears were *thinking* is necessary for understanding what they did.

Locke's ideas on human nature led him to recommend play when it could be put to good account, as well as to look for ways so to put it. Later, with Rousseau and particularly with Froebel, we shall see still a different attitude

---

[31] *Ibid.*, pp. 131–132. Italics in original.

toward play. But, though schools as Locke would have them would still be prisons in the sense of imprisoning the minds of children and casting them in preexistent moulds, the imprisonment would at least be pleasant.[32]

On Faculty Psychology and Formal Discipline

There is one final point in Lockean theory that ought to be examined. Should he, or should he not, be credited with supporting *faculty psychology* and *formal discipline?* From time to time, writers on educational history have almost gone so far as to make him a prime leader in that movement. For instance, although recognizing the validity of classifying Locke with the "sense realists" (or "sensationists") such as Montaigne, Bacon, and Comenius, Paul Monroe[33] insists that Locke's place is fundamentally with the disciplinarians.

This he does by dismissing Locke's *Thoughts Concerning Education* as not significant and quoting excerpts from *Conduct of the Understanding.* There are two reasons why we cannot agree with Monroe. First, it was to *Thoughts* rather than to *Conduct* that Franklin referred in his *Proposals* (*q.v.,* p. 70), and it is with *American* education that we are concerned. Second, even the quotations cited by Monroe carry the *habit-formation* context rather than the disciplinary one.

The difficulty seems to have arisen from Locke's extensive use of the term "faculty." But Locke went to considerable pains to make clear that he was not using it in the disciplinary sense. Let us pause for a moment to get straight this "faculty" idea.

During the late 1800s, the *faculty-psychology* and *formal-disciplinary* way of thinking had a rather firm grip on American educational theory. It was the basis of the famed report of the Committee of Ten (1892) in which formal geometry and Latin were defended as practical subjects in the high school curriculum because they gave training to the "logical faculty" as well as to the will power. Even as late as 1938, Bagley supported these two subjects as "exact and exacting studies" that toughened the moral fiber of American youth and counteracted the "softening" effects of "Progressive Education."[34] Following is an example of the argument as presented in 1865:

[32] See Agnes E. Benedict, *Progress to Freedom: The Story of American Education.* New York: Putnam, 1942, p. 213.

[33] Paul Monroe, *A Brief Course in the History of Education.* New York: Macmillan, 1914, pp. 261–266.

[34] Ernest E. Bayles, *The Theory and Practice of Teaching.* New York: Harper & Row, 1950, Chap. 6, especially pp. 85–91.

The study of Latin and Greek furnishes very good Intellectual Discipline.
A recitation in Latin or Greek, when well conducted, gives exercise to the
memory, the judgment, and the reason. No better culture for the intellectual
faculties can be found than that which comes from making nice discriminations
between the meaning of words; carefully comparing constructions; earnestly
searching the underlying thought in one language and the fit words to express
it in another; and closely studying the modifications and relations among words,
phrases, and clauses. It is not maintained that there are not other valuable
means of intellectual discipline. The polished Greek himself probably obtained
his culture without the study of language other than his own. But it is claimed
that the disciplinary advantages of the study of Latin and Greek have stood the
test of centuries, and nothing has been found that can be safely used to supersede
them. The amount of practical knowledge gained from the study of the classics
may not be equal to that which can be gained in the same time from other
sources; but the grand end of study is to increase mental power, to give general
efficiency; and no way has been found better suited to the accomplishment of
this end than the thorough study of the noble languages of Greece and Rome.[35]

In general, the idea was that the mind is made up of "faculties" just as the
body is made up of muscles; hence, faculties are the "muscles of the mind."
Therefore, faculties are trained by exercise just as are muscles, *and,* it doesn't
make much difference *what* they are exercised on just as long as they are
exercised. Since *logic* is one faculty and *will* another, according to the argument,
and since Latin and geometry are both logical and at the same time are not
likely to be learned without exercise of will, they are both very practical subjects
because both logic and will power are very practical and helpful qualities.

Now, Locke had this very concept in mind when he wrote the following:

Powers belong to agents. It is plain then that the will is nothing but one
power or ability, and freedom another power or ability: so that to ask whether
the will has freedom, is to ask whether one power has another power, one
ability another ability? a question at first sight too grossly absurd to make a
dispute, or need an answer. For who is it that sees not, that powers belong only
to agents, and are attributes only of substances, and not of powers themselves?[36]

He then continued,

However the name "faculty" which men have given to this power called the
"will," and whereby they have been led into a way of talking on the will as

[35] James Pyle Wickersham, *Methods of Instruction.* Philadelphia: Lippincott, 1865,
pp. 278–279.
[36] *An Essay Concerning Human Understanding, op. cit.,* pp. 169–170. Italics in original.

acting, may, by an appropriation that disguises its true sense, serve a little to palliate the absurdity; yet the will, in truth, signifies nothing but a power or ability to prefer or choose; and when the will, under the name of a "faculty," is considered as it is, barely as an ability to do something, the absurdity in saying it is free or not free, will easily discover itself. For if it be reasonable to suppose and talk of faculties as distinct beings that can act (as we do when we say, "The will orders," and "The will is free,") it is fit that we should make a speaking faculty, and a walking faculty, and a dancing faculty, by which those actions are produced, which are but several modes of motion; as well as we make the will and understanding to be faculties by which the actions of choosing and per-ceiving are produced, which are but several modes of thinking; and we may as properly say, that it is the singing faculty sings, and the dancing faculty dances, as that the will chooses, or that the understanding conceives; or, as is usual, that the will directs the understanding, or the understanding obeys or obeys not the will: it being altogether as proper and intelligible to say, that the power of speaking directs the power of singing, or the power of singing obeys or dis-obeys the power of speaking.[37]

And, a page or so later, he concludes,

. . . For "faculty, ability, and power," I think, are but different names of the same things: which ways of speaking, when put into more intelligible words, will, I think, amount to thus much; that digestion is performed by something that is able to digest; motion, by something able to move; and understanding, by something able to understand.[38]

What Locke evidently had in mind whenever he used the word "faculty" was a *potential* or a *possibility*—a structure (agent) of some kind that had the potential of being made into something if the right things were done to it. A piece of iron, for example, has the possibility (faculty?) of being made into a steel mainspring for a watch, whereas a piece of cotton has not. When Locke talked of studying mathematics because such study might be handled so as to develop the capacity to reason, he meant that it could, and should, be so handled. Then it would have a twofold value—the value of learning widely useful mathe-matical relationships themselves, and in addition the value of learning to think logically. But there was this vital difference between Locke and the *formal* disciplinists. The latter merely took it for granted that the study of geometry (since the *subject* was logical) would automatically promote the development of logical capacity. On the other hand, Locke made the point that pupils had

37 *Ibid.*, p. 170.
38 *Ibid.*, pp. 171–172.

to be made to see the logical principles at work, how they function in geometry, and how the same principles might be put to work in other ways. Otherwise, the study of geometry would *not* promote the development of logical capacity.

It was *specific habits* that Locke kept always in mind; not some vague disciplinary power. But, since the distinction is not obvious at first glance and also since both before and after Locke the word "faculty" was also used the other way, it seemingly was quite easy to make of Locke a formal disciplinist. Yet, when in 1902 Thorndike carried out his experiment that supposedly dealt the death blow to formal discipline, Thorndike turned to the Lockean idea itself, education as habit formation, his expression being "learning as habit formation."

To make Locke a formal disciplinist removes him from among those who led us away from the Puritan tradition and its *re-citation;* from those who pioneered in the development of "experience curricula." And, even though an apologist for the British class system of education and falling much short of the modernity of Comenius, Locke did exert a direct and important influence on the thinking of our Founding Fathers, both educational and political, and both in a liberal rather than reactionary direction. Hence, we present Locke as the arch promoter, at least for us, of the idea of *education as habit formation* and *for use,* and point to his *Thoughts on Education* as the book that represents him in this context. That his was a somewhat equivocal role is recognized, but as a nation we took from him his forward-looking aspect and disregarded the other.

Suggested Readings

Bayles, Ernest E., *The Theory and Practice of Teaching.* New York: Harper & Row, 1950, Chap. 6.

Benedict, Agnes E., *Progress to Freedom: The Story of American Education.* New York: Putnam, 1942, Chap. 4.

Benne, Kenneth D., *The Gentleman: Locke.* In Nash, Paul, Kazamias, Andreas M., Perkinson, Henry J., *The Educated Man: Studies in the History of Educational Thought.* New York: Wiley, 1965, Chap. 8, pp. 190–223.

Brubacher, John S., and Rudy Willis, *Higher Education in Transition.* New York: Harper & Row, 1958.

Butts, R. F., and Cremin, L. A., *A History of Education in American Culture.* New York: Holt, Rinehart and Winston, 1953, Chap. 3.

Cubberley, Ellwood P., *The History of Education.* Boston: Houghton Mifflin, 1920, Chap. 18.

Eby, Frederick, *The Development of Modern Education,* 2nd ed. Englewood Cliffs, N.J.: Prentice-Hall, 1952, Chap. 11.

Eby, Frederick, and Arrowood, Charles F., *The Development of Modern Education,* Englewood Cliffs, N.J.: Prentice-Hall, 1934, Chap. 12.

Locke, John, *An Essay Concerning Human Understanding.* Any unabridged edition.

Locke, John, *Of Civil Government.* Any unabridged edition.

Locke, John, *Some Thoughts Concerning Education, with Introduction and Notes by the Rev. R. H. Quick, M.A.,* 2nd ed. Cambridge: The University Press, 1889.

Locke, John, "Of the Conduct of the Understanding," in John W. Adamson (ed.), *The Educational Writings of John Locke.* New York: Longmans, 1912.

Locke, John, *The Second Treatise of Government.* Any unabridged edition.

Locke, John, "Some Thoughts Concerning Education," in John W. Adamson (ed.), *The Educational Writings of John Locke.* New York: Longmans, 1912.

Monroe, Paul, *A Brief Course in the History of Education.* New York: Macmillan, 1914, Chap. 9.

Parker, Samuel C., *A Textbook in the History of Modern Elementary Education.* Boston: Ginn, 1912, pp. 150–159.

Price, Kingsley, *Education and Philosophical Thought.* Englewood Cliffs, N.J.: Allyn and Bacon, 1962, Chap. 6.

Thayer, V. T., *The Misinterpretation of Locke as a Formalist in Education.* Madison: University of Wisconsin Press, 1921.

Ulich, Robert, *History of Educational Thought.* New York: American Book, 1950, pp. 200–210.

Wickersham, James P., *Methods of Instruction.* Philadelphia: Lippincott, 1865.

Franklin's Academy as it appeared in the 1700's—The College, Academy and Charitable School of Philadelphia—forerunner of what is now the University of Pennsylvania.

Benjamin Franklin, an American pioneer in employing the idea of learning as habit formation, as he appeared at about the time of establishing the first American academy. This portrait, painted in 1759 by B. Wilson, was presented to the nation in 1906 by the Right Hon. Earl Grey, G.C.M.G., and afterwards hung in the White House, Washington, D.C.

4 ❧ Our Early Nationalization Period

Colonial Versus Early National

The colonial period of American education was essentially one of *transplanta-tion,* in which Old World institutions were picked up bodily and with no essential alteration replanted in the soil of the New World.

We come now to our early national period, during which we were forming our own way of life—educational as well as political, economic, and social. Though we recognize the inexactitudes that result in almost any general categories mankind may set up, we also find many advantages growing out of them. Hence, we shall essay now to deal with what we may call our *period of nationalization*—of nation-building—and, even though our Declaration of Independence was made in July of 1776, we are going to set the dividing date at 1750 and consider that nation-building, at least educationally, began to take form with us at about that time.

From 1750 (even from 1700) until 1825, elementary schooling underwent a slow process of secularization. Religion dropped out as one of "the three R's," readin' and 'ritin' moved up to first and second, and 'rithmetic came into third place. Speaking of one of the better-equipped Massachusetts towns of around the 1780s, a writer of the time said:

In point of fact, the children were neither taught much, nor were they taught well; for through life the mass of them, while they could do little more in the way of writing than rudely scrawl their names, could never read with real ease or rapidity, and could keep accounts only of the simplest kind. As for arithmetical problems, the knowledge of them was limited to the elementary multiplication, division, addition, and subtraction. None the less, after a fashion and to a limited extent, the Braintree school child, like the school children of all other Massachusetts towns, could read, could write, and could cipher; and for those days, as the world then went, that was much.[1]

Moreover, as a result of the Revolutionary War and the subsequent efforts to pay off the national debt as well as to work out solutions to our political problems, educational matters were permitted to lag and schools of all kinds went into somewhat of a decline.

In discussing schooling in larger population centers, specifically, Philadelphia, New York, and Boston, Paul Monroe has this to say about the latter:

Boston had attained quite the highest degree of school efficiency of all the communities in the country, partly because of its unified population, more largely because of its century and a half of tradition and experience. In 1789 the town adopted a reorganized system of education. This consisted of a grammar school for the teaching of Latin and Greek; three writing schools, open to both sexes, for writing and arithmetic "including vulgar and decimal fractions"; three reading schools, one in each part of the town, for both sexes, for reading, spelling, English grammar, and composition. Children were admitted at the age of seven "having previously received the instruction usual at women's schools." Schools for elementary teaching were not supported by the town until 1819 and were not combined with the city system until 1855. Control was in the hands of a school committee on inspection. This committee gave specific direction concerning subjects to be studied, texts to be used, method to be adopted, hours of attendance and recitation, and even all the details of schoolroom management. However, as late as 1819 it was found that more than 500 of the 2800 children of elementary grade age did not attend schools of any character.[2]

[1] Charles Francis Adams, Jr., *Three Episodes in Massachusetts History*, p. 781, in Paul Monroe, *Founding of the American Public School System*. New York: Macmillan, 1940, Vol. 1, p. 205.
[2] Monroe, *op. cit.*, pp. 208–209. We may add that Monroe's entire Chapter 8, Vol. I, pp. 185–221, gives an excellent account of the American school situation of about 1770–1830, with monitorial schools treated on pp. 360–371.

Monitorial Schools

What we see as the one significant change in elementary schools of the early national period (1750–1825) was introduction of the monitorial or Lancasterian school idea. Called *Lancasterian* after its founder, Joseph Lancaster (1778–1838), this kind of school was capable of accommodating 500–1000 pupils at a time, in one large room and under one teacher. This was made possible by using *monitors,* older pupils who taught younger ones.

Since the monitors received little, if any, pay—remuneration was limited almost exclusively to remission of tuition fees—the costs of running a school of this kind were very low, only a few dollars per pupil per year. Consequently, in the cities the plan was rapidly adopted for establishing more or less publicly supported charity schools. Small tuition fees were collected for pupils whose parents could afford them, with no charge for those whose parents could not (the charity-school principle).

One large room was used to house the 500–1000 pupils composing a school. The pupils were seated on benches in regular rows, the younger (and smaller) on lower benches toward the front and the older (and larger) in a gradient toward the rear, typically ten to a bench. A higher stool at the end of each bench was for the monitor. Each monitor had charge of his row, with the schoolmaster and possibly a paid assistant in charge of all. In an open area extending the full length of each side of the room were semicircles painted on the floor. For recitation, each monitor's pupils would "toe the circle," facing him as he stood at the center with his back to the wall. Reading, spelling, and other oral recitations would be handled in this manner and written work (ordinarily on slates) would be shown at the seats.

As is perhaps obvious, this was "cheap" instruction, both financially and educationally. Since the monitors would be capable of judging only whether pupil answers were exact repetitions of accepted answers—they had to be verbatim—this was no whit of advance beyond Puritan *re-citation.* And curriculum content (subject matter) had to be such as would lend itself to such treatment (method). For example, "teaching the alphabet was tedious and required from one to two years to enable the child to 'learn his letters.' "[3] Hence, the monitorial plan, because of its low cost and seeming simplicity, sprang quickly into high popularity. But after about two decades, popularity about as

[3] Thomas E. Finegan, in *Encyclopedia Americana,* 1939, Vol. 16, p. 688.

suddenly turned into disillusionment and the life-span of the monitorial plan in the United States was only a scant quarter-century (approximately 1805–1825).

The effect, however, of the monitorial-school idea was, according to writers such as Ellwood P. Cubberley, to promote the cause of public education. Because of its low cost, appropriations from municipal tax funds were not hard to obtain in the name of providing schooling for workingmen's children (at that time a large percentage of whom would be in the category of paupers). Hence, the principle of public support for education obtained a foothold outside of New England. Afterwards, when the monitorial plan had fallen into disrepute, the taste of the public for free schools had been established and it continued to grow. Of this we shall see more when we come to our later nationalization period.

Joseph Lancaster promoted the monitorial idea along with Dr. Andrew Bell (1753–1832) who developed it in Madras, India; it was originally known as the "Madras System." Before he first came to the United States in 1818, Lancaster had for 20 years promoted the idea throughout Britain and Ireland and by 1811 "had founded 95 schools, attended by 30,000 children."[4] Upon arrival in New York, Lancaster was accorded the honors reserved for a distinguished guest. He afterwards went to Philadelphia, thence to Washington, D.C., receiving accolades at both places.

Tied essentially to Lancaster's monitorial plan, but important otherwise, was the New York Public School Society. Organized in 1805 under the leadership of DeWitt Clinton, on and off mayor of New York City from 1803 to 1815 and governor of the state from 1817 to 1828, it was semipublic, receiving moneys both from private subscriptions and from appropriations by the Board of Aldermen of the city. In 1806 it founded its first school, organized on the Lancasterian plan. Thereafter, until its termination in 1853, it organized and conducted many such schools and, until his death in 1828, Clinton was enthusiastic in extolling the virtues of the monitorial plan.

Franklin's American Academy

We have seen that during the early period of our nation-building little was done to change the nature of elementary education. That it became gradually, though slowly and incompletely, secularized was at least helped by the Lockean influence, even though we cannot point to specific or direct connections and

4 *Ibid.*, p. 686.

there may have been none. Let us now turn to secondary education, and therein we seem to find a clear and direct line of thought emanating from Locke and eventuating in distinct change.

As previously noted (see Chapter 1), the Latin grammar school was our first on the secondary level. With a curriculum almost exclusively of Latin and Greek reading and composition, its sole and only function was preparing students to pass college-entrance examinations. This, of course, was highly useful for those who would go to college, and during the early years of Harvard College they were mostly boys who contemplated going into the ministry.

By 1740–1745, however, two changes had transpired or were in process, both of which tended to reduce the "usefulness" of the Latin-Greek curriculum. First, the colleges—now William and Mary, and Yale, as well as Harvard—were attended by many students who did not have the ministry in mind and did not especially need to know Latin and Greek (and Hebrew) in order to read the Bible either in the original or in its early translations. Second, it is reported that at that time there were *more pupils entering* Latin grammar schools in one year *than there were students in college*. Hence, a curriculum that was solely *preparation for college* was a highly *nonuseful* one for all but very few. This, seemingly, was what Benjamin Franklin had in mind when he submitted his "Proposals Relating to the Education of Youth in Pennsylvania."[5]

As mid-eighteenth century approached, here and there schools began to appear that not only were nondenominational or nonsectarian but also were designed to give instruction in subjects of a distinctly useful or practical kind. These tended, too, to be supplemental to instruction in "the three R's," hence to be somewhat "secondary" in nature. Moreover, they were in no sense "town" schools, but were distinctly private; instruction provided by individual teachers in evening or day classes and supported solely by fees paid by the pupils. Often called "the private school" or "the advertized school," they had to offer attractive wares; hence subjects with popular appeal such as bookkeeping, surveying, gunnery, geography (maps and globes), algebra, geometry, trigonometry, astronomy, architecture, German, French, Spanish, and the like.

The word *Academy*, however, was applied to an organized school; a private one, but under the control of a board of trustees. And Franklin's was probably the first chartered academy in America. Moreover, Franklin's plan was well thought out; it was based on a rather clearly formulated program or philosophy. It was also distinctly American; it was no warmed-over version of something

[5] *Facsimile reprint of "Proposals Relating to the Education of Youth in Pensilvania"* [sic], issued by the Rosenbach Fellowship in Bibliography. Philadelphia: University of Pennsylvania Press, 1931.

British or European. Hence, we have in Franklin's Academy the beginnings of an "American" school system and, since his *Proposals* were published in 1749 and the institution opened its doors in January, 1751, we have chosen 1750 as a suitable date for marking the beginning of our national period as far as education is concerned. Indeed, it was in November of 1750 that the newly established board of trustees, with Franklin as chairman, ordered "that the academy be opened on the seventh day of January next."[6]

As early as 1740, Franklin was thinking along the lines of an Academy and in 1743 he actually talked over the matter with a friend.[7] In 1749, he published his *Proposals* and distributed copies free to those he thought he could interest in contributing money for the establishment of an "Academy, in which they [the youth of Pennsylvania] might receive the accomplishments of a regular Education."[8] Of the "Authors quoted in this Paper," the first was Milton and the second, "the great Mr. Locke, who wrote a Treatise on Education, well known, and much esteemed, being translated into most of the modern Languages of Europe."[9]

"As to their Studies," proposed Franklin, "it would be well if they could be taught *every Thing* that is useful, and *every Thing* that is ornamental: But Art is long, and their Time is short. It is therefore propos'd that they learn those Things that are likely to be *most useful* and *most ornamental*. Regard being had to the several Professions for which they are intended."[10] Then he goes on to enumerate handwriting, drawing, arithmetic, "accounts," geometry, astronomy, English grammar (with the quotation from Locke that we give on pp. 53–54), English writing style, oral reading, history (to which pages 19–26 are devoted, and through which geography, morality, oratory, and religions are to be studied), *natural* history (what we now call science), "the history of commerce," and "mechanics." In the rather voluminous footnotes to the *Proposals* are no less than a dozen direct quotations from Locke's *Thoughts* and, of other quotations, many (such as those from "Dr. Turnbull") are highly Lockean.

Thus, we see Franklin proposing a secondary school with a curriculum broad enough to cover much of what is covered by a typical high school in the United States today. Moreover, he wanted our own language studied, not Latin and Greek, whereas in the Latin grammar school it was the latter that were studied

[6] From H. G. Good, *A History of Western Education,* 2nd ed. New York: Macmillan, 1960, p. 391.
[7] Franklin, *op. cit.,* Introduction by William Pepper, pp. vii–xvii.
[8] *Ibid.,* p. 3.
[9] *Ibid.,* p. 4.
[10] *Ibid.,* p. 11. Italics in original.

and *not* our own. However, since money for support of the new school had to be obtained and since it could come only from those who had it, he had to bow to their wishes. And they wished Latin.

Franklin, therefore, made a compromise—to have both a "Latin School" and an "English School." But he retained until his death his basic preference for the English school, as is shown in a paper he wrote in 1789 entitled *Observations relative to the original founders of the academy in Philadelphia,* in which he says,

In 1749, I was encouraged to hazard another Project, that of a Public Education for our Youth. As in the Scheme of the Library, I had provided only for English Books, so in this new Scheme my Ideas went no farther than to procure the Means of a good English Education. A number of my Friends, to whom I communicated the Proposal, concurr'd with me in these Ideas; but Mr. Allen, Mr. Francis, Mr. Peters, and some other Persons of Wealth and Learning, whose Subscriptions and Countenance we should need, being of Opinion that it ought to include the learned Languages, I submitted my Judgment to theirs, retaining, however, a strong Prepossession in favor of my first Plan, and resolving to preserve as much of it as I could, and to nourish the English School by every means in my Power.[11]

Pepper then adds the comment:

Franklin complains of the partiality shown to the Latin School. He drew a simile between the fashion of wearing a hat and the study of the classics. He tells how hats first began to be worn, then how curls and powdering came into vogue and how then, though hats could not be worn on the head, every man of fashion still felt that he must carry one under his arm, and that hats were then called *chapeaux bras* and were of no use and attended with some expense, and were a constant trouble. He then says, "The still prevailing custom of having schools for teaching generally our children, in these days, the Latin and Greek languages, I consider therefore, in no other light than as the *chapeau bras* of modern Literature." He evidently searched carefully through the minutes of the trustees from 1751 to 1789 and quoted numerous actions taken by the Board favoring the *Latinists,* as he calls them. He was the only one of the original trustees living in 1789, and this paper of his was one of the last things which he wrote. He died within a year, on April 17, 1790, at the age of eighty-four years.[12]

[11] Pepper's Introduction to Franklin, *op. cit.,* pp. xv–xvi.
[12] *Ibid.,* pp. xvi–xvii. Italics in original.

Franklin's wish, thus, was for a secondary school that would prepare young people for *life* rather than for college alone—*education for use*. However, it was not to be narrowly utilitarian or vocational. He wanted the students to learn "those things that are likely to be most useful and most ornamental" (see quote on p. 70) and this included physical exercise "in running, leaping, wrestling, and swimming, etc."[13] Of course, for those going to college, *education for use* would indeed require college preparation; hence, he acquiesced in the Latin school but was far from enthusiastic in adding another such school to the apparent oversupply of the time. Moreover, Franklin was not necessarily opposed to foreign language instruction as such, for he included it in his proposed curriculum. But the languages were to be studied only if they were to be used and by such as would use them:

. . . All intended for Divinity should be taught the *Latin* and *Greek;* for Physick, the *Latin, Greek* and *French;* for Law, the *Latin* and *French;* Merchants, the *French, German,* and *Spanish;* And though all should not be compell'd to learn *Latin, Greek,* or the modern foreign Languages; yet none that have an ardent Desire to learn them should be refused; their *English,* Arithmetick, and other Studies absolutely necessary, being at the same Time not neglected.[14]

That the Academy would become an institution that would be broadly preparatory for life, however, was not to be. Although it rather quickly superceded and replaced the Latin grammar schools and indeed did not reach the peak of its popularity until 1860–1880 and though the curricula of the academies retained much of the original breadth of Franklin's school, such institutions soon reverted to the role of college preparation. In fact, in 1755 the Philadelphia Academy was rechartered and expanded into the *College, Academy, and Charitable School of Philadelphia,* so that the Latin school won out and college preparation became paramount. This for the Philadelphia Academy was virtually inevitable, for Provost Smith (the original head) turned out to be far more concerned with promoting the Anglican faith and the study of Latin than he was in providing "useful studies."

By perhaps 1800, Latin grammar schools had all but disappeared and the Academies had become so imbued with college preparation that lay sentiment (Franklin was, of course, educationally a layman) began again to grow in favor of a secondary school to emphasize preparation for life rather than for college. In 1821, by vote of the townspeople, the first public high school was established—

13 *Ibid.,* p. 10.
14 *Ibid.,* p. 25. Italics in original.

in the city of Boston and known as the English Classical School, later as the English High School. This school was for boys only—"sons of sea captains, small merchants, and small artisans"[15]—but in 1826 a similar (practical and public) school was opened for girls. The latter, however, immediately became too popular and in two years was discontinued because public sentiment was that the city treasury could not afford the cost. Boys, it was thought, would not stay in school long because they would soon enter the trades for which they were being prepared. But girls would stay in school until marriage and that might not be until after a number of years.

Higher Education

By 1750, higher education in English colonial America—confined to Harvard, William and Mary, Yale, and Princeton—had ceased to be solely professional training for the ministry and had become sufficiently secularized to merit being called liberal-arts education. It still followed, however, the pattern of Oxford and Cambridge, i.e., of English-type colleges. This meant *dissemination* of knowledge; perhaps not even that except in a limited way, limited to the "classical." It certainly did not mean research, or addition to knowledge. Thus, it followed the pattern rationalized by Locke as the capstone in the training of an English gentleman.

The colonial American college was in many ways a blood brother to its English model. Like the latter, it upheld the tradition of a prescribed liberal-arts curriculum, based upon a primarily classical preparatory course; it was more deeply concerned with the forming of character than the fostering of research; it placed great value on a residential pattern of life for students (what Cotton Mather called the "collegiate way of living"); and it was concerned primarily with training a special elite for community leadership. To these fundamental policies it held steadfastly and without important change for nearly 200 years.[16]

Nor had much further change occurred in the American college pattern by 1850, essentially the close of what we have chosen to call our period of nationalization. New colleges were founded between 1750 and 1850: the College of Philadelphia (Franklin's college, later the University of Pennsylvania), 1753;

15 Good, *op. cit.,* p. 500.
16 John S. Brubacher, and Willis Rudy, *Higher Education in Transition.* New York: Harper & Row, 1958, p. 25.

King's College (later Columbia), 1754; Rhode Island College (Brown), 1764; Queen's College (Rutgers), 1766; Dartmouth, 1769; 18 more by 1800, almost 50 more between 1800 and 1830, and 80 more between 1830 and 1850. Ninety were added between 1850 and 1860.[17]

During the late 1700s, specialized training for certain professions—professorships in law at William and Mary, Pennsylvania, and Columbia; in medicine at Pennsylvania, Harvard, and Dartmouth—had its beginnings. And, of course, although secularization was under way, courses in theology were offered to prepare for the ministry. But the apprenticeship system was mainly relied on, just as it was for merchants, artisans, mechanics, etc. A young man wishing to become a lawyer would work in a law office, doing various routine jobs while incidentally becoming familiar with a lawyer's work and when he could find time reading law books, necessary equipment in any law office. So it was in medicine and the ministry.

Next, in the early 1800s, certain practitioners began to take on more than one or two apprentices, then to give lectures, and finally to devote most of their attention to such training instead of to regular practice; hence, a "school" was established. Moreover, college professorships soon expanded into "departments" and finally into professional schools as we know them today—Harvard establishing a law school in the 1820s, and Pennsylvania one in medicine at about the same time.[18]

For teaching, as we shall see later, specialized professional training began in the "normal" schools. The first *state* normal school was established in 1839 at Lexington, Massachusetts, as a result of the efforts of Horace Mann. Such schools were at first little above secondary-school level, and not until the nineteen-teens did they become four-year, degree-granting colleges.

Training for engineering followed essentially the same pattern. Though academy curricula sometimes included surveying along with geometry and trigonometry, most of the arts of an engineer were learned on the job. Founding of the Rensselaer Polytechnic Institute in 1824 at Troy, New York, marked the beginning of professional engineering-training on the college level.

Thus, we see that during our midnationalization period the colleges were beginning to become much more than liberal-arts minded. They too were being affected by the way of thinking of Franklin—of *education for use*—and it is not at all surprising that his college (the name changed in 1777 to "University of the State of Pennsylvania") was in the vanguard of changes of this

[17] Frederick Eby and Charles Flinn Arrowood, *The Development of Modern Education.* Englewood Cliffs, N.J.: Prentice-Hall, 1934, pp. 558–570.
[18] See Brubacher and Rudy, *op. cit.,* chap. 10.

kind. This did not mean that a liberal-arts education was not considered useful. As previously noted, Franklin said "useful and ornamental"; and by ornamental he obviously had in mind the equipment to enable a person to carry himself as a broadly educated man, showing, perhaps, the American version of what Locke meant by his term, "breeding." A liberal-arts education was useful but not all that was needed. So, in conjunction with liberal-arts instruction, a college-trained person should also be broadly equipped vocationally. This was unquestionably the feeling of Franklin as well as of Jefferson, founder of the University of Virginia (1819). And it was why training in so many professions was tied in with the colleges and predicated on a liberal-arts background.

The Thinking of Our Founding Fathers

From about 1790 to 1825, there was considerable sentiment in favor of establishing a national university at Washington, D.C., under the auspices of the federal government. In fact, our first six presidents—Washington through John Quincy Adams—all recommended such action to Congress. Moreover, in his will Washington bequeathed 50 shares (par value $500 each) of stock in the Potomac River Company to be held in trust for starting an endowment for such a university. But no action ever was taken, and (incidentally) what became of those 50 shares of stock is unknown even today. State universities had their inception during this time, but never a national university—at least in the original sense. We indeed have the three "military academies" (really colleges)—Army at West Point, Navy at Annapolis, and Air Force at Colorado Springs—but their purpose and nature are far different from the national-university idea as envisioned by our early presidents.

Furthermore, during this time a number of plans for a unified, nationwide system of education were proposed. Spearheaded during the Revolutionary Period by the writings of Thomas Paine, the ideal of a government "of the people, by the people" was fresh in the minds of Americans. Moreover, they had experienced the ill effects of a weak central government under the Articles of Confederation and the Continental Congress, and had, in the new Constitution of 1787, set up a governmental arrangement in which the combined will of *all* of the people (the nation as a whole) would be a potent, unifying force. Actively encouraged by the American Philosophical Society, of which Franklin was president from 1769 to 1790 and Jefferson from 1796 to 1815, the 1780–

1800 period witnessed a rush of proposals regarding a national system of education for the United States. Chief proponents of plans were the following:

1. Benjamin Rush (1786)
2. Robert Coram (1791)
3. James Sullivan (1791)
4. Nathaniel Chipman (1793)
5. Samuel Knox (1797)
6. Samuel Harrison Smith (1798)
7. Amable-Louis-Rose de LaFitte du Courteil (1797)
8. Pierre Samuel Du Pont de Nemours (1800)
9. Noah Webster (Numerous writings from 1785 to 1835, particularly *On Education of the Youth in America*, 1788.[19]

The idea that seemingly permeated all these plans and was also implicit as well as explicit in the thinking of Franklin and Jefferson was that the success of democracy in the United States rested largely, if not wholly, on the education of the youth. Moreover, the nation as a whole needed to exercise continual surveillance over the program in order to avoid the divisive or fractionating forces that would very likely become dominant should so important a matter be left wholly to the states, to say nothing of leaving it to local communities or districts. Yet, probably because of the deep-seated fear of centralized authority on the part of so many—a holdover from our troubles with George III—and its expression in the difficulties attendant to the very adoption of the Constitution itself, we did not at that time set up a national ministry of education; and we have not since. In fact, since education is among the "unstated powers," it is constitutionally reserved to the states.

On the other hand, like these far-sighted "planners" of our early national period, those responsible since then for carrying on the American educational enterprise have recognized the necessity for surveillance at the national (or federal) level and have inaugurated ways and means for effecting it. Chief among these, perhaps, are the regional accrediting agencies—the North Central Association and others—which have in an extra-legal way done much to coordinate state and local efforts and accomplishments.

Actually, as is well known, the official national educational agency—the U.S. Office of Education—exercises practically no control over individual schools or school districts. It is principally a data-gathering agency. Therefore, the degree to which our educational efforts are coordinated nationwide is little short of

[19] For a definitive account of these plans, see Allen Oscar Hansen, *Liberalism and Education in the Eighteenth Century*. New York: Macmillan, 1926.

amazing. There are, of course, ways in which the federal government is active in nationwide coordination. Examples are the work of the U.S. Department of Agriculture in vocational agriculture and vocational home-economics education, and the Supreme Court ruling in opposition to segregation in the schools. But such action at the national level is itself unplanned, uncoordinated, and sporadic, to say the least, and this early concern of our Founding Fathers can hardly be said to have borne fruit.

Suggested Readings

Benedict, Agnes E., *Progress to Freedom: The Story of American Education.* New York: Putnam, 1942, Chaps. 4–7.

Brubacher, John S., and Rudy, Willis, *Higher Education in Transition.* New York: Harper & Row, 1958, Chaps. 5, 6.

Cubberley, Ellwood P., *Public Education in the United States.* Boston: Houghton Mifflin, 1934, Chap. 4.

Eby, Frederick, and Arrowood, Charles F., *The Development of Modern Education.* Englewood Cliffs, N.J.: Prentice-Hall, 1934, Chaps. 15, 19.

Edwards, Newton, and Richey, Herman G., *The School in the American Social Order,* 2nd ed. Boston: Houghton Mifflin, 1963, Chaps. 6–10.

Fisk, Franklin, G., *Is the National Science Foundation Becoming a New Federal Agency?* Unpublished doctoral dissertation at the University of Kansas, 1963.

Franklin, Benjamin, *Proposals Relating to the Education of Youth in Pensilvania.* Facsimile Reprint by the Rosenbach Fellowship in Bibliography. Philadelphia: University of Pennsylvania Press, 1931. Introduction by William Pepper, pp. vii–xvii.

Good, H. G., *A History of Western Education,* 2nd ed. New York: Macmillan, 1960, Chaps. 3–6.

Gross, Carl H., and Chandler, Charles C., *The History of American Education Through Readings.* Boston: Heath, 1964, Part II.

Hansen, Allen O., *Liberalism and Education in the Eighteenth Century.* New York: Macmillan, 1926.

Meiklejohn, Alexander, *Education Between Two Worlds,* 3rd ed. New York: Harper & Row, 1942.

Meyer, Adolphe E., *An Educational History of the American People.* New York: McGraw-Hill, 1957, Chaps. 5, 6.

Monroe, Paul, *Founding of the American Public School System.* New York: Macmillan, 1940, Vol. I, Chaps. 8–15.

ÉMILE,
OU
DE L'ÉDUCATION.

LIVRE PREMIER.

Tout eſt bien, ſortant des mains de l'Auteur des choſes : tout dégénere entre les mains de l'homme. Il force une terre à nourrir les productions d'une autre, un arbre à porter les fruits d'un autre : il mêle & confond les climats, les élémens, les ſaiſons : il mutile ſon chien, ſon cheval, ſon eſclave : il bouleverſe tout, il défigure tout : il aime la difformité, les monſtres : il ne veut rien, tel que l'a fait la nature, pas même l'homme : il le faut dreſſer pour lui, comme un che-

Tome I.   **A**

The first text page, Volume I, of the first edition of Rousseau's Emile, originally printed in four volumes. (Rare Book Room, New York Public Library)

5 ᷒ *ROUSSEAU: Education as Unfoldment*

In the preceding chapter, we noted that early in our century of nation-building secondary education underwent a distinct change, though difficulties were encountered in holding it. The colleges multiplied in number but, except for rather hesitant ventures into professional training, changed little. And elementary education changed even less, if it did not even somewhat retrogress.

The Great Awakening

In the latter part of our century of nationalization we shall find elementary education undergoing rather thorough modification. But, since vital changes in institutions and procedures ordinarily come only as a result of changes in ideas, we shall need first to look into the latter and afterwards return to what transpired educationally during our later nationalization period. Moreover, the work of two men will have to be examined before we can get a very clear notion of the way the minds of Horace Mann and Henry Barnard (as well as others) were working as they labored for educational reform during what has come to be known as our Great Educational Awakening.

Between 1835 and 1845, both Barnard and Mann visited western Europe to investigate schools, and returned enthusiastic with what they had seen, especially in Germany. Early in the century, German elementary-school people had become imbued with the ideas of the little Swiss educational reformer, Johann Heinrich Pestalozzi, one of the great teachers of the Western world. Pestalozzi, in turn, originally received his inspiration from the Swiss-French genius, Jean-Jacques Rousseau, whose educational treatise, *Emile,* he had read a few years after its publication in 1762. Therefore, let us also take a look at Rousseau's *Emile,* then at what Pestalozzi made of it, then at what the Germans and finally what we did about it. Possibly in following this thread we may have to indulge in a bit of oversimplification. We believe, however, that even though we do we shall be holding true to the major current of cause and effect, and that is what really counts in the unraveling of man's destiny.

Rousseau

Jean-Jacques Rousseau was born June 28, 1712, at Geneva, in the French-speaking region of Switzerland. After living most of his life in France, he died at Ermenonville in 1778. As with Comenius and Locke, we feel that for our purpose a chronicle of more than a few of the events of Rousseau's life is not important. Such information is widely available; either *Encyclopedia Americana* or *Encyclopedia Britannica* is quite satisfactory.

Intellectually brilliant but emotionally unstable, Rousseau blossomed late into the philosophical-political-educational-literary genius that he is credited with having been. His mother died at his birth; he grew unhappily to the age of 16, first with his father and later with relatives when, returning one Sunday evening from a walk in the country, he found the city gates of Geneva closed for the night. He turned and left for years of dissolute vagabondage, never again returning to Geneva except for rare occasions when he merely passed through; seemingly he was not mourned by any with whom he had lived.

Until he was 37, he was unknown to the world at large, but he had read widely, was an accomplished musician-composer, had become a close friend and colleague of Diderot, one of the French Encyclopedists and a leader in the Enlightment, and was helping with the Encyclopedia.

In 1749, while on his way to visit Diderot in Vincennes, he noticed an announcement of a prize to be awarded by the Academy on the Arts and Sciences of Dijon for the best essay on the question: "Has the restoration of the arts and sciences had a purifying effect upon morals?" According to his own account, he was suddenly so struck with the idea that science and civilization were a curse to humanity, instead of a blessing, that he even fainted by the roadside. At once he wrote such an essay, submitted it, and, although it was exactly opposite in sentiment to the expectations of the Academy members, was awarded the prize.

Fame was immediate, and during the next 12 years he came to write the treatises that have won for him top recognition in the Western world, both in political science and in education. Those two were *The Social Contract* and *Emile,* both published in 1762; never again did Rousseau produce anything that has been recognized as the equal of either. Since our concern is with education, we shall focus our attention on *Emile,* the book read a few years later by Pestalozzi while in college, which served for him as the first inspiration toward his educational reforms. Suffice it to say of *The Social Contract* that years later Napoleon was to characterize Rousseau as "the evil spirit of the French Revolution." Thus, Rousseau's *Social Contract* teamed with Locke's *Of Civil Government* to furnish a rationale for the American and the French Revolutions. And, though in certain ways opposed to one another, Rousseau's *Emile* and Locke's *Thoughts Concerning Education* also have teamed together to point toward the revolution in education for which the United States have during the past century made significant contributions.

Emile—Unfoldment and Negative Education

"Everything is good as it comes from the hands of the Creator of Nature; everything deteriorates in the hands of man." So goes the opening sentence of *Emile.*[1] The first paragraph continues:

God makes all things good; man meddles with them and they become evil. He forces one soil to yield the products of another, one tree to bear another's fruit. He confuses and confounds time, place, and natural conditions. He

[1] From the book *Emile; or, Education* by Jean Jacques Rousseau. Everyman's Library. Reprinted by permission of E. P. Dutton & Co., Inc. The first sentence is from the Payne translation; the remaining quotations will be from the translation by Barbara Foxley. New York: Dutton, 1911.

mutilates his dog, his horse, and his slave. He destroys and defaces all things; he loves all that is deformed and monstrous; he will have nothing as nature made it, not even man himself, who must learn his paces like a saddle-horse, and be shaped to his master's taste like the trees in his garden.[2]

Then Rousseau declares the natural tendencies in a child to be "like a sapling chance sown in the midst of the highway, bent hither and thither and soon crushed by the passers-by,"[3] and counsels a parent, "From the outset raise a wall round your child's soul"[4] lest it be overwhelmed by "the crushing force of social conventions."

This is the heart of Rousseau's "naturalism." To him, the word "nature" did not mean the great outdoors. It meant the child's own natural soul; the innate quality of his being, before it has been affected for good or for ill by what surrounds him. Hence, his appeal for a "return to nature" was not to get out into the fields, the meadows, and the forests. It was, instead, so to protect a child from his man-made surroundings—science and civilization—that his innate tendencies would have opportunity to grow and unfold in accordance with their own nature.

Emile is composed of five "books," or parts. Each of the first four deals with one of the stages or "epochs" assumed by Rousseau as the way in which a child grows from infancy to adulthood. In other words, he assumed what is known as the *culture-epochs* theory of child development; that child development is in stages (or epochs) and goes by *leaps* from one to the next. Hence, this is the *saltatory* (leaping) theory, as opposed to the *gradual* theory generally held today. The saltatory theory is that the various stages are sharply demarcated, *qualitatively* different from one another; that a child at a later stage is a person different from what he was at an earlier one. The only connecting link is the child's innate destiny, *en*folded within him at birth and destined to *un*fold in the stage-order predestined at birth. Growth, therefore, is *unfoldment, development from within.*

The "culture" aspect of the "culture-epochs" theory is that these epochs or stages are a *recapitulation* of the child's racial or cultural history. This is an extension of the theory of biological recapitulation—the latter dealing with prenatal (before birth) development and the former postnatal (after birth). Prenatal recapitulation is predominantly biological and is a well-established scientific principle, whereas postnatal recapitulation is predominantly cultural

[2] *Emile,* Everyman's Library edition, p. 5.
[3] *Ibid.,* p. 5.
[4] *Ibid.,* p. 6.

and is a theory that is now rather generally rejected by authorities in the field of cultural anthropology.

Rousseau's culture-epochs theory embraces four individual stages—infancy, childhood, youth, and adulthood—and it is on these that the first four books of *Emile* are based. The corresponding culture stages are: beasthood, savagery, civilized-solitary, and civilized-social. Hence, Book I deals with the baby as a little animal, not yet human, and extends from birth to age 5; Book II deals with the child as a human savage, and includes ages 6–11; Book III deals with the adolescent as a reasoning being—during the *"Age of Reason"* (12–15) he is civilized but concerned only with himself; Book IV deals with the youth or young adult as a *social* being, aware and thinking of others, and takes him from postpuberty to the end of formal education.

As the reader may suspect, a close reading of *Emile* shows the dividing lines between these stages to be not only far from sharp but also rather confused or confusing. That, of course, is a major reason for today's rejection of the culture-epochs theory; it necessitates overlooking much of what can readily be observed in careful child-study. Actually, Rousseau evinces some vacillation and self-contradiction as to stage-characteristics and stage-distinctions. Yet he holds rather tenaciously to these distinctions, as when almost out of context he drops the comment, "childhood is the sleep of reason,"[5] meaning that before 12 a child is not a reasoning being at all—only instinctive—but, with the unfoldment, very quickly becomes rational.

Book V of *Emile* deals not with Emile but with Sophy, whom Emile is to marry; hence with the education of girls. However, since Rousseau's ideas regarding women's education were quite different from what he proposed for Emile, we shall in our treatise disregard it. Rousseau's impact on Western education is tied irrevocably to Emile; therefore, to depart therefrom is to depart from the thought line that it is our purpose to follow. Let us now return to Rousseau's plan for Emile's upbringing.

Emile is a rich man's son, a scion of the aristocracy. He is so because, as Rousseau says,

The poor man has no need of education. The education of his own station in life is forced upon him, he can have no other; the education received by the rich man from his own station is least fitted for himself and for society. Moreover, a natural education should fit a man for any position. Now it is more unreasonable to train a poor man for wealth than a rich man for poverty, for in proportion to their numbers more rich men are ruined and fewer poor men be-

[5] *Ibid.*, p. 71.

come rich. Let us choose our scholar among the rich; we shall at least have made another man; the poor may come to manhood without our help.[6]

This is presumably so because the rich are able to take advantage of the products of science and civilization, whereas the poor are not, and these products are debilitative because

Our wisdom is slavish prejudice, our customs consist in control, constraint, compulsion. Civilised man is born and dies a slave. The infant is bound up in swaddling clothes, the corpse is nailed down in his coffin. All his life long man is imprisoned by our institutions.[7]

And Rousseau continues:

I am told that many midwives profess to improve the shape of the infant's head by rubbing, and they are allowed to do it. Our heads are not good enough as God made them, they must be moulded outside by the nurse and inside by the philosopher. The Caribs are better off then we are. "The child has hardly left the mother's womb, it has hardly begun to move and stretch its limbs, when it is deprived of its freedom. It is wrapped in swaddling bands, laid down with its head fixed, its legs stretch out, and its arms by its sides; it is wound round with linen and bandages of all sorts so that it cannot move. It is fortunate if it has room to breathe, and it is laid on its side so that water which should flow from its mouth can escape, for it is not free to turn its head on one side for this purpose."[8]

The next page is devoted to a polemic against the use of "swaddling clothes," a practice (as the reader knows) dating from before the birth of Christ. Let the infant be free to exercise his body as he wishes; he will not be emotionally frustrated by restraints and he can develop the healthy body of nature's design. Moreover, mothers are themselves to suckle their own children *as nature intended,* not to turn them over to others.

Not content with having ceased to suckle their children, women no longer wish to do it; with the natural result—motherhood becomes a burden; means are found to avoid it. They will destroy their work to begin it over again, and they thus turn to the injury of the race the charm which was given them for its increase. This practice, with other causes of depopulation, forbodes the

6 *Ibid.,* p. 20.
7 *Ibid.,* p. 10.
8 *Ibid.,* p. 10.

coming fate of Europe. Her arts and sciences, her philosophy and morals, will shortly reduce her to a desert. She will be the home of wild beasts, and her inhabitants will hardly have changed for the worse.[9]

And, so it is reported, Rousseau was to a degree successful in making both these reforms fashionable among the higher circles of the Paris of his day.

What is this education according to nature? How is Emile to be brought up? Rousseau replies, "We can do much, but the chief thing is to prevent anything being done."[10] "The only habit the child should be allowed to contract is that of having no habits."[11] "When our natural tendencies have not been interfered with by human prejudice and human institutions, the happiness alike of children and of men consists in the enjoyment of their liberty."[12] "Nature provides for the child's growth in her own way and this should never be thwarted. Do not make him sit still when he wants to run about, nor run when he wants to be quiet. If we did not spoil our children's wills by our blunders their desires would be free from caprice."[13] "Nature would have them children before they are men. If we try to invert this order we shall produce a forced fruit immature and flavourless, fruit which will be rotten before it is ripe; we shall have young doctors and old children.[14] "Give him ["your scholar"] *no orders at all, absolutely none.*"[15] The plot builds climactically:

Give your scholar no verbal lessons; he should be taught by experience alone; never punish him, for he does not know what it is to do wrong; never make him say, "Forgive me," for he does not know how to do you wrong. Wholly unmoral in his actions, he can do nothing morally wrong, and he deserves neither punishment nor reproof.[16]

Let us lay it down as an incontrovertible rule that the first impulses of nature are always right; there is no original sin in the human heart, the how and why of the entrance of every vice can be traced. The only natural passion is self-love or selfishness taken in a wider sense. This selfishness is good in itself and in relation to ourselves; and as the child has no necessary relations to other people he is naturally indifferent to them; his self-love only becomes good or bad by the use made of it and the relations established by its means. Until the

9 *Ibid.*, p. 12.
10 *Ibid.*, p. 9.
11 *Ibid.*, p. 30.
12 *Ibid.*, p. 49.
13 *Ibid.*, p. 50.
14 *Ibid.*, p. 54.
15 *Ibid.*, p. 55. Italics ours.
16 *Ibid.*, p. 56.

time is ripe for the appearance of reason, that guide of selfishness, the main thing is that the child shall do nothing because you are watching him or listening to him; in a word, nothing because of other people, but only what nature asks of him; then he will never do wrong.[17]

> *May I venture at this point to state the greatest, the most important, the most useful rule of education? It is: Do not save time, but lose it.* I hope that every-day readers will excuse my paradoxes; you cannot avoid paradox if you think for yourself, and whatever you may say I would rather fall into paradox than into prejudice. The most dangerous period in human life lies between birth and the age of twelve. It is the time when errors and vices spring up, while as yet there is no means to destroy them; when the means of destruction are ready, the roots have gone too deep to be pulled up. If the infant sprang at one bound from its mother's breast to the age of reason, the present type of education would be quite suitable, but its natural growth calls for quite a different training. The mind should be left undisturbed till its faculties have developed; for while it is blind it cannot see the torch you offer it, nor can it follow through the vast expanse of ideas a path so faintly traced by reason that the best eyes can scarcely follow it.[18]

Then comes the climax: "*Therefore the education of the earliest years should be merely negative. It consists, not in teaching virtue or truth, but in preserving the heart from vice and from the spirit of error.*"[19]

Thus, we have Rousseau's principle of *negative education*—not what you do but what you refrain from doing. Let nature take her course; just see that neither you nor any other would-be teacher interferes. Let what is *en*folded *un*fold; preserve the innate virtue of humanity; foster the natural man. This is not a new principle; it harks back intermittently to antiquity. But it was given a tremendous rejuvenation by Rousseau. It affected literature for a century and a half after him, as with Wyss's *The Swiss Family Robinson* and Barrie's *The Admirable Crichton*. And it hit American education broadside during the early twentieth century though not, contrary to popular belief, under the aegis of John Dewey. "By doing nothing to begin with," Rousseau says, "you would end with a prodigy of education."[20] And again, "Zealous teachers, be simple, sensible, and reticent; be in no hurry to act unless to prevent the actions of others."[21]

We shall not go further in documenting Rousseau on *negative education*.

17 *Ibid.*, p. 56.
18 *Ibid.*, p. 57. Italics ours.
19 *Ibid.*, p. 57. Italics ours.
20 *Ibid.*, p. 58.
21 *Ibid.*, p. 60.

But this is the basis for his fame and this is his impact on education, in America and elsewhere. Let those who will, including himself as we shall soon see, take what steps they will to protect Rousseau from Rousseau—for this is his weakness as well as his strength. It was *negative education* that made Rousseau an educational giant; that so impressed the young Pestalozzi that even though he early discovered its shortcomings, he never lost its impact and never ceased to deal with children as children, not as miniature adults. Unquestionably, Rousseau made it clear that he had different ideas for the education of women (Book V of *Emile*), for the education of "the poor" (see our pp. 83–84), and for the total educational system of a nation (as in his plan for Poland). But what is "Roussellian" is, in common parlance, what grows out of the impact of *negative education*.

What does negative education mean in terms of assumptions regarding the original nature of man? "Everything is *good* as it comes from the hands of the Creator of nature." Human beings become evil only as they are misled by depraved human adults who themselves were in turn misled by their predecessors, and so back to Adam. On the other hand, the assumption that each child, unless prevented, will recapitulate his racial history has in it the principle of self-propulsion; no outside push is needed; hence, *active*. Thus, Rousseau's negative education means a *good-active* child, one whose growth pattern should in no wise be affected by outside forces. This is *education as unfoldment;* "growth from within."

The *bad-active* assumption of the Puritans meant that play, being natural (hence vicious), was not to be permitted except only to avoid a blowup—the "safety valve" principle. The *neutral-passive* assumption of Locke meant that play, being natural and of itself neither good nor bad, might readily be used provided it is directed toward "good" ends. Therefore, we found Locke going so far as to advice the use of dice for helping children learn to read.

The *good-active* assumption of Rousseau means that play, being natural and therefore *good*, is what children must be permitted to do, under peril of provocation to depravity should interference be tolerated. And that is exactly what we have seen Rousseau recommending with high enthusiasm. And later, when we come to Froebel (Chapter 9), we shall find him, especially in kindergarten, enthroning play as the heart of the curriculum. As Rousseau said, "Do not make him [Emile] sit still when he wants to run about, nor run when he wants to be quiet."

And the reader should further note that the *good-active* assumption is in full theoretical opposition to *supervised* play; for that represents adult interference, nonetheless effectual because it is veiled. It is the *neutral-passive* assumption of Locke that theoretically justifies *supervised* play, for only then, as Locke advised, can we be assured that good ends will be achieved through the play of the children under our care.

Denial of Negative Education

At this point, we need to inform the reader that we have been doing a lot of "picking and choosing" in the quotations from *Emile* that have so far been presented. We have done this intentionally, therefore acknowledging it is no admission of guilt. For it is only by approaching our subject in this way that we can promote what would seem to be a clear understanding of Rousseau. Otherwise, we shall be guilty of helping to continue the confusion in educational theory that has very actively continued for the full two centuries since publication of *Emile*.[22] Pestalozzi, Froebel, and Kilpatrick all made practical recognition of the educational futility of full permissivism in connection with play or with any other activities of childhood, but none of them set up a *theory* that would avoid the dilemma of *good-active* permissivism on the one hand and *neutral-passive* dominance on the other—the Rousseau-Locke dilemma. To avoid this, we have to resort to the genius of John Dewey, to which we shall eventually come.

And Rousseau himself, in *Emile*, fell into this very dilemma. As soon as he says that "the only habit the child should be allowed to contract is that of having no habits,"[23] he immediately continues (in the next paragraph):

As soon as the child begins to take notice, what is shown him must be carefully chosen. The natural man is interested in all new things. He feels so feeble that he fears the unknown: the habit of seeing fresh things without ill effects destroys this fear. Children brought up in clean houses where there are no spiders are afraid of spiders, and this fear often lasts through life. I never saw peasants, man, woman, or child, afraid of spiders.[24]

And in the second following paragraph:

All children are afraid of masks. I begin by showing Emile a mask with a pleasant face, then some one puts this mask before his face; I begin to laugh,

[22] It may be of interest to note that this volume is published shortly after the second centennial year of the publication of *Emile* (1762–1962).

[23] *Op. cit.,* p. 30.

[24] *Ibid.,* p. 30. Italics ours.

they all laugh too, and the child with them. By degrees I accustom him to less pleasing masks, and at last hideous ones. If I have arranged my stages skilfully, far from being afraid of the last mask, he will laugh at it as he did at the first. After that I am not afraid of people frightening him with masks.[25]

Then this paragraph follows:

If Emile must get used to the sound of a gun, I first fire a pistol with a small charge. He is delighted with this sudden flash, this sort of lightning; I repeat the process with more powder; gradually accustom him to the sound of the gun, to fireworks, cannon, and the most terrible explosions.[26]

In this *exemplification* of what Rousseau would like to have done, it is obvious that there is a lot of *choosing* on the part of the tutor; hence, supervision. This is clear violation of negative education, and is exactly what Locke would have us do. Moreover, this is not an exceptional case; we have not found a single illustration in *Emile* of what Rousseau says he would do, were he to do the job himself, that is at all different in principle from this. Rousseau's examples consistently show selection by the tutor. In fact, at one place Rousseau actually says:

To select these objects, to take care to present him constantly with those he may know, to conceal from him those he ought not to know, this is the real way to training his early memory; and in this way you must try to provide him with a storehouse of knowledge which will serve for his education in youth and his conduct throughout life.[27]

Then:

Take the opposite course with your pupil; let him always think he is master while you are really master. . . . No doubt he ought only to do what he wants, but he ought to want to do nothing but what you want him to do. He should never take a step you have not foreseen, nor utter a word you could not foretell.[28]

25 *Ibid.*, p. 30. In this footnote we cannot refrain, for the literary touch, from including the next paragraph (italics ours):
When Hector bids farewell to Andromache, the young Astyanax, startled by the nodding plumes on the helmet, does not know his father; he flings himself weeping upon his nurse's bosom and wins from his mother a smile mingled with tears. What must be done to stay this terror? Just what Hector did; put the helmet on the ground and caress the child. In a calmer moment one would do more; one would go up to the helmet, play with the plumes, let the child feel them; at last the nurse would take the helmet and place it laughingly on her own head, *if indeed a woman's hand dare touch the armour of Hector.*
26 *Ibid.*, pp. 30–31.
27 *Ibid.*, p. 76.
28 *Ibid.*, pp. 84–85. Italics ours.

Later he twits Locke for first proposing this principle, then momentarily forgetting it:

Locke, in the midst of the manly and sensible advice he gives us, falls into inconsistencies one would hardly expect in such a careful thinker. The same man who would have children take an ice-cold bath summer and winter, will not let them drink cold water when they are hot, or lie on damp grass. But he would never have their shoes water-tight; and why should they let in more water when the child is hot than when he is cold, and may we not draw the same inference with regard to the feet and body that he draws with regard to the hands and feet and the body and face? If he would have a man all face, why blame me if I would have him all feet?[29]

And on page 178 Rousseau says, "Nothing must be left to chance."

There are numerous lengthy examples in which Rousseau shows to what lengths he would go *to get Emile to want to do what he* (Rousseau) *wants Emile to want to do*. For example, on pages 135–138 a complicated arrangement is made with a conjuror at a county fair in order that Emile may learn how magnets work. On pages 98–101 games are played in the dark to help Emile learn how to judge distances without measuring instruments. On pages 62–64 he describes how Robert, the gardener, helps Emile find that he must be considerate of both the property and the feelings of others. We quote the following example because it is not as lengthy as most:

But Emile is educated in a simpler fashion. We take so much pains to teach him a difficult idea that he will have heard nothing of all this. At the first word he does not understand, he will run away, he will prance about the room, and leave me to speechify by myself. Let us seek a more commonplace explanation; my scientific learning is of no use to him.

We were observing the position of the forest to the north of Montmorency when he interrupted me with the usual question, "What is the use of that?" "You are right," I said. "Let us take time to think it over, and if we find it is no use we will drop it, for we only want useful games." We find something else to do and geography is put aside for the day.

Next morning I suggest a walk before breakfast; there is nothing he would like better; children are always ready to run about, and he is a good walker. We climb up to the forest, we wander through its clearings and lose ourselves; we have no idea where we are, and when we want to retrace our steps we cannot find the way. Time passes, we are hot and hungry; hurrying vainly this way and that we find nothing but wood, quarries, plains, not a landmark to

[29] *Ibid.,* p. 93.

guide us. Very hot, very tired, very hungry, we only get further astray. At last we sit down to rest and to consider our position. I assume that Emile has been educated like an ordinary child. He does not think, he begins to cry; he has no idea we are close to Montmorency, which is hidden from our view by a mere thicket; but this thicket is a forest to him, a man of his size is buried among bushes. After a few minutes' silence I begin anxiously—

Jean Jacques. My dear Emile, what shall we do to get out?

Emile. I am sure I do not know. I am tired, I am hungry, I am thirsty. I cannot go any further.

Jean Jacques. Do you suppose I am any better off? I would cry too if I could make my breakfast off tears. Crying is no use, we must look about us. Let us see your watch; what time is it?

Emile. It is noon and I am so hungry!

Jean Jacques. Just so; it is noon and I am so hungry too.

Emile. You must be very hungry indeed.

Jean Jacques. Unluckily my dinner won't come to find me. It is twelve o'clock. This time yesterday we were observing the position of the forest from Montmorency. If only we could see the position of Montmorency from the forest—

Emile. But yesterday we could see the forest, and here we cannot see the town.

Jean Jacques. That is just it. If we could only find it without seeing it.

Emile. Oh! my dear friend!

Jean Jacques. Did not we say the forest was—

Emile. North of Montmorency.

Jean Jacques. Then Montmorency must lie—

Emile. South of the forest.

Jean Jacques. We know how to find the north at midday.

Emile. Yes, by the direction of the shadows.

Jean Jacques. But the south?

Emile. What shall we do?

Jean Jacques. The south is opposite the north.

Emile. That is true; we need only find the opposite of the shadows. That is the south! That is the south! Montmorency must be over there! Let us look for it there!

Jean Jacques. Perhaps you are right; let us follow this path through the wood.

Emile. (Clapping his hands.) Oh, I can see Montmorency! there it is, quite plain, just in front of us! Come to luncheon, come to dinner, make haste! *Astronomy is some use after all.*

Be sure that he thinks this if he does not say it; no matter which, provided

I do not say it myself. He will certainly never forget this day's lesson as long as he lives, while if I had only led him to think of all this at home, my lecture would have been forgotten the next day.[30]

Rousseau as Follower of Comenius and Locke

We see how thoroughly, in his examples, Rousseau forsakes negativistic permissivism and adopts the Lockean principle of closely supervised play. The last paragraph of the preceding excerpt ends with the admonition, "Teach by doing whenever you can, and only fall back upon words when doing is out of the question." This is in line with both Comenius (*Orbis Pictus*) and Locke in their insistence on ideas as the outgrowth of personal observation, with words arbitrarily applied after the ideas have been established. Moreover, "We learn to do by doing" is an expression highly familiar to twentieth-century readers, commonly but erroneously attributed to Dewey—who never said it—but in exact accord with Thorndike's psychology and pedagogy (Chapter 10). As we shall see when we come to him, Thorndike is a very faithful twentieth-century counterpart of Locke as this learning-by-doing (habit formation) principle attests, and herein we find another aspect of Rousseau that is Lockean rather than "Roussellian." Furthermore, Rousseau's insistence that Emile shall learn only *useful* things also conforms to a Lockean principle; that of *education for use*. Actually, the whole pattern represented by the practical examples given by Rousseau is thoroughly Lockean—education as habit formation and for use.

Rousseau's Theory Versus Rousseau's "Practice"

For the foregoing reasons, it seems that we must make a distinction between Rousseau's theory and Rousseau's "practice,"[31] and we shall ask the reader to bear with us in so doing. As for Rousseau as educator, this seems to be his significant inconsistency or self-contradiction. To set forth a theory that points in one direction (permissivism) and to intersperse with it a set of illustrations that employ a thoroughly different theory (planned and supervised manipula-

---

[30] *Ibid.*, pp. 143–144. Italics ours.
[31] Even though we recognize that Rousseau never really did any actual practicing.

tion) is indeed self-contradictory, as well as quite confusing. It is confusing, however, only to those who do not realize what is being done; to those not sensitive to the requirements of theoretical thought or logic. It is loose-minded individuals of this kind who find it frequently necessary to offer the apology, "Well, that's my theory but don't take it too seriously." And to this we feel that the proper rejoinder is, "If you can't take a theory seriously, don't take it at all." For straight or logical thought and scientific procedure are unachievable otherwise.

There would seem to be no question, however, that Rousseau's *theory,* even though itself going so far as to justify license and even licentiousness, has in actual fact been a great force in promoting the freedom for children in classrooms that they sorely need if their latent potentialities are to be given maximal development. It seems to be a "fact of life" that, in order to get a hearing, a pioneer has to overstate his case; otherwise, people pay him no mind. It is those who follow who must instill order into what may for a time seem, and perhaps actually be, chaotic.

The distinction between liberty and license is an old one and, if Rousseau's *good-active* assumption were indeed in true accord with human nature, then certainly would Rousseau's theory promote liberty and not license. But down-to-earth experience with youngsters seems not to support the *good-active* assumption. And merely to say that children are to have liberty but not license is not a clear directive to teachers; it fails to tell them when to do what, even in generalized terms. Although what we are saying in this paragraph may not do much at this time toward clarifying and ordering the matter, we believe that heightened understanding will come as we follow American educational thought and practice from the first quarter of the nineteenth century into the second half of the twentieth. The direct impact of Rousseau's thinking did not seem to hit us until the second decade or so of the present century, and it is that impact which seemingly is so distressing to present-day critics of American education, at least of the lay variety. It is *educational permissivism* that they decry—Rousseau's *theory.* If that is what American teachers had been practicing for the past half-century, we should agree with them heartily. But is it?

However, since the wave of Roussellian reform reached us first by percolating through the work of Pestalozzi, we shall temporarily terminate consideration of the one and shift to the other. In the meantime, let us doff our hats for a moment as we pay tribute to one who contributed so much to what we have already achieved in making schools and schooling more educative than they used to be.

Suggested Readings

Ballinger, Stanley E., *The Natural Man: Rousseau*. In Nash, Paul, Kazamias, Andreas M., and Perkinson, Henry J., *The Educated Man: Studies in the History of Educational Thought*. New York: Wiley, 1965, Chap. 9, pp. 224–246.

Brumbaugh, Robert S., and Lawrence, Nathaniel M., *Philosophers on Education*. Boston: Houghton Mifflin, 1963, Chap. 4.

Cassirer, Ernst, *The Question of Jean Jacques Rousseau*, translated and edited by Peter Gay. Bloomington: Indiana University Press, 1963.

Davidson, Thomas, *Rousseau and Education According to Nature*. New York: Scribner, 1898.

Eby, Frederick, *The Development of Modern Education*, 2nd ed. Englewood Cliffs, N.J.: Prentice-Hall, 1952, Chap. 13.

Eby, Frederick, and Arrowood, Charles F., *The Development of Modern Education*. Englewood Cliffs, N.J.: Prentice-Hall, 1934, Chap. 13.

Morley, John, *Rousseau*, 2 vols. London: Macmillan, 1886.

Parker, Samuel C., *A Textbook in the History of Modern Elementary Education*. Boston: Ginn, 1912, Chaps. 8, 9.

Price, Kingsley, *Education and Philosophical Thought*. Englewood Cliffs, N.J.: Allyn and Bacon, 1962, Chap. 7.

Rousseau, J. J., *Emile*, translated by Barbara Foxley. New York: Dutton, 1911; reprinted in Everyman's Library, 1955.

Rousseau, J. J., *Jean-Jacques Rousseau on Education*, R. L. Archer (ed.). London: E. Arnold, 1928.

Rousseau, J. J., *The Minor Educational Writings of Jean Jacques Rousseau*, translated and edited by William Boyd. New York: Bureau of Publications, Teachers College, Columbia University, 1962.

Ulich, Robert, *History of Educational Thought*. New York: American Book, 1950, pp. 211–224.

Wynne, John P., *Theories of Education*. New York: Harper & Row, 1963, Chap. 2.

Pestalozzi was concerned with the problem of educating abandoned, destitute children, out of which grew his educational philosophy. Switzerland honors her great citizen by having created and now maintaining Pestalozzi Village in Trogen where, since World War II, displaced children have found a beautiful home as well as a fine education. (Courtesy of the Swiss National Tourist Office, New York)

6   *PESTALOZZI: The Art of Sense Impressionism*

> There is a strange contrast between the men Rousseau and
> Pestalozzi. Rousseau was a voice, and nothing else. Everything
> he did tended to lessen the influence of everything he wrote.
> But Pestalozzi taught mainly by action. In him the most in-
> teresting thing is *his life*.[1]
>
> R. H. QUICK

Johann Heinrich Pestalozzi was born in Zurich, Switzerland, on January 12,
1746, and died in Brugg, Aargau, on February 17, 1827. A reader may find
it significant to compare these dates with those of the American Revolution
(1776–1781), the French Revolution (1789–1799), and the life-span of
Napoleon (1769–1821), for these events certainly bore significantly on the life
of Pestalozzi. And it is not inconceivable that his life and work may some day
be recognized as having exerted an effect on Western civilization at least as
widespread and as permanent as the other events.

[1] Roger de Guimps, *Pestalozzi; His Life and Work,* translated by J. Russell, Introduction
by R. H. Quick. New York: Appleton-Century-Crofts, 1895, p. xv. Italics in original.

It is said that once, when asked after a visit to Paris whether he had seen Napoleon, Pestalozzi replied (of course, in jest), "No; and, what is more, Napoleon did not see me." Suffice it to say that on Sunday, August 26, 1792, the National Assembly of France honored Pestalozzi—along with George Washington, Thomas Paine, and James Madison of the United States, Jeremy Bentham, Thomas Clarkson, and William Wilberforce of Britain, Thaddeus Kosciuszko of Poland, Friedrich Gottlieb Klopstock of Germany, and other eminent humanitarians or lovers of freedom by the title of Citizen of the French Republic.

A peculiar person from childhood—an "impractical," idealistic dreamer—the story of Pestalozzi's life is a chronicle of failures. Yet, though he may be said to have lost every battle, the campaign he waged against the emptiness and the inconsequentiality of the schooling of his day was, without question, eminently successful. In fact, he has been characterized as one of the world's most successful failures.

Brought up in a home atmosphere of self-abnegation by a widowed mother and a dedicated nurse, he was so timid and clumsy in the presence of other children that they pinned upon him the sobriquet of Harry Oddity of Foolstown. Yet he got along with them, seemingly not greatly minding their jibes. He went through college at Zurich at a time when its faculty included advanced thinkers in religion, history, and political economy, with his own thinking so distinctly drawn in that direction that he early acquired the reputation of being a "radical." Here too he read the newly published *Emile* of Rousseau, this being in the mid-1760s.

During college, he was preparing to follow in his grandfather's footsteps by becoming a minister but, with his first sermon, he decided that the ministry was not for him and turned to the study of law. However, as a result of active participation in the promotion of reforms in behalf of the peasantry (fostered, in fact, by Rousseau's *Social Contract*), he became identified by the citizens of Zurich as a "dangerous revolutionary." In consequence, he could not hope for a public appointment that would enable him to work toward his life long objective—established perhaps even before college—of seeking to ameliorate the lot of downtrodden humanity. Therefore, he soon gave up law.

He then turned to farming, hoping not only to gain a livelihood but mainly to show the surrounding peasantry how to use the newly developing knowledge of intensive agriculture to achieve the profitable returns that we now know are possible from well managed market gardening. He spent a year in work and study on the farm of Tscheffeli, a noted agriculturist of the time, then (1768) bought 100 acres of swampland near Zurich on which he planned to grow madder, a plant at that time used mainly in the manufacture of certain dyes.

His plans, however, were grandiose when compared with his financial resources—anticipation of his own and his prospective wife's inheritances and a
loan by a mercantile firm of Zurich. In 1769 he and Anna Schulthess were
married, in 1770 their son, Jacobli, was born, and shortly thereafter an imposing
house was built, thenceforth called *Neuhof* (new household or home). But
barren swampland could not be reclaimed overnight and creditors (the merchants) became impatient, so in 1775 all was lost but the home and a small surrounding area. However, within a century the dream of Pestalozzi became indeed
a reality, these lost acres themselves yielding several luxuriant crops of market-
able vegetables every year.

As Jacobli reached 4 and 5 years of age, his father gave a thorough tryout to
Rousseau's educational "theory" as embodied in *Emile*. His diary of these
experiences shows clearly how Pestalozzi rapidly reached a realization that a firm
hand must be maintained even though Jacobli needed always to be dealt with as
a little boy; not as a man in miniature. He had to learn things on the basis of his
own findings, not through the behests of his father; yet his father had to
maintain a firm directive. This, of course, represented Rousseau's "practice"
rather than his theory (negative education), yet it was part of Rousseau (the
Lockean part).

Contrasting what he was learning about the upbringing of children with
what was then being done with (and to) children in the schools, Pestalozzi's
conviction of the urgent need for a complete renovation of educational practice
grew apace. And, in face of what perhaps to anyone but "Harry Oddity of
Foolstown" would be recognized as insuperable obstacles, he decided to do
something. He turned Neuhof with its little plot of ground into an orphanage
that could care for about 80 homeless waifs, gathered from near and not so
near, wherein he (and his family) "lived like a beggar in order to learn how to
make beggars live like men."

Working from hand, through head, and to heart, the orphanage was conducted as a cooperative enterprise, to be ultimately self-supporting, wherein
each child would progressively learn and perform the various tasks needed in
the maintenance of a home for all. And, by way of the experiences so gained,
they would learn how to make a life as well as a living. By the work of their
hands they would get the "sense impressions" out of which ideas (*head*) would
form. Ideas, the assumed precursor of actions, hence habits, would then coalesce
into habit patterns—Pestalozzi seeing, of course, that they were *right* ones—
thereby begetting character (*heart*). This was Pestalozzi's theory of how children learn—as he later called it, *The Art of Sense Impressionism*—a thoroughly
Lockean theory.

As a by-product of the learning process but a necessity for the plan by which the orphanage had any promise whatever of becoming self-supporting, the children would perform the labors required for carrying on the affairs of the "household." In an appeal (early 1776) for subscriptions to enable him to get his venture on its feet, Pestalozzi had this to say:

I beg the friends of humanity to entrust me for six years with a few florins yearly. I shall return them in annuities, beginning from the tenth year, which will be easy for me to do from the gains of the workmen whom I shall have trained.

If I succeed in obtaining this help I promise to devote all my time and strength to the education of poor forsaken children. I promise to proportion the number of admissions to the amount that is allowed me, I promise to teach all the children to read, write, and count; and the boys the chief occupations of farming and tillage as far as I can, the care of meadows and pasture; the different kinds of grasses, care of fruit and forest trees, &c. The care of the house also will teach the girls gardening, domestic work and sewing.

The occupation for winter will chiefly be the spinning of cotton.[2]

But the 50–80 little and not-so-little "beggars" that Pestalozzi gathered around him provided neither the determination nor the manpower needed to maintain a venture of such dimensions, even when first supplemented by money from private donors, much of which was supposed to be repaid after 10 years. Hence, though a marked success in terms of human rehabilitation, by 1780 the orphanage had to be abandoned. The donors were never repaid, including Madame Pestalozzi who contributed most of her own inheritance. For almost 20 years, though they still had Neuhof, the Pestalozzis lived in direst poverty, supported almost wholly by what little he received from his writings.

And during those years he did write; six books were published, chief of which was *Leonard and Gertrude* (1782). A simple novel depicting the life of a Swiss peasant family in which the mother, Gertrude, not only brought up and taught the children in Pestalozzi's way but also succeeded in rehabilitating a kind but drunkard husband, the book became immediately popular. For Pestalozzi, however, it was a treatise on education and that aspect was essentially unrecognized by its many readers. Hence, for him it was a failure—so much so that 20 years later (1802) he published a sequel, *How Gertrude Teaches Her Children,* in which he made very clear his educational intent. But this book had little sale. Moreover, since as a royalty for *Leonard and Gertrude* Pestalozzi had received only a specified lump-sum payment and not a large one at that, he received no financial advantage from its popularity.

[2] Roger de Guimps, *Pestalozzi: His Aim and Work.* Syracuse: C. W. Bardeen, 1889, p. 31.

Mainly due perhaps to his writings during this period, however, Pestalozzi became widely known and respected through central Europe, as is partially attested by the honor bestowed upon him in 1792 by the French National Assembly. The reader is also reminded that these years (1780–1798) encompassed some of the American Revolution as well as the first quarter-century of the national life of the United States, all of the French Revolution, and the beginnings of the period of Napoleon—heady years in American and European history. Moreover, if in reading *Leonard and Gertrude* the reader should wonder at its lack of present-day sophistication, he should be reminded of Hawthorne's *House of Seven Gables* or Stowe's *Uncle Tom's Cabin*, both written many years later, to say nothing of today's Westerns on television.

By 1798, Pestalozzi's thinking about education had reached the point that he felt he had to do something about it. The barrenness of learning by rote, whether of a catechism or of anything else, trained neither head nor heart—neither intellect nor character. And the almost universal feeling of enmity and hatred between teacher and pupils—breaking as it did into frequent open revolt and, at least by the big boys, into knock-down fights—distressed Pestalozzi as the very antithesis of anything genuinely educational. His desire to establish a school for destitute children became little short of an obsession; in this school kindness and love would reign, and the intellectual powers of children would be fostered; beggars would grow into men and brutishness would give way to humaneness. He wanted to show the world that it could be done and how to do it.

In September of 1798, Pestalozzi's opportunity came. Following is an account of its coming:

The new French Republic wished to improve its neighbour the old Swiss Republic by centralization. Unterwalden, one of the three cantons which founded the Republic, proud of its own self-government, objected, and refused to take the oath of allegiance to the new Unitary Constitution imposed by France. The French army marched on Stanz, its chief town. It was resisted and repelled, but eventually it reached Stanz, and, exasperated by the vigorous and unexpected resistance, massacred the inhabitants and burnt the town, September 9th, 1798. There were 169 orphans, excluding 77 provided for by private charity and 237 other children practically homeless. The central Swiss Government, November 18th, determined to found an Orphans' Home at Stanz, and Pestalozzi was appointed manager, December 5th. He arrived two days later and opened the orphanage January 14th, 1799.[3]

---

[3] J. H. Pestalozzi, *How Gertrude Teaches Her Children,* edited and with an Introduction by Ebenezer Cooke. Syracuse: C. W. Bardeen, 1894, p. xix.

With the help of one lone servant, Pestalozzi opened the institution to the 50 most needy children, even before repairs had been completed. The building was a mess; the children were filthy, clothed in rags, infested with vermin, starved and scrawny, many immoral, and perhaps all mentally distraught. In an incredibly short time the establishment was set in order, the children clothed, fed, and on the road to health, and the educational program under way. One contemporary report reads: "It fairly bewilders one to see all that this excellent man does, and the improvement that he has made in such a short time on his pupils who are full of zeal to learn."

But the project was short-lived. The foregoing account of its beginning concludes with the following:

In five months there was war again. The convent was wanted for a military hospital, and on June 8th, 1799, sixty children were sent away, and Pestalozzi, almost dead, went to Gurnigle for a little rest.[4]

As to the idea underlying Pestalozzi's educational program, here is the way he himself spoke of it at Stanz:

I wished to combine study with work, the school with the workshop and in a measure to blend them. But I could not realise my plan for want of the means, materials, and tools. . . . Meanwhile, in the work of the children I attached less importance to the actual gain than to the bodily exercise, which, while developing their strength and skill, would one day enable them to win their bread.

I sought less in the beginning to teach my children to spell, read, and write, than to profit by these exercises to develop the powers of their mind as much as possible and in all directions. I made them spell by heart before having learnt their A B C, and the whole class could spell the most difficult words without knowing the letters. . . . I went rapidly over the fragments of geography and natural history in Gedilke's reading book. . . . They showed much intelligence in quoting the personal experiences they had with plants and animals. . . . I learned, myself, with the children. Our way was so simple and wanting in art, that I could not have scorned to learn and teach as I did.

My aim was so to simplify the means of teaching that the most ordinary man could easily grasp them and educate his children himself.[5]

Thus, approaching the turn of the century and past 50 years of age, this man, recognized today as one of the greatest of teachers of the Western world, had

[4] *Ibid.*, p. xx.
[5] de Guimps, *Pestalozzi: His Aim and Work*, pp. 94–95.

never taught in a regular school. After a short rest at Gurnigel, he cast about and after some difficulties received an appointment to teach a class of about 35 elementary school children in the "lower-class" section of the small town of Burgdorf (its French name, Berthoud), near Berne. This was perhaps in August, 1799.

Physically awkward, himself unschooled, fearful lest he should not give satisfaction to the authorities but convinced of the efficacy of his own ideas, Pestalozzi dispensed with Catechism, with Psalms, and, in fact, with all books. Here is his own account of what he did:

. . . I began again to say my a.b.c. from morning to night, following without plan the empirical course interrupted at Stans. I was indefatigable in combining syllables, in disposing them in graduated series; I did the same in numbers; I filled whole copy books in this way; I sought in every way to simplify the elements of reading and counting and to reduce them to a psychological connection; so that the child could pass easily from the first step to the second, from the second to the third, &c. But instead of letters it was lines, arcs, angles, and squares, that the pupils had to draw upon their slates.[6]

After quoting the above, de Guimps goes on to say,

At the same time Pestalozzi placed before the children large drawings representing various objects which he wished them to observe and describe. One day, he made them study in this way a drawing of a window: the children had to count the number of panes, sashes, &c. During this exercise, one of them kept his eye constantly fixed on the window of the room and ended by saying: "Could we not learn as well from the window itself as from the picture?"

To Pestalozzi this was a ray of light. "The child is right," he cried, "he wants nothing to intervene between himself and nature." Immediately he put his drawings aside and made the pupils observe the objects which were in the room.[7]

After eight months of such teaching, the children were given an examination by the school commission, which under date of March 31, 1800, issued a most laudatory public statement (addressed ostensibly to Pestalozzi), the third paragraph of which reads as follows:

Whilst by the laborious method hitherto pursued children from five to eight years of age only learn the letters, to spell and read, your pupils have not only accomplished this task with such a degree of perfection as we have not met with

[6] *Ibid.,* p. 100.
[7] *Ibid.,* pp. 100–101.

before, but the cleverest among them distinguished themselves by their beautiful writing, their talent for drawing and counting. You have succeeded with all in arousing and cultivating the taste for history, natural history, measuring, geography, &c., in such a way that their future masters will see their work incredibly simplified if they are able to take advantage of this preparation.[8]

So did recognition of the efficacy of his pedagogical ideas finally come to this indefatigable man. Actually, his classroom procedures would harly be tolerated today. Here is a description by Ramsauer—first a pupil of Pestalozzi at Burgdorf and later a teacher at Yverdon—of class work during the summer of 1800:

There was no regular school plan nor order of lessons; and Pestalozzi did not limit himself to any fixed time, but often went on with the same subject for two or three hours. We numbered about sixty boys and girls from eight to fifteen years of age; our lessons lasted from eight o'clock in the morning till eleven; and in the afternoon from two o'clock till four, and the teaching was limited to drawing, arithmetic and exercises in language.

There was neither reading nor writing; the pupils had no text-books nor copy books and they learned nothing by heart. We had neither drawing models nor directions but slates only and red chalk, and whilst Pestalozzi made us repeat sentences about natural history as language exercises, *we could draw whatever we liked*: some drew little men and women; others houses; others again traced lines and arabesques according to their fancy. Pestalozzi never looked at what we drew or rather scribbled; but by the cuffs and elbows of our coats one could see that the scholars had made use of the red chalk. As for arithmetic we had between every two scholars a little frame divided into squares in which were points that we could count, add, multiply, subtract, and divide.

. . .

Our master had not patience to go back, and in his excessive zeal he troubled himself little with the individual pupil. The exercises in language were the best, those especially upon the paper of the schoolroom, which were true exercises in intuition. We spent hours before that old and torn paper, occupied in examining the pattern, holes and tears, in reference to number, form, position, and colour, also in formulating our observations into sentences more and more developed.

Then he said to us:

Boys! What do you see? (He never mentioned the girls.)

Answer: A hole in the paper.

         A tear in the paper.

Pest: Well! Repeat after me:

[8] *Ibid.*, pp. 101–102.

> I see a hole in the paper,
> I see a long hole in the paper,
> Behind the hole I see the wall,
> I see figures on the paper,
> I see black figures on the paper,
> I see round and black figures on the paper,
> I see a square yellow figure on the paper.

Beside the square yellow figure I see a round black one. The square figure is joined to the round figure by a wide black stripe, &c.

The exercises on natural history were not so well understood.

As Pestalozzi, in his zeal, did not notice the time he often went on from 8 o'clock till 11 with the same subject.[9]

Ideas on Teaching—"Experience Curricula"

As to Pestalozzi's major ideas about teaching, perhaps two are crucial; both represent what to him was the meaning of the Roussellian principle of "following nature." The first was that of understanding and sympathizing with children's wants, wishes, and desires; the second was following the plan that he called "The Art of Sense Impressionism" (*The ABC of Anschauung*). Of the former we have already spoken. It was not maudlin permissivism; it was, rather, what might be expressed as sympathetic but stern understanding. The latter led to his idea later expressed by Louis Agassiz in the motto "Study Nature, not Books," and tended to promote classroom practices such as those described by Ramsauer in the passage just quoted. Here is the way Pestalozzi himself once stated the principle:

. . . But we are not yet so far advanced as the Appenzell woman, who in the first weeks of her child's life, hangs a large, many-coloured, paper bird over his cradle, and in this way clearly shows the point at which the Art should begin to bring the objects of Nature firmly to the child's clear consciousness.

Dear friend! Whoever has seen how the two and three-weeks old child stretches hands and feet towards this bird, and considers how easy it would be for the Art to lay a foundation for actual sense-impressions of all objects of Art and Nature in the child by a series of such visible representations, which may then be gradually made more distinct and extended—Whoever considers all this and then does not feel how we have wasted our time on Gothic monkish educa-

[9] John Ramsauer in de Guimps, *ibid.*, pp. 104–105. Italics in original.

tional rubbish, until it has become hateful to us,—truly cakes and ale are wasted on him.

To me the Appenzell bird, like the ox to the Egyptians, is a holy thing, and I have done everything to begin my instruction at the same point as the Appenzell woman. I go further. Neither at the first point, nor in the whole series of means of teaching, do I leave to chance what Nature, circumstance, or mother-love may present to the sense of the child before he can speak. I have done all I could to make it possible, by omitting accidental characteristics, to bring the essentials of knowledge gained by sense-impression to the child's senses before that age, and to make the conscious impressions he receives, unforgetable.[10]

As is perhaps obvious, Pestalozzi's *ABC of Anschauung,* or Art of Sense Impressionism, is highly reminiscent of, if not identical with, the Artistotelian-Comenian-Lockean principle of *tabula rasa* with its principle that there is nothing in the mind except what is first received by way of the senses. Hence, in Pestalozzi we have a follower of Rousseau who espouses Lockean strategy. This, however, was not new, for a writer of almost a century ago made the suggestion that Rousseau's *Emile* was the story of a youngster actually brought up and educated by none other than John Locke himself. We do not vouch for the validity of this assertion; we merely repeat it. Rousseau, therefore, in essence adopted Lockean (*neutral-passive*) *practice* and explained it as if it exemplified Roussellian (*good-active*) *theory.* This we have already noted. Now, we see it reappearing. In Pestalozzi, we find that we must follow nature, but we must assume that nature starts with "atomistic" sense impressions and out of them builds concepts as broad and far-reaching as human imaginations have flown, or can fly. And in Comenius' *Orbis Pictus,* we find little that is different from Pestalozzi's *ABC of Anschauung,* also based supposedly on the dictum of "following nature." But with both Pestalozzi and Comenius we find conscious rejection of Rousseau's principle of "negative education." They assumed that, in order to *follow* nature, we must first know nature—know what constitutes the natural order of child development—and, by using such knowledge, organize curricula that will take advantage of nature by working *with* her. We must know child psychology; we must not assume that children are merely adults in miniature.

We hope, from this, it is evident that we are not short-selling Comenius, Locke, Rousseau, or Pestalozzi. They all tend to "add up" to much the same educational strategy—*experience curricula.* But their various formal assumptions regarding human nature—*good-active, neutral-passive,* or whatever they may be—

10 Pestalozzi, *op. cit.,* p. 146.

do not provide a clear, consistent *rationale* for educational theory. For the present, we must pay our respects to the *intuitions* of these pioneers, note both their strengths and their shortcomings, and see what has come of both in terms of educational practice, especially in the United States.

To say that Pestalozzi had the "feel" for teaching as today we think it should be done is seemingly a fully justified statement. His *empathy* for children in learning situations seemed to be so keen that whatever methodological devices he employed were successful. But many were successful only in the hands of Pestalozzi; in the hands of others the outcomes were often quite the contrary. Moreover, as recognized by many of his contemporaries and even by himself, Pestalozzi's written theory suffered the fault of virtually all theories-in-the-making; it embodied points or aspects of confusion and even of self-contradiction. Hence, those who sought to follow him were far from agreement among themselves as to what to follow and, naturally, each thought what he saw and did was the real Pestalozzi. The confusion and consequent discord were seemingly a major cause for the slow but steady decline and final failure during the last two-thirds of the 20-year existence of the world-renowned school at Yverdon.

Burgdorf and Yverdon

Returning to our narrative, by midyear 1800 steps were being taken by Pestalozzi's friends to help him achieve wider dissemination of his reforms. By late October of that year, he was able to announce the opening of an educational Institute at the castle of Burgdorf, which was to be a boarding school for children and at the same time a demonstration or normal school for training teachers. The Institute opened early in 1801. Hermann Krüsi was the first fellow teacher to aid Pestalozzi in this undertaking and, soon afterwards, he was joined by Johannes Niederer, Johannes Buss, Gustav Tobler, and Joseph Neef.

It was during the three and one-half years of the Institute at Burgdorf that Pestalozzi is generally credited with doing his best work. His colleagues were able and dedicated men, all of whom seem to have caught the true spirit of his attempts at reform. Reports by supporters were highly favorable and visitors— men of eminence—came from many countries of western Europe. These, in turn, gave glowing reports at home and the fame of the Institute spread rapidly. Applications for enrollment soon exceeded capacity and further ones had to be denied.

However, in 1803 Swiss political affairs began to change, culminating in 1804 by the cantonese government of Berne requisitioning the castle as a residence for the prefect of the district. In June, 1804, Pestalozzi moved his school to an old convent at Munchenbuchsee, three or four miles outside the city of Berne. There it remained only until the following October, when the move was begun that brought Pestalozzi to his most famous school, in another old castle—this time at Yverdon.

It was while at Burgdorf that Pestalozzi published what is probably his most important book, *How Gertrude Teaches Her Children*—though the title is a bit misleading since the book was mostly a presentation of Pestalozzi's ideas on teaching rather than on how Gertrude taught. Careful reading of this book could well be made a requirement for all students of educational theory, since it has much of significance even for mid-twentieth-century thinking. In it, "intuition" (*The ABC of Anschauung*) is vital. As stated by de Guimps, intuition is "what Pestalozzi calls direct and experimental perception, whether in the domain of the physical or moral; intuitive ideas are those that result immediately from perceptions. All descriptions, explanations, and definitions are ineffectual upon the mind of the child if they do not rest upon already acquired ideas.[11]

One of Pestalozzi's leading biographers has summed up his pedagogical principles as follows:

1. Intuition is the basis of instruction.
2. Language should be linked with intuition.
3. The time for learning is not the time for judgment and criticism.
4. In every branch, teaching should begin with the simplest elements and proceed gradually according to the development of the child, that is, in psychologically connected order.
5. Sufficient time should be devoted to each point of the teaching in order to ensure the complete mastery of it by the pupil.
6. Teaching should aim at development and not dogmatic exposition.
7. The educator should respect the individuality of the pupil.
8. The chief end of elementary teaching is not to impart knowledge and talent to the learner, but to develop and increase the powers of his intelligence.
9. Power must be linked to knowledge; and skill to learning.
10. The relations between the master and the pupil, especially as to discipline, should be based upon and ruled by love.
11. Instruction should be subordinated to the higher aim of education.[12]

In principles 1, 2, and 6, we see the Comenian-Lockean order of sensation-idea-word. In 4 and 5 is the Comenian-Lockean idea of progression from par-

[11] *Pestalozzi: His Aim and Work,* p. 147.
[12] H. Morf in de Guimps, *Pestalozzi: His Aim and Work,* pp. 154–155.

ticular to general, or from simple to complex; essentially the process of *induction* in its strict philosophical sense. In 7 and 10 we see a reflection of the Roussellian concept of following or respecting child nature, and in 8, perhaps less clearly, that of "development from within." Thus, in his own way Pestalozzi was carrying forward, modifying, and making additions to an outlook on teaching that already had a long history in the thinking of progressive-minded men—men ahead of their times.

The first years at Yverdon were an extension of Burgdorf. Eminent visitors came in increasing numbers, and also young persons who were sent or who came voluntarily for the purpose of observing and studying firsthand the Pestalozzian way. In fact, entertainment of and demonstrations for visitors came to take up so much of Pestalozzi's time that, together with other diversions, it became impossible for him to do much, if any, teaching himself.

Of the many young persons who, either as pupils or as observers, came to Yverdon during the early years of the school, one individual and one group deserve special mention. The former was Friedrich Froebel[13] who made a two-week visit in August, 1805, and later returned for a two-year stay (1808–1810). During this time he was both pupil and teacher but in either role he was studying Pestalozzianism. The latter was a group of 17 young Germans, sent at various times by Frederick William III of Prussia under the instigation of the German philosopher, Fichte. These young Germans were explicitly instructed to look, not for the detailed procedures followed at the school, but for the basic spirit of the teaching. And successful they seem to have been for they returned to Germany, later to occupy various positions of responsibility in the educational system of the new Prussia, at that time recovering from its disastrous conflict with Napoleon (October, 1806).

Full success for the school, however, was short-lived. As noted above, Pestalozzi could do little teaching himself, so it had to be done by others and, when the master himself did not have clearly in mind what he would have done, it is understandable that others would also be unclear. Krüsi, Niederer, and Tobler went with Pestalozzi from Burgdorf to Yverdon, Tobler to remain for less than five years. Niederer devoted more effort and time to writing than to personal contacts with pupils, his philosophical bent fitting him especially for that role. Of the original coworkers at Burgdorf, Krüsi alone remained primarily a teacher, accompanied however by the young John Ramsauer who had been an older pupil at Burgdorf and became the teacher on whom Pestalozzi relied most heavily for conducting demonstration classes when especially important visitors were being entertained at Yverdon.

[13] See Chapter 9.

One other—Joseph Schmid—completed the core of those responsible for Yverdon. Schmid was a pupil at Burgdorf, coming there from a peasant home in the Tyrolean mountains. At Yverdon he quickly became proficient in the Pestalozzian way of teaching arithmetic, algebra, geometry, and trigonometry, but a systematic mind and a determined will soon gained for him Pestalozzi's confidence as the one to administer the school. However, in this capacity he soon became so domineering toward the other teachers that in 1810 he was faced with open revolt, led by Niederer, and had to be dismissed.

Thus, from even before 1810 but especially from then on, the Institute began to decline, both instructionally and administratively. The newer teachers had neither the knack nor the understanding of the early ones and Schmid's administrative capacities were sorely missed. Finally, early in 1815 Schmid was requested, by Niederer himself, to return and take charge. According to de Guimps,

Schmid returned to the castle of Yverdon at Easter, 1815, Pestalozzi received him as a saviour, a son who was sacrificing himself for his father, and he vowed eternal gratitude to him.

As soon as he arrived, Schmid set about quietly and coldly all the necessary reforms; he worked nearly all day and all night. He dismissed useless masters, lowered the salary of others, checked waste, re-established the order and regularity of the lessons, as well as the discipline of the pupils. All the good fellow-workers willingly seconded him in these reforms, which they felt to be necessary.[14]

But Schmid was seemingly not content merely to put things in order. He proceeded ruthlessly and persistently to become master of all, including Pestalozzi, who by then was almost 70 years old and occasionally ill. Moreover, in December of that year (1815) Madame Pestalozzi died, a severe blow to her devoted husband.

The year 1816 might be deemed the beginning of the end, though the Institute continued for another 10 years. Schmid's hold on Pestalozzi had become seemingly complete; so much so that the latter turned against even his old colleagues. Ramsauer left during the spring, after repeated slightings by Schmid. Later, 16 German teachers—masters, undermasters, and student teachers —headed by Blochmann wrote a letter of protest and, after receiving no satisfaction in a conference with Pestalozzi and Schmid, left Yverdon and returned

---

[14] *Pestalozzi: His Aim and Work,* p. 201.

to Germany. By then, of the "old guard" only Niederer and Krüsi remained; hence the teaching further deteriorated, enrollments decreased, and financial difficulties increased.

Hoping to obtain more money for the Institute, Schmid decided to publish a subscription edition of Pestalozzi's writings. A printed appeal for subscribers, ostensibly by Pestalozzi but believed by Niederer and Krüsi to be the work of Schmid and deemed by them to be unworthy of Pestalozzi, was so odious to those two longtime associates and devoted friends that they could remain no longer. Niederer and his wife opened a boarding school for girls, which remained at Yverdon for 20 years and afterwards was moved to Geneva where Niederer died in 1843. Krüsi also established a school of his own at Yverdon but in 1822, even though the school was flourishing, accepted a call to take charge of the cantonal school at Trogen, Canton Appenzell. Here he was so successful that in 1833 a normal school was established at his native village of Gais and he was made principal. There he served till his death in 1844.

The rest of the Pestalozzian story must be told quickly. The publication of his works was a financial success, supported by grants from old friends such as the Kings of Prussia and of Bavaria and the Emperor of Russia. In all, it netted about 50,000 francs. But Schmid took charge of these proceeds for the support of the Institute, so that at his own death Pestalozzi was again almost penniless.

Meanwhile Niederer and Schmid entered into a bitter controversy, through newspapers, pamphlets, and even an extended lawsuit, all of which reflected unfavorably on both. Also, by the middle of 1817, practically all remaining experienced teachers—Boniface, Stern, Knusert, Hagnauer, and Lange—had departed to carry Pestalozzianism elsewhere.

So far, we have said nothing of Emmanuel von Fellenberg, the world-famous Swiss educator who early founded a school based on Pestalozzian ideas. After about four years of travel through France and Germany studying the conditions of the agricultural poor and, like Pestalozzi, deciding that education was sorely needed, Fellenberg decided to establish an institute in which he would combine general education with the learning of a trade. Returning to Berne, he purchased the nearby 600-acre estate of Hofwyl and, beginning in 1799, set up a school for children of the poor, a seminary for children of the higher classes, and a normal school. In 1804 when Pestalozzi was having to abandon the castle at Burgdorf and go elsewhere, Fellenberg invited him to become a partner at Hofwyl. This led to Pestalozzi's short stay at Munchenbuchsee, close to Hofwyl. But Fellenberg's was a dominating personality and Pestalozzi decided that a partnership would not work out satisfactorily, so chose Yverdon.

Now again in late 1817 while Pestalozzi was still in low spirits and poor health after the defections of his closest friends and co-workers, Fellenberg invited Pestalozzi to join him in establishing a school for middle-class children, to be run by Pestalozzi and located at a place chosen by him. But Schmid convinced Pestalozzi that he would be completely under Fellenberg's power, so for a second time a partnership with the latter was declined.

Finally, however, in 1818 Pestalozzi was successful in realizing a dream of a lifetime—to establish a school for poor children, to be run as he had attempted to run Neuhof and Stanz. In the tiny village of Clendy, near Yverdon, he started the school with 12 children, mostly orphans, devoting all his time to them and with the same success (even at age 72) as at Stanz. Such success again drew wide recognition and attracted visitors as well as more than doubling the enrollment. However, the old story of meddling by Schmid led in July, 1819, to amalgamation of the Clendy school into the Institute at Yverdon and its essential demise as a separate institution.

From then on, events went rapidly from bad to worse until in March, 1825, Pestalozzi left Yverdon to return to his old home at Neuhof, and the Institute was closed. At Neuhof, now the home of his grandson, Pestalozzi continued writing and even tried to start another school for the poor. But hard work, certain new disappointments, and a cold winter finally took their toll, and during the evening of February 17, 1827, the old man died. After a simple funeral ceremony, he was buried in the nearby village of Birr.

Suggested Readings

Barnard, H., *Pestalozzi and his Educational System.* Syracuse: C. W. Bardeen. No date.

de Guimps, Roger, *Pestalozzi: His Aim and Work.* Syracuse: C. W. Bardeen, 1889.

de Guimps, Roger, *Pestalozzi: His Life and Work,* translated by J. Russell and with an Introduction by R. H. Quick. New York: Appleton-Century-Crofts, 1895.

Eby, Frederick, *The Development of Modern Education,* 2nd ed. Englewood Cliffs, N.J., Prentice-Hall, 1952, Chap. 17.

Eby, Frederick, and Arrowood, Charles F., *The Development of Modern Education.* Englewood Cliffs, N.J.: Prentice-Hall, 1934, Chap. 17.

Krüsi, H., Jr., *Pestalozzi, His Life, Work, and Influence.* New York: American Book, 1875.

Monroe, W. S., *The Pestalozzian Movement in the United States.* Syracuse: C. W. Bardeen, 1907.

Parker, Samuel C., *A Textbook in the History of Modern Elementary Education.* Boston: Ginn, 1912, Chaps. 13–16.

Pestalozzi, J. H., *How Gertrude Teaches Her Children,* edited and with an Introduction by Ebenezer Cooke. Syracuse: C. W. Bardeen, 1894.

Pestalozzi, J. H., *Leonard and Gertrude,* translated and edited by Eva Channing. Boston: Heath, 1906.

Ulich, Robert, *History of Educational Thought.* New York: American Book, 1950, pp. 258–270.

Plate of School when in Draughts.

By the monitorial system, a teacher "taught" as many as 500 or more pupils in one room. He drilled a small group of older students in a lesson-segment. These students each then drilled a group of younger students. The aim was worthy: more education, cheaper, for more children, regardless of financial status. But it did not accomplish widespread literacy as had been hoped. New York City followed the system from 1806 to 1853. (Courtesy of The New-York Historical Society, New York City)

7 ᴙ *Our Later Nationalization Period*

We have noted previously the changes undergone by American education—elementary, secondary, and higher—to about 1825. The "three R's" had changed from "religion, readin', and ritin' " to "readin', ritin', and 'rithmetic." Secondary education had forsaken the Latin grammar school, had attempted to "go on its own" and prepare for life instead of for college but had been brought up short by college-entrance considerations, and had tried its first public high school. Higher education had turned from theological training to the liberal-arts idea and was in process of inaugurating professional education in medicine, law, and engineering.

The year 1825 is taken as the beginning of what is known as "The Great Educational Awakening," a period that, though witnessing gradual development of what had already been established in secondary and higher institutions, represented thoroughgoing change in elementary schooling, as well as the inauguration of systematic teacher-training, of educational administration and supervision, and of open recognition and adoption of the public-school idea. In short, this was the period of Horace Mann and Henry Barnard. By the time of the Civil War, most of the major aspects of today's school system had been inaugurated. Our whole national educational program was set, and ready to expand.

Growth of American educational thought and practice during the first half of the nineteenth century was not a simple, one-line affair. The almost complete autonomy of local school-districts made anything approaching it an impossibility. Westward expansion of the nation and the industrial revolution with its encouragement of urbanization introduced new factors effectual in shaping educational programs. Increasing urbanization, for example, by taking children off of farms where they work and play side by side with adults, eliminated the built-in opportunity for them automatically to absorb adult outlooks on life as well as adult skills. Hence, whole new fields of instructional obligations gradually devolved upon the schools, making three-R curricula wholly inadequate, certainly for areas classed as urban.

First, however, let us examine the effects that changing ideas regarding education had upon American educational practices. And in this regard the work of Pestalozzi seems to have been influential in a number of ways or through a number of different channels.

Pestalozzianism Enters the United States—The Neef-Maclure Channel

The earliest introduction of Pestalozzianism into the United States was by Joseph Neef and William Maclure. Neef, it will be recalled, was one of the teachers at Burgdorf. With the termination there, Neef set up a private school in Paris following Pestalozzian lines.

William Maclure (1763–1840), a Scotsman, made a fortune in his homeland, retired, came to Philadelphia, and turned to personal interests, particularly geology but also education. Traveling through Europe in 1804–1805, he heard of Pestalozzi and Fellenberg and visited both Yverdon and Hofwyl. Impressed especially with the spirit of cooperation and fraternity that he found at Yverdon, he tried to get Pestalozzi to set up a school in Philadelphia. Pestalozzi decided against it, but recommended Neef. Neef accepted, came to Philadelphia in 1806, and spent the next three years learning English. During this time he also wrote and published his *Sketch of a Plan of Education,* a book in English presenting the Pestalozzian idea. In 1809, he set up the school, underwritten by Maclure who also paid his expenses to America and probably supported him until the school's opening.

For the first three years, while in Philadelphia, the school was highly successful, but removal to the nearby town of Village Green turned it into a financial failure and, after a year, Neef moved the school to Louisville, Kentucky, at the invitation of certain interested citizens. However, since Louisville was then a town of only about 5000 population, it was hardly large enough to support such a school and, after two years, Neef purchased a nearby farm where he lived until 1826 when Maclure found him and invited him to New Harmony.

The New Harmony movement is historically important in ways other than educational, but our treatise must be confined to the latter. Robert Owen and William Maclure, both Scotsmen of wealth, decided to collaborate in sponsoring a socialistic community at New Harmony, Indiana. Maclure, besides making a considerable financial contribution, assumed responsibility for the educational program. Having lost track of Neef but thinking of him at once, Maclure finally located him and convinced him to set up the school system and take charge. Neef arrived with his family in March, 1826, and, until abandonment of the experiment in 1828, had a thoroughly Pestalozzian school in full swing. Following is an excerpt from what Maclure wrote about the instruction:

The great or fundamental principle is, never to attempt to teach children what they can not comprehend, and to teach them in the exact ratio of their understanding without omitting one line in the chain of ratiocination, proceeding always from the known to the unknown, from the most easy to the most difficult; practising the most extensive and accurate use of all the senses; exercising, improving, and perfecting all the mental and corporal faculties by quickening combination; accelerating and carefully arranging comparison; judiciously and impartially making deductions; summing up the results free from prejudice, and cautiously avoiding the delusions of the imagination, a constant source of ignorance and error.[1]

Conflict between Maclure and Owen, however, coupled perhaps with midwestern antipathy to something as rankly socialistic as the New Harmony idea, soon terminated the movement and Neef's school.

As to the Neef-Maclure channel by which Pestalozzianism came to the United States, it seems not to have been influential. It set up demonstrations of rather thoroughgoing Pestalozzianism in Pennsylvania, Kentucky, and Indiana, but America paid it little mind. It was too early. The right people were not touched and little came of it.

[1] George B. Lockwood, *The New Harmony Movement*. New York: Appleton-Century-Crofts, 1905, p. 236. For a most illuminating account of Pestalozzian principles and of "The Educational Experiment" at New Harmony, read the whole of Chapter 20, pp. 209–293.

The Mann-Barnard Channel

The second of the major channels—Mann-Barnard—was seemingly the vital one. Coupled with the names of Mann and Barnard are those of James G. Carter, John Griscom, Samuel Read Hall, William C. Woodbridge, Lowell Mason, and others.

John Griscom, a schoolman in the Philadelphia–New York region, visited European schools in 1818–1819 and in 1823 published a widely read report on what he saw, including a visit at Yverdon during which he talked with Pestalozzi. James G. Carter, a Massachusetts teacher who in 1835 was elected to the state legislature, was chiefly responsible for passage in 1837 of the bill establishing the Massachusetts State Board of Education. He was then appointed by the governor to the committee responsible for securing Horace Mann as Board secretary. As early as 1827, Carter had presented to the Massachusetts legislature a bill to establish a normal school but, although the bill received favorable consideration in the House, it lost by one vote in the Senate.

In 1823 at Concord, Vermont, Samuel Read Hall, minister in the local Congregational Church, set up what is credited as the first teacher-training school in the United States; a private school, conducted on a part-time basis. Distinctly Pestalozzian in outlook, he accepted women for training as well as men. He wrote a number of textbooks on teaching and on other aspects of school work, the leading one being *Lectures on School Keeping*. William C. Woodbridge, a New Englander, taught in an elementary school for deaf mutes from 1817 to 1820, visited Europe, and after his return published two textbooks in elementary geography (1822 and 1824) both distinctly Pestalozzian. On a return trip to Europe, he visited Swiss and German schools, especially those of Pestalozzi and Fellenberg. During the 1830s he edited and published the *American Journal of Education,* later named the *American Annals of Education and Instruction,* which carried many articles on Pestalozzianism.

Having become interested in music teaching as conducted at Yverdon and Hofwyl, Woodbridge influenced Lowell Mason to adopt it, first in the Boston Academy of Music and then in certain of the public schools of Boston. From about 1830 until his death in 1872, Mason worked to perfect and popularize his ideas. He stressed the singing of songs that children would learn and sing for the very love of it. First learning the songs by rote, the singers would later be introduced to musical notation, thereby gradually coming to know the technical aspects and achieving the various degrees of musicianship that their varying interests and capacities would make possible—simple to complex, known to un-known, concrete to abstract. From about 1840 to the close of his life Mason labored within Boston and without, but it was not until the year of his death (1872) that vocal-music instruction as conceived by him was finally introduced into all levels of the Boston public-school system.

Others who were active before the Civil War in encouraging the kind of teaching espoused by Pestalozzi if not Pestalozzianism itself were Bronson Alcott, father of Louisa May Alcott, who wrote *Little Men* and *Little Women;* Alexander D. Bache, great-grandson of Benjamin Franklin and president of Girard College; David P. Page, principal of the Albany Normal School (New York) and author of *Theory and Practice of Teaching,* the first American text-book to bear that title; Calvin E. Stowe, husband of Harriett Beecher Stowe, author of *Uncle Tom's Cabin,* who worked in Ohio and made a report on Prussian education that appeared when Mann was just entering the educational field; Warren Colburn, author of the famous textbook, *First Lessons in Arith-metic on the Plan of Pestalozzi* (1821); Karl Ritter and Arnold Guyot on the teaching of geography; Thomas H. Gallaudet, early promoter of schools for handicapped children; William Russell, founder of the *American Journal of Education* (not Barnard's *Journal* [see p. 123]), in which were published nu-merous articles by many of the aforementioned; and Louis Agassiz, Swiss natural-ist who became professor of natural history at Harvard University in 1848 and, though never directly connected with Pestalozzi, was instrumental in introducing sense-perceptionist (laboratory) principles into college and university science in-struction.

But to Horace Mann (1796–1859) and Henry Barnard (1811–1900) has gone credit for taking the lead in promoting the changes that transpired in elementary education between 1825 and 1860. Born on a small Massachusetts farm the fourth of five children, Mann's early years were much occupied with hard work helping to make the farm produce enough to support the family, and until he was 16 he attended school only from eight to ten weeks per year. In 1819, however, he graduated from Brown University as valedictorian of his class. After graduation he spent a year studying law in a lawyer's office at Wrentham, Massachusetts, then served two years as librarian and tutor in Latin at Brown. Afterwards he returned to the study of law, this time in Litchfield, Connecticut, and later established his own office at Dedham, Massachusetts, where he de-veloped a successful practice. In 1827 he was elected to the House of Representa-tives of Massachusetts and in 1833 to the state Senate where, in 1836 and 1837, he served as president. In April, 1837, sponsored in the House by Carter (see p. 118), the law was passed that established a State Board of Education. This

Board in turn would appoint a secretary to serve as the state school-officer who would report periodically to the Board and the Legislature. Neither Board nor secretary had administrative control of the schools of the state; they could only investigate, report, and recommend. Contrary to general expectation that Carter would become secretary, the Board instead appointed Mann and, though it meant giving up the much more lucrative practice of law, he accepted the appointment.

Though Mann had been interested in the improvement of education since his college days, when appointed secretary he knew little of its professional literature or of classroom methodology. Hence, his early attention was focused upon two rather obvious needs—institutions for training elementary-school teachers and a system of free, public (or "common") schools. Within six months after taking office in June, 1837, in the first of his 12 Annual Reports, he stressed the necessity of competent teachers and an adequate system of public schools. Two years later, at Lexington in September, 1849, the doors of the first *state* normal school to be established in the United States were opened, financed by an appropriation of $10,000 by the state legislature to match an equal amount given by Edmund Dwight, the Board member mainly responsible for Mann's appointment and for convincing him that he should accept.

Quickly setting about remedying his lack of technical knowledge in matters educational, Mann began reading professional books and visiting the schools themselves. Almost at once, too, he started delivering lectures to influential groups throughout the state, marshaling support for his anticipated reforms. Mann was an orator of the first rank, in a time when American oratory was in full flower. And in November, 1838, he initiated publication of his *Common School Journal,* which was continued until his resignation from the secretaryship in 1848.

In May, 1843, Mann sailed for a six-month trip to Europe, to serve as a vacation, an opportunity to observe European schools at first hand, and a wedding trip.[2] On this trip he visited schools in England, Ireland, Scotland, France, Belgium, and Holland; but most of all in Germany, including Hamburg, Magdeburg, Berlin, Potsdam, Halle, Weissenfels, Leipsig, Dresden, Erfurt, Weimar, Eisenach, Frankfurt am Main, the Grand Duchies of Nassau, Hesse-Darmstadt, and Baden, and the Rhenish province of Prussia. This entire trip was at his own expense.

Let us digress for a moment and return to Pestalozzi's school at Yverdon.

---

[2] This was his second marriage, his first wife having died in 1833. This bride was Mary Peabody, sister of Elizabeth Peabody, who later established the first English-speaking kindergarten in the United States; the third sister later became the wife of Nathaniel Hawthorne.

It will be recalled from the preceding chapter that, at Fichte's instigation, Frederick William III of the newly forming Germany had in 1808–1812 sent many German youths to study the Pestalozzian way, with strict injunctions to disregard detailed devices in favor of the basic atmosphere or spirit of the instruction. Recall also that the faculty breakup of 1816 led to the return to Germany of a number of able teachers and assistants. Spread across the resurgent German nation and under governmental encouragement, this personnel had done much to incorporate the ideas of developmental (inductive) teaching, sympathetic or empathetic handling of school children, and thorough mastery of subject matter by teachers, which Pestalozzianism represented. This is doubtless what Horace Mann was seeking in his visitations, and it is what he saw in Germany. The growing Prussian militarism after 1850 that led to the dominance of Bismarck, Mann perhaps saw but ignored. What he did not ignore and what he brought home and reported in his famed Seventh Annual Report (1844) was what can with seeming justification be considered the true spirit of the Swiss master—Yverdon before 1815.

Let it be said here that Pestalozzianism did not necessarily represent democracy in education. His was a benevolent paternalism, which was a thorough reversal of the almost sadistic discipline of the time. His was an understanding-level (inductive or developmental) type of instruction in contrast with the rote of long-established tradition. His was impartation by teachers of the thorough knowledge of content that enabled them to teach without textbook and in a way other than the slavish question-answer, question-answer type of oral quizzing that required only *lesson-hearers—not teachers*. This is what Mann seemingly found in Germany and brought home to Massachusetts and beyond. It was an admixture of the *neutral-passive* assumptions of *tabula rasa* (or *education as habit formation*) and the *good-active* assumptions of *education as unfoldment*. But it did not embody the genuine fusion of the conflict between active and passive (or reactive) assumptions regarding childhood (or learners) that in the twentieth century has been achieved by John Dewey's concept of *interaction* (see Chapter 12). Even today, however, more than a century after Horace Mann's visit, we are still confronted with educational *practice,* if not *theory,* that has found no real harmonization of the commonly recognized necessity, on one hand, for guidance by competent and empathetic teachers and, on the other, for responsible freedom on the part of students without sinking to anarchistic license. This, we believe, is today's fundamental problem of democratic educational theory.

Mann's Seventh Annual Report was so full of enthusiasm for German-Pestalozzian teaching that he immediately incurred the wrath of the "Boston school-masters"—specifically, 30 or more principals. Especially irritating was his indictment of corporal punishment, calling it a practice that had to be employed by inferior men to compensate for professional incompetence. They attacked; Mann replied; and for more than a year the altercation was vehement, with Mann finally emerging largely victorious. Though it attracted attention, however, Mann's Seventh Report should not be taken as overshadowing his others. All were significant, and rightly deserve their place as American educational classics of the nineteenth century.

Moreover, it should not be thought, either that Mann's actual reforms were universal, even in Massachusetts, or that all reforms that he promoted were Pestalozzian. As to the latter, public education was not a point of concern to Pestalozzi and, though Pestalozzian teaching required trained teachers, Mann had inaugurated his normal school program before his European trip, though he consulted the Pestalozzian-minded Henry Barnard and Thomas H. Gallaudet before so doing. The same question might be raised regarding Mann's Teachers' Institutes, started in 1845 after his return, since Barnard had first organized them in Connecticut in 1839. At any rate, in the Institutes many of the lecturers were distinctly Pestalozzi-inspired; e.g., Agassiz, Mason, Barnard, Krüsi (Jr.), Guyot, and Ritter.

School libraries, which Mann sponsored early, were hardly to be credited to Pestalozzi, whose dictum was "Study nature, not books," though it would hardly be just to imply that there was no place for books in a Pestalozzian system. In fact, it may be noted that the thoroughgoing Pestalozzian William Maclure was America's "first great founder of libraries," not only at New Harmony but in scores of other communities in Indiana and elsewhere.

Mann held the secretaryship for 12 years, until 1848, when he resigned to enter the United States House of Representatives, succeeding John Quincy Adams, who died in office. Here he served for five years, promoting humanitarian causes including the antislavery movement. In 1852 he ran for governor of Massachusetts but was unsuccessful and, in 1853 when his term in Washington expired, he accepted the presidency of a new school, still under construction—Antioch College of Yellow Springs, Ohio. This was to be (and still is) a distinctly forward-looking school—nonsectarian, coeducational,[3] and nonracial—and, as was to be expected, incessant labor and the overcoming of many difficulties were the order of every day in every year. Finally, during the hot August of 1859 after a period of ill health, Mann died, but not without fulfilling a behest

---

[3] Although Oberlin College was previously coeducational, Antioch was the first to admit men and women to the same classes.

in his last baccalaureate address in June of that year, "Be ashamed to die until you have won some victory for humanity."

Like Mann, Henry Barnard was born on a New England farm—near Haverford, Connecticut, on January 24, 1811—but in more favorable circumstances than was Mann. He attended a dame school, then a grammar school, and finally Yale, where he graduated in 1830. He taught school in the winter of 1830–1831 and in the spring of 1831 began the study of law. Admitted to the bar in 1835, he then took a six-month trip through Europe. Having heard, while at Yale, of Maclure's efforts to spread Pestalozzianism and of Fellenberg's work as well, he visited the latter at Hofwyl. During 1837–1840, he served in the Connecticut House of Representatives, securing passage in 1838 of a bill providing for establishment of a state Board of Commissioners of Common Schools and serving from 1838 until 1842 without pay as secretary of the Board.

In 1842 for political reasons, the Legislature discontinued the Board and shortly afterwards Mann offered Barnard the principalship of his second normal school, at Barre. Barnard declined, however, and later became State Superintendent of Schools of Rhode Island (1843–1849) before returning to Connecticut, this time as State Superintendent of Education (1850–1855). Failure of health both in 1849 and 1855 accounted for relinquishment of the latter two positions. In 1858 he became Chancellor of the University of Wisconsin but ill health again caught him and in 1860 he had to resign. In 1866–1867 he was President of St. John's College (Annapolis, Maryland) and in 1867 became the first United States Commissioner of Education. In 1870 he resigned, to devote the next 11 years to writing, finally retiring in 1881 and remaining in retirement until his death in 1900.

Even though Barnard was long an active school administrator and did much in addition to promote better schools in New England and elsewhere, it was as writer, editor, and publisher that he is recognized as doing his most important work. And chief among such publications was his *American Journal of Education*.

First issued in August, 1855, the *Journal* was continued for 32 years, even though operating continually at a financial loss. Barnard's own estimate was that this loss totalled about $30,000, or close to $1000 per year; at a subscription price first of three dollars and later of four dollars per year, the total number of paid subscriptions never exceeded 500. Yet it was considered by Barnard's contemporaries and has been by historians since then as in the top rank of American educational publications.

Barnard's purpose in the *Journal* was to make available to school people writings that would help them in their work. Articles covered practically the entire range of school concerns—building architecture; histories of various state, regional, and national associations dealing with education; growth of high schools and colleges, of kindergartens and the kindergarten idea, and of adult education; biographies of American and European educators; accounts of European school practices; selections from both Stowe's and Mann's reports on German schools; articles on educational matters by most of the leading educators of the time, many by Barnard himself. But ranking high, if not first, in attention were the ideas and the work of Pestalozzi. Pestalozziana included, besides excerpts from Mann's Seventh Annual Report, many articles by Barnard himself; works on Pestalozzi by European authorities such as Diesterweg and von Raumer; articles by William Russell (who in 1826–1830 published the first periodical bearing the name, *American Journal of Education,* afterwards purchased by William C. Woodbridge but soon given a different name and in no way connected with Barnard's *Journal*); numerous excerpts in translation from Pestalozzi's own writings; and so many others that the titles alone would occupy several pages. So important was this *Journal* considered that in 1892 the U.S. Office of Education prepared and published an index of the entire 32 volumes.

Pre-Civil War Changes in American Education

As for ideas and the people sponsoring them, the foregoing account brings us essentially to the time of the Civil War (1861–1865), which we have taken as the close of our *period of nationalization.* During that period (1750–1860) we not only established ourselves politically as an independent nation but we also built an educational system that was our own and had the basic characteristics of our system of today: free, public, tax-supported schools, with parochial or other private schools permitted but not to be supported by public moneys; graded schools of the ladder type wherein completion of one grade or level opens the way to the next (at that time on the 8–4–4 plan); school architecture to provide on the elementary level a separate room for each grade, with classes in the neighborhood of not more than 25–30 pupils; women teachers coming to take the place of men, especially in the lower and middle elementary grades; strong state and municipal supervision of elementary and secondary schools by superintendents and/or boards of education; formal teacher training in state-supported, college-level institutions (state normal schools); higher education provided in many states by state-supported, state-controlled universities and colleges; complete elimination of the pauper school principle. Without going into detail, we can elaborate a bit on each of the foregoing aspects.

We have already noted how the monitorial school movement, because of its low cost, gave the public school idea a chance to get its foot in the door. Public moneys being once appropriated for schools—even though, as in Philadelphia and New York City, essentially for "pauper schools"—gave the public a taste for that mode of financing and, after the educational tawdriness of the monitorial plan was realized, provided the precedent needed to use such moneys for school support even though the monitorial plan was rapidly losing public esteem.

But this transition did not come without the combination of a variety of forces.[4] There was the American Lyceum movement, sponsored by Josiah Holbrook, that was not only a matter of adult education but was also designed for "the advancement of education, especially common schools." We have noted the efforts of Horace Mann in behalf of "common schools," to which many others, including Barnard, contributed. Important was the early and continuous work of the movement to organize or unionize labor. From its major beginnings during Jackson's campaign for the presidency of the United States, organized labor has worked for public education of a general (nonvocational) kind. There were also the efforts of various organizations of professional school-people and interested laymen, such as the Western Academic Institute in Ohio, the New Jersey Society of Teachers and Friends of Education, and similar organizations in New York State, Pennsylvania, North Carolina, Florida, etc. Special meetings or conventions, both local and statewide, petitioned state legislatures to enact legislation providing for public schools. And it should be remembered that in New England, especially Massachusetts, the precedent for public education had been long since established—the Old Deluder Satan Law of 1647—even though leaders such as Mann and Barnard saw much still to be accomplished in their own time.

The mandatory "rate bills" of colonial times represented private school-financing even though the school itself might be essentially a community enterprise. Moreover, such bills were to be paid by parents or guardians as part of the total cost of raising children; childless persons incurred no obligations for financing schools, since schooling was thought to be essentially a matter of personal advantage—not a general advantage to community, commonwealth, state, or nation.

---

[4] See Ellwood P. Cubberley, *Public Education in the United States*. Boston: Houghton Mifflin, 1919; rev. ed., 1934, Chap. 6. This excellent report gives both details of the process and bibliographical source material.

When childless or wealthy persons did give additional financial support for schools, it was voluntary—a matter of private philanthropy such as crown grants or private subscriptions to charitable organizations like SPG, SPCK (see p. 15), or the Public School Society of New York City. Moreover, when moneys provided by philanthropy, or by those who paid their own rate bills, were used to pay rate bills for the children of self-declared paupers, we had at work what is known as the "pauper school" principle. Although this principle had its major beginnings in the southern colonies, it later spread northward and, with the advent of monitorial schools, became widely used for the presumed benefit of laboring people in the cities. Private gifts and bequests also were frequently made to provide school buildings and other facilities.

When public moneys first came to be used for support of schools, they were derived from a variety of sources. Land grants to the various colonies were begun early, proceeds from the sale of which were used to established endowments; current income from these being applied on current expenditures. Beginning with Ohio in 1802, National Land Grants to newly admitted states were inaugurated. These represented the sixteenth section of every range or township to be used for support of "common schools," and two townships for support of a state university. Following Ohio's lead, the new western states that benefited from the land grants dedicated them to the support of free, common (public) schools.

Direct local appropriations of public tax moneys were rather common in the New England colonies, and this was a source of substantial funds used by the Public School Society of New York City from 1805 till its disbandment in 1852. Such public appropriations were sometimes supplemented—as with the New York (City) Public School Society—by private subscriptions.

During the first half of the nineteenth century, lotteries and license taxes were widely used for raising school funds. Moneys from liquor, theatre, and lottery licenses were often designated for support of schools, together with taxes on banks and insurance premiums and other taxes that might be termed occupational. Even public lotteries were practiced for a time, the proceeds devoted to school support—until public sentiment was aroused against the "immorality" of such public approval of gambling.

It gradually became evident, however, that halfway or partially hidden financial measures such as the foregoing would not long support the widespread demand for schooling that conditions of the mid-nineteenth century fostered. The population was rapidly increasing; industrialization was causing a shift from rural to urban living; all classes of people were becoming conscious of the educational need, both from the individual standpoint and from that of the increasingly complicated group or social needs of a democratic society, such consciousness being fostered and promoted by the propaganda efforts of lyceum, labor, and professional groups, as previously noted.

Consequently, public taxation for school purposes came progressively to the fore, with legislation necessary for its authorization. At first such legislation was permissive, various local and state legislative bodies granting permission for groups within their jurisdiction to levy taxes for public schools. In passing, it should be noted that a taxing unit must have legal permission to levy a tax even when a majority of its voting population is favorable, because otherwise any taxpayer who wishes may bring court action to secure release from the obligation to pay such a tax. However, for a number of reasons, permissive legislation—either citywide or statewide—soon proved infeasible; its spottiness made it too hard to initiate and too easy to evade. Hence, gradually and step by step the various states took the legislative and judicial actions necessary to establish compulsory local-and-state taxation for public-school support.

Adoption of the principle of free public schools, supported by tax moneys levied for that purpose, had its counterpart in rejection of the pauper-school principle and charity schools. In fact, the fight for free schools—and an extended fight it was, often a bitter one—was simultaneously a fight *against* charity or pauper schools, and against rate bills as well.

The fuller argument or outlook ran somewhat as follows. A free, democratically-governed people is hardly a possibility unless the citizenry is an educated and informed one. Hence, the education of youth is as important to the nation as a whole as to each person; its benefits are social as well as individual. Moreover, education is as needful for the poor as for the rich, and vise versa, not only as a personal right but also as a nationwide benefit or necessity. There should not be one kind of education for one class and another for another; not as far as "class" is concerned. (The problem of differentiation of instruction to care for individual differences was not recognized at the time.) Rate bills for those who can pay and charity education for those who cannot means that those who have children in school and are unwilling or ineligible to declare themselves paupers pay for the destitute as well as for themselves; thus, both the destitute and the childless do not pay, yet receive the *social* or *common* benefits of an educated citizenry the same as whose who do pay. The expense of a public educational system should seemingly be distributed as equitably among the entire citizenry as any other common benefit for which tax moneys are appropriated; hence, it should be financed by public taxation.

From colonial beginnings to the present, private and parochial schools have existed, have been recognized or authorized either officially or unofficially, and have played a more or less prominent role in our educational efforts. With the nationwide advent of free-public-school dominance during the mid-nineteenth century, there was no cessation of private-and-parochial-school attendance and enrollees in these schools were always recognized as complying with the truancy laws. In fact, comparing 1860 and 1940 as to the ratio of pupils enrolled in public schools to total pupil enrollments, we find about the same—approximately nine out of ten, or 90 percent—in both cases,[5] although the term "public school" was used somewhat more loosely in the 1860 data than in those of 1940. More-over, between 1940 and 1960 enrollments in private and parochial schools gained by three or four percentage points, due largely to increases in Catholic parochial schools.

In light of the mid-twentieth-century efforts by parochial-school representatives to secure federal appropriations for private and parochial schools, it may be well here to note that this probably was a hotter issue during the second quarter of the nineteenth century than it is now. Cubberley's account of what happened in New York City typifies what was thought and what was done at that time.

After the beginning of the forties, when the Roman Catholic influence came in strongly with the increase in Irish immigration to the United States, a new factor was introduced and the problem, which had previously been a Protestant problem, took on a somewhat different aspect. Largely through the demands of the Catholics one of the most interesting fights in the whole process of secularizing American education was precipitated in the City of New York.

It will be remembered that the Public School Society, founded in 1805, had become the greatest single educational organization in the city, and had received state money, after 1807, to assist it in its work. In 1820 the Bethel Baptist Church, which had opened a school for poor children of all denominations, was admitted by special act to a share in the state appropriation. To this the Public School Society objected, and the legislature in 1825 turned over the quota of New York City to the city council, to divide as it thought best. The council cut off the Baptist schools, three of which were by that time running, and refused to grant public money to any religious society. In 1828 the Public School Society was permitted to levy a local tax to supplement its resources, it being estimated that at that time there were 10,000 children in the city with no op-portunities for education. The Society was regarded as a non-denominational organization, though chartered to teach "the sublime truths of religion and morality contained in the Holy Scriptures" in its schools.

In 1831 the Roman Catholic Benevolent Society applied to the city council

---

[5] Newton Edwards and Herman G. Richey, *The School in the American Social Order*, 2nd ed. Boston: Houghton Mifflin, 1963, pp. 377–382.

for a grant of funds for their Orphan Asylum School, which was allowed. The Methodists at once applied for a similar grant, in behalf of the orphan and destitute children attending the school under their management, and were refused.* The religious question now became more and more prominent, though without any progress being made toward its settlement. By 1840 the Massachusetts conflict was on, and in that year Governor Seward, of New York, urged the establishment of schools in the cities of the State in which the teachers should be of the same language and religion as the foreign patrons. This dangerous proposal encouraged the Catholics, and they immediately applied to the New York City council for a division of the city school fund, and, on being refused, carried their demand to the legislature of the State. A Hebrew and a Scotch Presbyterian Church also applied for their share, and supported the Catholics in their demands. On the other hand, the Methodists, Episcopalians, Baptists, Dutch Reformed, and Reformed Presbyterians united with the Public School Society in opposing all such division of the funds.

The legislature deferred action until 1842, and then did the unexpected thing. The heated discussion of the question in the city and in the legislature had made it evident that, while it might not be desirable to continue to give funds to a privately organized corporation, to divide them among the quarreling and envious religious sects would be much worse. The result was that the legislature created for the city a City Board of Education, to establish real public schools, and stopped the debate on the question of aid to religious schools by enacting that no portion of the school funds was in the future to be given to any school in which "any religious sectarian doctrine or tenet should be taught, inculcated, or practiced." Thus the real public school system of New York City was evolved out of this attempt to divide the public funds among the churches. The Public School Society continued for a time, but its work was now done, and in 1853 it surrendered its buildings and property to the City Board of Education and disbanded.[6]

It is not likely that the foregoing line of thought and action is any less cogent today than it was then. For about a century, the matter was considered settled, only to become again an issue because of efforts at securing federal assistance toward equalization of educational opportunity throughout the nation.

Along with establishment of public schools, free and open to all and indeed with attendance at some kind of school a requirement, came the principle of

---

[6] *Op. cit.*, pp. 236–237. Footnote in original. Reprinted by permission of the publisher.

* The request was about to be granted by the council, when the Public School Society entered so vigorous a protest, with legal reasons, that the council at first hesitated and later refused. The Society reiterated its conviction, previously expressed in 1825, "that the school fund ought not to be diverted, in whole or in part, to the purposes of sectarian instruction, but should be kept sacred to the great object, emphatically called COMMON EDUCATION."

gradation and of separating children into groups based on the number of years they have been in school, completion of one grade being prerequisite to entrance upon the next.

Prior to monitorial schools, elementary-school practice had been essentially that of the one-room rural schools that are well within the memories of many adults living today. It was individualized instruction (even possibly programmed because each child had his book which he followed minutely), each child going as fast as he could and reporting (reciting) individually to the teacher. The teacher was a hearer of lessons; much of the remainder of his work, as with Ichabod Crane in Irving's *The Legend of Sleepy Hollow,* being whittling quill pens and hickory sticks.

The monitorial schools, however, instituted group process, seating the youngest and smallest—the beginners—on the low benches in front and those who had been longer in school on gradually higher benches toward the rear. Pupils sat in groups and recited in groups, a monitor being assigned to each. But all was mechanical—recitation by rote—as before.

With Mann, Barnard, and their co-workers, however, things began to change. The changes, of course and as always, were opposed by many practitioners because they did not understand what to change to, nor did many see any particular need to change. But the ideas of Comenius, of Locke, of Rousseau, and of Pestalozzi were part of the cultural climate, making it impossible for the empty verbalisms of *re*-citation by rote to be educationally convincing, as they once were. With more children coming to school and with the slowly spreading realization that children's mental or thinking processes needed progressive development, among other things the conviction grew that children should be gathered together into equally advanced groups and given opportunity to listen to one another as they talked with teacher on matters of mutual concern. We probably did not consciously copy this from Germany, but Mann saw it there and described it in his famed Seventh Annual Report, leading to establishment in 1847 of what is said to be our first fully graded school—the Quincy Grammar School in Boston under the principalship of John D. Philbrick who in 1856 became superintendent of the Boston schools. By 1860, much progress had been made in the larger cities toward graded elementary schools.

Separation of elementary-school children into grades based on the number of years they had been in school also necessitated a change in school architecture. Where the monitorial plan had taken over, the "Little Red Schoolhouse" had had to be replaced by a large structure consisting mainly of a single room of sufficient size to house 300, 500, or even a thousand pupils. Transitionally, subsequent to the monitorial plan, a two- or three-story building might have

on each floor a large room seating 200 or more, with probably two small recitation rooms adjoining where assistants, known as ushers, would conduct small
groups by turns and hear their recitations. These recitation groups would each
be composed of pupils at about the same stage of advancement so that they
could recite together. The large room, presided over by the "master," housed
children of diverse ages. In some cases, the lower story might house the primary
school and the upper the "grammar" or intermediate school, the masters of the
two being entirely independent of one another with no particular thought that
the lower should be preparatory for the upper. It might even be that each floor
represented a complete school, in and of itself, as independent of the other
as if in another part of town. In this connection, it should be noted that at
this time there were few local school-coordination officers, even in cities. By
1850, there were only 12 city school superintendents, by 1861 only 26, and by
1870 only 29.

In 1848, however, the year after Philbrick organized his graded school, he
designed a building to house 660 pupils. A four-story building, each of the
first three floors was to house four classrooms for 55 pupils each, and the fourth
or top floor to be an assembly room. This architectural style became immediately
popular and, with variations, was dominant until well past 1900. For smaller
communities or districts, the two-story, square, eight-rooms-for-eight-grades type
of building became standard.

It has been claimed that the German *Volkschule* (people's school), which
Mann observed, served as the pattern for our eight-year elementary school. This,
however, may perhaps be legitimately questioned, because we did not at first
settle on an eight-year elementary school, but varied from seven grades to nine.
Moreover, the German *Volkschule* was a terminal school for the lower classes of
people; after graduation, there was only apprenticeship or possibly trade-school
training, if there was any continuation at all. From our colonial beginnings,
however, all our schools were open to any who could afford to attend and could
satisfy entrance requirements. Prior to the first public high school (Boston,
1821), all levels were self-contained—college, secondary, and primary—each
higher level administering its own entrance requirements, regardless of attendance or nonattendance at a lower level. From its beginning, however, the American public high school was predicated upon completion of a common or
grammar-school course and its own courses designed accordingly. Hence, our
fully-graded, eight-year elementary schools were never of the terminal type, as
was the German *Volkschule*.

With these qualifications, however, it is probably not unduly stretching the
point to acknowledge some influence by Germany on the design of our graded

elementary school as it came into being between 1840 and 1860. It was a school in which each successive grade was predicated on its preceding one and which in turn was preparatory for the following one, in which each grade was taught by a single teacher supposedly specially trained for that grade, in which class size was gradually reduced to be ideally not more than 25–30 pupils, and in which oral group-instruction was to be a mainstay. And to say that this was Pestalozzianism, brought to us by way of Germany, is seemingly also not stretching the point unduly. We were not making these changes because Pestalozzi said so, but because these ideas were part of the intellectual climate and we saw them as good. Pestalozzi and his predecessors had much to do with making them part of that climate, and for that we honor them.

This principle of continuity, too, of admission to successive grades predicated on completion of the preceding ones, was during the Great Educational Awakening carried through to include high school and college. Because of such continuity, it has become known as the "ladder-type system." Originally, Latin grammar schools admitted pupils even as young as 8 years on the basis of their being able to read and write, and the academies did little different except that 10 years was ordinarily the minimum age of admittance. From the beginning, the colleges admitted students on the basis of their own entrance examinations, mainly capacity to read and compose in Latin and Greek. But with high schools and elementary schools both as parts of city school systems, and with city school systems becoming coordinated into single units by virtue of inauguration of city school superintendencies, it rapidly became accepted practice that completion of elementary school constituted a ticket of admission to high school.

With college admission contingent on passing a college's own entrance examinations, any articulation between them and secondary schools was purely subservient on the part of the latter. This was the function of colonial Latin grammar schools; and of American academies in their role of "prep schools," a role quite at odds with Franklin's original intention. This role continued through the Awakening, but was somewhat modified with the advent, about 1870, of acceptance of high-school credits in specified courses (in lieu of entrance examinations) as qualification for college entrance, an innovation spearheaded by the newly appointed president of Harvard University, Charles W. Eliot. This kept preparation for college as a dominating function of secondary education, but it did per se represent a higher degree of respect by college faculties for high-school instruction. It led, of course, to high-school accreditation by the colleges, so that the latter might have some assurance of the quality of credits granted by the former, and, in turn, to regional accreditation associations: the New England Association (1885), the Middle States and Maryland (1892), the North Central Association (1894), etc.

Thus, by the time of the Civil War or what is taken roughly as the close of the Awakening, the United States had developed the structure for a full, "ladder-type" system of schools, from grades one through sixteen, now known as the 8–4–4 plan: eight years of elementary, four of secondary, and four of college or university (higher). With the exception of the step from grade 12 to 13 which came shortly thereafter, completion of the work represented by one rung of the ladder opened the way (at least in theory) for making an attempt at the work of the next rung. Neither race, nor class, nor sex, nor creed was to stand in the way of anyone. Educational opportunity was to be open equally to all, to go as far as interest and capacity led.

This open road was, of course, little more then than aspiration, plan, and commitment. As we all know, now only a century later determined efforts are being made to achieve complete elimination of the race barrier, though all through the past century in a large percentage of our best educational institutions neither race, class, creed, nor color has, in and of itself, been an obstacle to enrollment. Even inadequacy of facilities—faculty, plant, equipment—to care for all who desired to continue schooling can hardly be said to have been a limiting factor, because ever since we have become committed to the public-school principle we have accepted consciously the consequent obligation to tailor the facilities to the demand. Not for us has been the attitude of keeping enrollments within the bounds of existing facilities. What we might have done at any given time had all young persons of school age actually demanded admission is a matter for conjecture; but, as they did come they were taken, even though it meant and still means rapid expansion.

Seemingly, the only limiting factor that we have not tried fully to eliminate is the economic one. Yet, this observation must be severely qualified. We have had compulsory-attendance laws since 1852, when, encouraged by Mann, Massachusetts passed the first one. Child-labor legislation and increases in the remuneration of those gainfully employed have grown steadily and rapidly over the past century. The seeds for these developments had been sown and first harvests gathered before 1860. For public elementary and secondary schools, rate bills and tuition fees were largely eliminated during the Awakening; but they are still levied for higher education, though in amounts far below per-student costs even in nonpublic colleges and universities.

During the present century, further steps have been taken on elementary and secondary levels to ease the financial strain of schooling. The large movement of the population from farms to urban communities has made possible the placement of schools within easy walking distances from homes, and free daily automotive transportation is being supplied for those further away. In many localities, textbooks are now being loaned to students, and school libraries furnish access to other books. School lunches and other food services are widely available at low cost and, under certain conditions, at no cost. A wide variety of health services, largely free, is available in most if not all urban, village, and rural-consolidated schools.

For higher education, low-cost food service has become common practice. Health and medical services, even hospitalization, are widely furnished as a regular item included in tuition fees. Textbooks are loaned in some cases. Low-rental student housing is being increasingly supplied, in dormitories for single students and even in one- and two-bedroom apartments for married students; financed often by private gifts and federal loans, the latter gradually retired as part of the rental charge. Nonprofit student bookstores effect some saving on textbook costs. Many cultural and entertainment features, open to the public with admission charges, are open to students at low blanket rates that are included in tuition fees; including concerts, lectures, theatricals, and inter-collegiate athletic contests.

Finally, there is the rapidly expanding supply of fellowships, scholarships, and student-loan funds. Financed for decades by private gifts and limited legislative appropriations, funds for this purpose were greatly enhanced by the GI Bills, which established educational grants for veterans of World War II and of the Korean conflict. Although these grants represented, perhaps, a feeling of obligation by the nation to reimburse young veterans for educational time lost, they also represented a realization that highly trained manpower is a national asset as well as a personal one. Then in the late fifties with the post-Sputnik scare over Soviet scientific, military, and technical growth, the National Science Foundation was activated and empowered to spend millions of dollars to up-grade our scientific and technical manpower capacity. This, among other things, meant scholarship and other grants to individuals for further training and education—additional recognition that this is a national asset as well as a personal one. And very quickly came the further recognition that such upgrading of manpower competence must be cultural as well as technical; it cannot stop with science and mathematics, but must include linguistics, the humanities, and social science as well. And athletic scholarships should not be forgotten, for, as long as we demand entertainment of this kind, it is only common decency that it be paid for; moreover, such scholarships do indeed represent an additional contribution to upgrading the competence of the nation's manpower.

Hence, although the United States may be somewhat laggard—in comparison, say, to the U.S.S.R., Britain, and even France—in subsidizing individual students to enable them to reach higher levels of higher education, nevertheless we have gone much beyond the steps taken during the Awakening toward reducing the economic as a limiting factor in providing educational opportunity for all. And, what we may not yet have done in terms of personal subsidies is doubtless more than outweighed by the very existence of more than 2000 colleges and universities, filled to overflowing, and the fact that, proportionately, attendance in the United States is many times what it is elsewhere. Indeed, is it not more than likely that, in our way, we are providing much greater opportunity and assistance toward enabling all our young people to go higher up the educational ladder than is possible in any other nation?

Previously, we have noted the beginnings of coordination of educational effort; of departure from the traditional high degree of local autonomy in the conduct of schools. Theoretically, local autonomy does not mean democracy, because an entire people speaking as a unit may not be gainsaid by any subgroup or groups within it. If it is, then a small group is contradicting the larger one, and the principle of equality of opportunity (by individuals) to participate in policy formulation is denied; a smaller number is gainsaying a larger number. The high degree of local autonomy characteristic of our colonial and early national school-policy was seemingly not greatly to be questioned when schooling amounted mainly to the three-r's and any advancement beyond was considered essentially a personal matter; when, as in 1800, we were 3 percent urban and 97 percent rural.

During our between-wars nation-building period, however, urbanization was getting under way and more and more educational demands were being placed on schools. School curricula were expanding, due to growing demand for additional subjects of instruction. As towns and cities grew and multiplied, coupled with the public-school idea, citywide coordination of the schools became seemingly needful with a superintendent in charge. City superintendencies were slow in coming—there were only 26 in 1861 and only 29 in 1870—but they were on the way. County superintendencies began about 1830 and were quite common in 1860. State superintendencies were inaugurated in 1812 with the appointment of Gideon Hawley in New York State, but he became more active or aggressive than the legislature had in mind and in 1821 the office was abolished, not to be reinstated until 1854. From 1830 on, however, state school-offices and officers came to be permanently established, incumbents chosen mostly by popular election. Horace Mann, however, was not so chosen. James G. Carter's foresight had led him to incorporate in the Massachusetts enactment of 1837 the appointment of a State Board of Education, which in turn would select a secretary who would be the state school officer, Mann being their first choice. Because high professional competence is much more likely to be obtained by this latter method over the former, the latter is today the method much preferred by the educational profession. From the beginning, city superintendencies have been handled by the latter method—appointment by the Board of Education.

Finally, in 1867 Congress established a Department of Education (but not with Cabinet rank) in the federal government, in charge of a Commissioner of Education to be appointed by the President. Henry Barnard was the first appointee, serving 1867–1870. The following year (1868), Congress, fearful of federal domination, reduced the Department to "Office of Education," and made sure that its power would be limited essentially to gathering statistics and distributing information.

Thus, we see that during the Awakening the framework for our present form of educational administration was worked out, even though several decades elapsed before it might be said to have been inaugurated. At the federal level is an office or bureau with little administrative power. At the state level, the degree of power exercised varies among the states, to be strengthened or weakened pretty much at the discretion of each state legislature. At the county level, the school officer's duties have to do mainly with rural schools and, with consolidations actively going on, generalizations about the significance or the functions of the county superintendency, especially where it is publicly elective, may not readily be made.

At the local or district level, much power and discretion are still in the hands of boards of education. It probably is not too much to say that here is where the bulk of school-control power lies. Licensing of teachers, a certain amount of accreditation of schools (shared with the regional associations), some influence in establishment of course syllabi and in textbook selection, some (though not many) conditions attached to disbursement of state school-funds; these represent perhaps most of the controls exercised at the state level. Much of what is left— and that is a great deal—is in local hands. Local-district autonomy on school matters is a long-standing tradition in the United States; inroads by state or nation are doggedly resisted; usually with truculence.

Suggested Readings

Barlow, Thomas A., *Channels of Pestalozzianism into the United States*. Unpublished doctoral dissertation, University of Kansas, 1963.

Barnard, Henry, *Henry Barnard on Education*, John S. Brubacher (ed.). New York: McGraw-Hill, 1931.

Butts, R. F., and Cremin, L. A., *A History of Education in American Culture*. New York: Holt, Rinehart and Winston, 1953, Chaps. 7, 8.

Cubberley, Ellwood P., *Public Education in the United States*. Boston: Houghton Mifflin, 1934, Chaps. 6–9.

Curoe, P. R. V., *Educational Attitudes and Policies of Organized Labor in the United States*. New York: Teachers College, Columbia University, 1926.

Curti, Merle, *The Social Ideas of American Educators*. Paterson, N.J.: Littlefield, Adams, 1961, Chaps. 3, 4.

Edwards, Newton, and Richey, Herman G., *The School in the American Social Order*, 2nd ed. Boston: Houghton Mifflin, 1963, Chaps. 10–17.

Gish, Lowell A., *Local, Central, and Professional Control of Education*. Unpublished doctoral dissertation, University of Kansas, 1964.

Gordy, J. P., *Rise and Growth of the Normal-School Idea in the United States*. Washington, D.C.: Government Printing Office, 1891.

Graves, Frank P., *A History of Education in Modern Times*. New York: Macmillan, 1914, Chap. 6.

Gross, Carl H., and Chandler, Charles C., *The History of American Education Through Readings*. Boston: Heath, 1964, Part III.

Lockwood, George B., *The New Harmony Movement*. New York: Appleton-Century-Crofts, 1905, Chap. 20.

Mann, Horace, *The Republic and the School: Horace Mann on the Education of Free Men*, L. A. Cremin (ed.). New York: Bureau of Publications, Teachers College, Columbia University, 1957.

Mann, Mary Peabody, *Life of Horace Mann*. Washington, D.C.: National Education Association, 1937.

Meyer, Adolphe E., *An Educational History of the American People*. New York: McGraw-Hill, 1957, Chaps. 7–9.

Williams, E. I. F., *Horace Mann, Educational Statesman*. New York: Macmillan, 1937.

Scene in a Classroom of 1897. Although Herbartianism had done much to improve American educational practice during the 1890s, this picture seems to capture the Herbartian ideal of "good" students, children who are quiet and passive as teacher marshals their ideas into well-organized apperceptive masses using the Five-Formal-Steps teaching method.

8 ᴥ *HERBART* and *Herbartianism*

The Oswego Movement—Decline of "Pestalozzianism"

In the preceding chapter, we noted two channels through which Pestalozzian ideas flowed into American educational thought: Neef-Maclure and Mann-Barnard. As to modification of practice, the former constituted little more than a trickle whereas the latter might be characterized as a wide-flowing stream, even though by no means all developments during the Great Educational Awakening should be thought of as Pestalozzian. The Neef-Maclure channel may be taken as coming from Switzerland direct, even though Neef did make a short sojourn in France between Burgdorf and Philadelphia. The Mann-Barnard channel came largely by way of the burgeoning German nation, so deeply impressed during the early nineteenth century by the ideas of the Swiss educator.

Informed readers, however, will now be wondering why what is known as the Oswego Movement has so far gone unrecognized in this treatise. The reason is twofold: First, it came after the Civil War period, hence was not within the period of the Awakening; second, though it experienced a rapid rise to high popularity, popular recognition and approval were only short-lived, just as rapidly subsiding and giving way to the Herbartianism of the nineties.

In the summer of 1859, Edward A. Sheldon, superintendent of schools at

Oswego, New York, was visiting in Toronto, Canada. In a museum there he saw a set of Pestalozzian teaching materials and publications currently in use by the Home and Colonial Infant Society of England, purchased the set for $300, took it back to Oswego, and put it to work. The materials, to be used in what was called "object teaching," were largely developed by the brother-sister team of Charles and Elizabeth Mayo, Charles having spent some time around 1820 with Pestalozzi at Yverdon. However, that was during the sharply declining years of both Pestalozzi and his school, so it is not surprising that the Mayo version was a far cry from what was carried to Germany and there developed by the masters who had worked side by side with Pestalozzi during Yverdon's prime.

What our leaders seemingly caught, through what were largely German contacts, was a vision of what education might become if children's minds were encouraged and helped to develop *ideas,* by way of their own observations of the objects and the events constituting the world of which they were a vital part; through their own experiences, gained under the surveillance of well-prepared teachers working according to carefully laid but flexible plans. First came ideas, to which words would later be tied. This was what may well be called *developmental teaching,* and quite authentically represented the process philosophically known as *induction* or the truth-getting process of Newtonian science. This was the true vision or spirit of Pestalozzi, something that he could himself do and that could in greater or lesser degree be "caught" by many who worked with him or who discerningly watched him teach.

What Charles Mayo seemingly caught, however, and his sister through him, was mainly a set of procedures or methodological devices—"methods." These were worked out in sets of "object lessons," and incorporated by Elizabeth in a manual for teachers. Prospective teachers could then be instructed to follow these procedures, a "practical" and quick type of training and such as might enable trainees to conduct classes that would be highly impressive to unsophisticated observers. Quick popularity was therefore possible, though in England object teaching came at a time when monitorial schools were still very much in vogue and popular appeal was not as great as it might otherwise have been.

Though Edward Sheldon of Oswego appears to have comprehended considerably more than the mere form of object teaching, the immediate effects of the instruction that he inaugurated seemed to focus on form. First, Sheldon set up an instructional program in object teaching for the teachers in the Oswego system. Then, in 1861, the city Board of Education created a city normal school and, for its first year, brought over from England a teacher in the Training College of the Home and Colonial Infant Society—Miss Margaret E. M. Jones—to introduce and establish the formal instructional program. The following year (1862) on Miss Jones' return to England, Hermann Krüsi, Jr., took her place, and the year following that (1863) Sheldon spoke before the National Teachers' Association (now the N.E.A.) on the subject, "Object Teaching."

Early in Sheldon's address, he had this to say:

We will not stop now to consider in detail the method best adapted to the development of the infant faculties, but will advert to them after considering briefly a few of the more prominent obstacles that lie in the way of the most successful progress of these improved methods of teaching. And in this connection we remark first, that the very title by which these methods are popularly designated is open to serious objection. It is true that the term "Object Teaching" is, to a certain extent, suggestive of the real character of these early processes, in that we are continually dealing with tangible objects and illustrations, but it is liable to be taken in a too limited sense. Instead of embracing a large number of subjects, and covering the entire field of the early culture of the faculties, many have taken it to mean nothing more than miscellaneous lessons on objects. These lessons often clumsily given by those who have no knowledge of correct principles, and who therefore continually violate them, have led many to condemn the whole system, and thus in certain quarters to bring it into disrepute.

Again, book speculators are continually making use of the term as a catch word, for the purpose of disposing of their wares; thus imposing upon the uninitiated, and bringing into discredit methods of which these books are the farthest possible from being the representatives. In this way old books have received new title pages, and new books with old methods have been christened with the catch word, "Object Lessons," or "On the Object Plan"; and what is lamentable, multitudes know not the difference between the *name* and the *thing*. In this way much mischief has already been done, and much more is yet to be experienced.[1]

It is thus evident that Sheldon himself saw the danger of failing to differentiate between "the *name* and the *thing*." Moreover, Krüsi was the son of one of Pestalozzi's ablest assistants, was born at Yverdon in 1817, studied in Germany where he experienced German education firsthand, and aided in his father's Swiss normal school, 1841–1846. Then for four years he was associated with

[1] Sheldon, E. A. "Object Teaching," *American Journal of Education*, 14:93–102, March, 1864. Reprinted from C. H. Gross and C. C. Chandler, *The History of American Education Through Readings*. Boston: Heath, 1964, p. 242. Italics in original.

the Mayos in and near London. Coming to the United States in 1852, he served for 10 years in Massachusetts as a normal school and teachers' institute lecturer before going to Oswego. Hence, Krüsi knew even better perhaps than Sheldon the difference between the form and the substance of "object teaching," and continually inveighed against the popular illusion that developed in the minds of those who got hold of the "practical" but missed the "theoretical." In 1866, the state took over, and Oswego became the second New York State Normal School, with Sheldon as head. However, of the approximately 1400 who graduated from Oswego during the first quarter-century of its existence and who went from there to almost every state in the Union, many were those who took with them the "methods" but not the spirit of Pestalozzi.

The first phase of the "Oswego Movement," therefore, was a burst of popularity that swept the nation. Oswego graduates became normal-school instructors, critic teachers, and city-school supervisors all over the country, though predominantly in the east and the midwest. But disillusionment almost inevitably follows illusionment, and the combined efforts of Sheldon and Krüsi were insufficient to overcome our obsession with the methodology of object teaching and our failure to grasp the basic theory that underlay developmental or inductive teaching. The second phase or the denouement of the Oswego Movement, therefore, was about as rapid deflation as the first phase had represented inflation. With the advent of the 1890s, the Froebelianism of Harris, Parker, and Hall and the Herbartianism of the McMurrys and DeGarmo were ready to take over.

Thus it seems that the third channel through which Pestalozzian doctrine flowed into the United States, although for the first time making the name of the Swiss pioneer widely known in this country, actually was the one that finally shut off the flow. It is for this reason that we have taken the Great Educational Awakening as the major contribution of Pestalozzi to the growth of American educational thought and practice. The Oswego Movement was seemingly of the panacea variety; salvation by means of a gadget. The work of Mann and Barnard was not blessed (or plagued?) with a neat device that could overshadow and from many conceal its basic substance. Moreover, the Awakening built not only on Pestalozzi but also on much that was not in Pestalozzi's thinking at all; for example, public education, which should subject the children of rich and poor alike to the discipline of thoroughly democratic educational principles, and the principle of grouping in "grades" of approximately equal educational attainment, which was Pestalozzian but was developed in America even before Neef and Maclure.

Thus, to make a long story short, that little unprepossessing but single-minded person, who was so impractical that he could seemingly make sense out of nothing, provided a "leaven that leavened the whole lump" of American educational thought and practice during the nineteenth century—albeit tending to make it Lockean rather than Roussellian.

Herbart and the Herbartians

Toward the close of the century, another European pedagogical movement, Herbartianism, entered American educational thought and practice. Introduction of this new movement, based on the writings of Johann Friedrich Herbart, a German professor of philosophy, was primarily the work of Charles DeGarmo, Charles A. McMurry, and Frank M. McMurry. These men studied at the University of Jena during the 1880s, when Herbartianism was the prevailing theory in Germany. Jena was its leading center and attracted students from all over Europe, the British Isles, and North America.

In 1889, DeGarmo published *The Essentials of Method,* a book based on the psychology and the teaching method of Herbart. Charles A. McMurry's *The Elements of General Method,* which is concerned with Herbartian principles and their bearings on curriculum, was published in 1892. Then, in 1897, the two McMurrys (who were brothers) published *The Method of the Recitation,* basically a follow-up to Charles'. *General Method.* Through these and other writings, DeGarmo and the McMurrys exerted considerable influence on the course of American education. But this influence was not confined to their writings alone. All three began their careers at Illinois State Normal University, at Normal. DeGarmo later became president of Swarthmore College and after that served as professor of education at Cornell University. Frank McMurry went from Normal to the University of Illinois, then to Teachers College, Columbia University. Charles McMurry went to the George Peabody College for Teachers, at Nashville, Tennessee, afterwards to become known there as "The Grand Old Man of Peabody." In 1892, through the efforts of these three, the National Herbart Society was formed. The purpose of the Society was to promote study of Herbartian ideas and ways in which these ideas might be adapted to American education.

Interest in the movement grew rapidly and Herbart's own writings were translated into English, as were those of two who carried on his work in Germany after his death—Tuiskon Ziller (1817–1883) of the University of Leipsig, and William Rein (1847–1929) of the University of Jena. Numerous books and articles on Herbartianism were written in this country, mostly between 1890 and 1900. In 1896, William J. Eckoff, one of the many translators of Herbart, wrote:

We have outgrown the limits of Petalozzianism [sic] just as our free-school system will no longer brook the restriction to the three R's. Many who know our public-school system best and love it most are persuaded that Herbartianism is the proper solution for the difficulties of to-day, as Horace Mann was rightly convinced that the doctrines of Herbart's predecessor, Pestalozzi, offered the true remedial agent for the difficulties at an earlier stage. It is hardly possible to attend an educational gathering of fair pretensions to magnitude or dignity without hearing Herbart's name at least. It is almost impossible to take up a catalogue of teachers' books without noticing publications based mediately or immediately on his principles.

Already many teachers are guided by Herbart's ideas who never heard of him. . . . American educators have begun to live, move, and have their being in an atmosphere of Herbartianism. It is coming to be the pedagogic spirit of the times.[2]

What are these ideas that were changing the character of American education? For an answer to this question let us turn first to Herbart's views, then to those of his followers.

Johann Friedrich Herbart (1776–1841) was born in Oldenburg, Germany. From 1794 to 1799, he attended the University of Jena. Upon leaving, he became tutor to the household of Herr von Steiger-Reggisberg, governor of Interlaken, Switzerland. In 1799 while in Switzerland, Herbart visited Pestalozzi at Burgdorf and was impressed by what he saw. Many of Herbart's early writings were on Pestalozzi's methods. In 1805, Herbart went to the University of Göttingen as professor of philosophy. In 1809 the University of Königsberg offered him the chair of philosophy, and he accepted. For political reasons, he returned to Göttingen in 1833 and remained there until his death.

Part of his duties as professor of philosophy were to give a series of lectures on psychology and pedagogy. In 1816, he published *A Textbook in Psychology*. A revised edition of this book was issued in 1834. In 1806 *The Science of Education* was published, and in 1835 his other major work on pedagogy, *The Outlines of Educational Doctrine*. During his stay at Königsburg, Herbart organized a pedagogical seminary for advanced study of educational problems. He also organized a small experimental school in which he taught mathematics.

2 William J. Eckoff (ed.), Preface to *Herbart's ABC of Sense-Perception and Minor Pedagogical Works*. New York: Appleton-Century-Crofts, 1896, pp. xiii–xiv.

Herbartianism: the Active-Reactive Dilemma

Because of certain similarities in their theories, Herbart has been presented at times as a disciple of Pestalozzi. However, if by disciple one means merely a follower, he can hardly be considered as such. Herbart saw flaws in Pestalozzi's theory and offered suggestions for their correction. According to Herbart, Pestalozzi's major contribution to education

. . . consists in having laid hold more boldly and more zealously than any former method of the duty of building up the child's mind, of constructing in it a definite experience in the light of clear sense-perception; not acting as if the child had already an experience, but taking care that he gets one; by not chatting with him as though in him, as in the adult, there already were a need for communicating and elaborating his acquisitions; but, in the very first place, giving him that which later on can be, and is to be, discussed.[3]

In Comenius, Locke, and Rousseau, we have seen variations of this theory—that mind is "constructed" by ideas derived from sense perception. But, as previously noted, Comenius and Rousseau did not use the theory consistently and, although Pestalozzi used it, he seemingly did not understand it thoroughly. Locke worked out the theory in detail but, assuming an originally passive or reactive mind, made it somehow become active once it received ideas. Herbart's task was to develop a consistent psychology; one that avoided the active-reactive dilemma that plagued his predecessors. If once this were accomplished, a correct as well as consistent method of instruction should be deducible. Because Herbart's psychology is fundamental to his educational theory, we shall discuss it first.

According to Herbart:

The soul has no innate natural talents nor faculties whatever, either for the purpose of receiving or for the purpose of producing. It is, therefore, no *tabula rasa* in the sense that impressions foreign to itself may be made upon it; moreover, in the sense indicated by Leibniz, it is not a substance which includes in itself original activity. It has originally neither concepts, nor feelings, nor desires. It knows nothing of itself, and nothing of other things; also in it lie no forms

---

[3] J. F. Herbart, "On the Proper Point of View for Judging the Pestalozzian Method of Instruction," in Eckoff (ed.), *op. cit.*, p. 61.

of perception and thought, no laws of willing and action, and not even a remote predisposition to any of these.[4]

Here we see Herbart ridding himself of faculty psychology and of Locke's assumption that mind has the power or capacity to combine and to analyze ideas.
But, if mind does not have power to act upon its ideas, how are we to explain
the facts of mental life? How are we to explain such phenomena as memory,
thinking, and interest?

Herbart's answer to this question was that *ideas* are active, and their activity
accounts for the flow of mental life. Mental activity is not a process independent
from, and performed upon, ideas. Such activity is inherent in ideas themselves.
By attributing activity to ideas, Herbart sought to avoid the dilemma of assuming first a reactive then an active mind. Adams wrote, "It is obvious that, on
this view, the soul sinks into comparative insignificance compared with the ideas.
The ideas really make up the mind. The soul is regarded as little else than the
battleground of contending ideas."[5]

The Conscious and the Subconscious

Herbart assumed that soul is "composed" of two "regions," which we may
designate as the *conscious* and the *subconscious*.[6] The two regions are separated
by a dividing line called the *threshold of consciousness*. The goal of every idea
is to maintain itself in, or to gain entry into, the conscious. Ideas vie with one
another for a place in the conscious, in a way analogous to the boys' game of
"king of the hill." Just as the "king" tries to keep the other players off the top
of the hill, ideas in the conscious try to prevent other ideas from taking their
place. At any given time there may be four or five ideas in the conscious. Some
will be receding into, and some will be emerging from, the subconscious. Essentially only one will be the object of attention.

[4] J. F. Herbart, *A Text-Book in Psychology,* translated by Margaret K. Smith. New
York: Appleton-Century-Crofts, 1895, p. 120.
[5] John Adams, *The Herbartian Psychology Applied to Education.* Boston: Heath, 1897,
pp. 49–50.
[6] Although Herbart's translators use the terms, "consciousness" and "subconsciousness"
or even "unconsciousness," we feel that the above are a better rendition of Herbart's meaning. The "-ness" terms represent process, whereas Herbart's concept of the mind was that
of a *locale;* a place where ideas reside. The expressions, "the conscious" and "the subconscious," convey the notion of place rather than process; hence their use.

All ideas are active, but some are more active than others. The more active are able to enter into the conscious more frequently and to remain longer. The power of an idea to enter into the conscious and to remain there is what Herbart meant by *interest*. Whenever an idea succeeds in entering the conscious, a feeling of pleasure or satisfaction results. Whenever an idea is suppressed, there is a feeling of pain or annoyance. Feeling originates in activity of ideas.

Herbart accepted the principle that frequency of repetition is the key to habit formation. Each time an idea enters the conscious its interest is increased. However, ideas seek out companions and allies. Just as "birds of a feather flock together," similar ideas seek to band together. In some unknown way, a conscious idea sends "messages" into the subconscious, calling similar ideas to it. At the same time dissimilar ideas are trying to enter the conscious, but are suppressed below the threshold by the idea dominant in the conscious. By combining forces, similar or compatible ideas increase their "foothold" in the conscious just as the "king of the hill" may increase his staying power by teaming up with close friends. Moreover, in calling similar ideas into the conscious, the old idea promotes an increase of interest in the whole coterie. Thus, one interest leads to another, and a "circle of thought" is created; like leads to like, and back again.

Herbart, of course, rejected the doctrine of innate ideas. All knowledge originates in sense perception. Sense organs are stimulated by environmental forces that in turn cause reactions in the soul. These reactions produce ideas. In this respect Herbart was substantially in agreement with Locke. Herbart also agreed with Locke that a complex idea, say of a snowball, is composed of several simple ideas such as "white," "cold," and "round." But Herbart differed from Locke in assuming that simple ideas are capable of combining themselves into complex ideas. A complex idea, derived from sense perception, he called an observation. Consequently, an observation is always of a particular thing—*this* snowball, *this* table. Whenever a group of simple ideas is presented simultaneously to the conscious, these ideas may combine.

The simple ideas that constitute our idea of a snowball (cold, white, round, etc.) are not analogous. They are *disparate*. The idea of "white" derived from a snowball is essentially identical to that derived from a white piece of paper. These are *identical* ideas. There is one more class of ideas: those that are *contrary* or *contradictory*. For example, the idea that a snowball is cold is not compatible with the idea that it is hot. The importance of these three classes is that they explain the interaction of ideas. Identical ideas tend to blend or fuse when co-present in the conscious, thereby forming one stronger, clearer idea. Co-present, disparate ideas combine to form a complex idea. Contrary ideas neither fuse nor combine, but attempt to prevent the other from entering the conscious. An idea can gain entrance only if it is not contrary to the idea dominant in the conscious.

Apperception

Psychologists long have recognized that we tend to see what we expect to see. In Herbartian terms, this means that ideas in the conscious control our observations and that what we observe is interpreted through them. An idea has meaning or significance only as it can be related to other ideas. Herbart called this process, of interpreting new ideas in light of old ones, *apperception*. He wrote, "Apperception, or assimilation, takes place through the reproduction of previously acquired ideas and their union with the new element [or idea] . . ."[7] DeGarmo explained the process as follows:

To illustrate further, let us construct a figure of three lines, one straight and perpendicular, one broken and oblique, and one curved, thus:

Sight gives us the figure as it stands, but the apprehension that we get at first view is unsatisfactory. We have perhaps had experience enough with lines to enable us to relate each one to its appropriate class, but we see no idea, no purpose in the whole. Remembering, now, however, that a painter once boasted that he could, by means of three lines, represent a soldier and his dog entering an inn, we can at once associate the hitherto meaningless marks with a system of ideas, and when this is done, the process of apperception may be said to be complete.[8]

Once an idea has been apperceived, we have the beginnings of an *appercep-*

7 J. F. Herbart, *Outlines of Educational Doctrine*, translated by Alexis F. Lange. New York: Macmillan, 1901, pp. 63–64.

8 Charles DeGarmo, *The Essentials of Method.* Boston: Heath, 1897, p. 25.

tive mass. Learning takes place through apperception, and results in the building up of apperceptive masses (or the apperceptive mass). These masses then determine future learning, for it is only by being apperceived by these masses that a new idea can be apprehended. As Lange points out, ". . . we see and hear not only with the eye and ear, but quite as much with the help of our present knowledge, with the apperceiving content of the mind."[9]

When a child comes to school, he already has a large number of ideas. These may be well organized, or they may not. For Herbart:

Of equal importance with the inner organization of the pupil's ideas are, for the teacher, the degree of ease or difficulty with which a given mass of ideas is called into consciousness, and its relatively long or brief persistence in consciousness. Here we are face to face with the conditions of efficient instruction and training.[10]

Teachers should observe pupils to determine (1) what ideas pupils have; (2) how well those ideas are organized; (3) what pupil ideas require correction and supplementation; and (4) what masses of ideas tend to dominate pupil consciousness and therefore constitute pupil interests. Once a teacher has determined how his pupils stand in these matters, instruction may proceed efficiently and effectively.

The Five-Step Plan for Teaching

Herbart divided his method of instruction into four steps: (1) *clearness,* or presentation of new ideas; (2) *association,* or relating of new ideas to old, compatible ideas; (3) *system,* or arrangement of associated ideas in logical order; and (4) *method,* or application of the new ideas to some problem or new situation. However, Herbart's steps are not clearly consonant with the principle of apperception or with his view that a teacher should utilize pupil interest. Tuiskon Ziller, professor at Leipzig and one of Herbart's followers, made a significant contribution in this connection. Ziller divided "clearness" into two steps—*preparation* and *presentation.* Wilhelm Rein, professor at Jena and also a Herbartian, later described the method as consisting of these steps: (1) preparation,

[9] Karl Lange, *Apperception,* DeGarmo edition. Boston: Heath, 1902, p. 21.
[10] *Outlines of Educational Doctrine,* p. 21.

(2) presentation, (3) association, (4) generalization, and (5) application. Rein also added a step subordinate to "preparation" called *aim.*

Rein meant by *aim* what today is called the objective of a given lesson, or what a teacher proposes to accomplish through a particular period of instruction. The teacher introduces the lesson by telling the pupils what is to be done and what is to be accomplished. The first step in instruction, *preparation,* is an interest-raising step and refers to preparing pupil's minds to receive new ideas. In this step old ideas, deemed compatible with the ideas to be presented, are raised to the conscious. By raising old ideas into the conscious, previous learning is strengthened and interest in the anticipated lesson induced. *Presentation* is next. Teacher presents the new ideas by lecturing or conversation, or students may do the presentation by reading silently or aloud, giving reports, and so on.

After the new ideas are presented in light of the old, the class is ready for *association.* New and old ideas are compared and contrasted. Teacher may point out similarities and differences, or may allow students to do so, or both. The next step, *generalization,* grows out of association. Common elements or characteristics of the new and the old provide the basis for formulating general principles or rules. The last step, *application,* relates these principles to new situations, or it may be used to deepen understanding of familiar situations. Application is assumed to clinch the learning, because it tests understanding and promotes clarity.

Correlation and Concentration: Forerunner of "Core Curricula"?

In light of the preceding discussion of apperception and of the Herbartian method of instruction, we see how Herbart and his followers worked out in detail the idea of *going from the known to the unknown.* We should start with what the child knows; then organize, correct, and build on it. Instruction thus constructs the mind by building apperceptive masses, which in turn condition future learning. Lesson plans become important, as do courses of study. Curricula must be planned in advance—to each smallest detail. Moreover, curricula should be coordinated, to make efficient use of the principle of apperception. Thus, emphasis on a coordinated curriculum leads to the Herbartian principles of *correlation* and *concentration.*

For Herbart:

The ultimate purpose of instruction is contained in the notion, virtue. But in order to realize the final aim, another and nearer one must be set up. We may term it, *many-sidedness of interest.* The word *interest* stands in general for that kind of mental activity which it is the business of instruction to incite. Mere information does not suffice; for this we think of as a supply or store of facts, which a person might possess or lack, and still remain the same being. But he who lays hold of his information and reaches out for more, takes an interest in it. Since, however, this mental activity is varied, we need to add the further determination supplied by the term *many-sidedness.*[11]

Scattering no less than one-sidedness forms an antithesis to many-sidedness. Many-sidedness is to be the basis of virtue; but the latter is an attribute of personality, hence it is evident that the unity of self-consciousness must not be impaired. The business of instruction is to form the person on many sides, and accordingly to avoid a distracting or dissipating effect. And instruction has successfully avoided this in the case of one who with ease surveys his well-arranged knowledge *in all of its unifying relations* and holds it together as *his very own.*[12]

Ideas spring from two main sources—experience and social intercourse. Knowledge of nature—incomplete and crude—is derived from the former; the later [sic] furnishes the sentiments entertained toward our fellow-men. . . .

Hence we have two main branches of instruction—the historical and the scientific. The former embraces not only history proper, but language study as well; the latter includes, besides natural science, mathematics.[13]

Because ideas may be divided into two groups, interests may be divided accordingly. There are interests directed toward things, and interests directed toward people. Under those directed toward things, Herbart included the following as broad classes: (1) empirical, (2) speculative, and (3) aesthetic. Those directed toward people are (1) sympathetic, (2) social, and (3) religious. Education is to develop interest in all these areas.

Herbart's position, growing out of thinking such as this, was later developed by Rein into the doctrine of correlation of studies. A person who has developed many-sided interests is able to survey "his well-arranged knowledge *in all of its unifying relations.*" This position is based on the assumption that different subject matters are interrelated and that instruction should promote student

[11] *Outlines of Educational Doctrine,* p. 44. Italics in original.
[12] *Ibid.,* p. 49. Italics in original.
[13] *Ibid.,* p. 24.

understanding of such relations. Commenting on Rein's doctrine of correlation of studies, DeGarmo writes:

If each subject is to be an errant comet, pursuing its path independent of the others—if, in other words, disorganization and isolation of topics is to rule our instruction—it is plain that the desirable unity of knowledge will not only not be promoted, but will actually be hindered; that consequently the teacher, in spite of his pious wish for the highest welfare of the pupil, may aid in making him a dependent being whose unrelated knowledge does him little or no good. Our desire to develop the individuality and power of the pupil can find its best realization, so far as instruction is concerned, in the best possible coordination of all the subjects that we teach. The first purpose of the coordination of studies is, therefore, the promotion of true unity and consistency in our mental life through instruction. . . . Now, the coordination of studies means their correlation; that is, it means that it shall enable the pupil in one way or another to become conscious of useful and interesting relations among the various topics of the various studies. Every child is sure to be interested in something, so that if he can see that other things are related to his favorite ones, life at once broadens before him. This basis of interest in study is laid when the child finds in the subject-matter of instruction that which appeals to his own thinking as valuable. He must understand it, therefore, primarily, in its relation to himself. . . . Coordination of studies promises to increase rapidly the pupil's power of apprehension and to promote his direct interest in what the school has to offer him. . . .[14]

Because ideas lead to action, another reason for correlation of studies is that it will "bring about unity or consistency in our volitional acts, therefore, it would seem that the body of knowledge in which volition has its roots should be unified to the greatest practical extent.[15] Finally, in DeGarmo's own view,

There is, in addition to these theoretical grounds, a practical reason for the proper coordination of studies, that should cause us to listen to all serious propositions looking to that end. It is universally acknowledged that our present curriculum, if not already badly congested, is likely soon to become so. Subject after subject has been added, not from any demonstrated pedagogical need, but in obedience to popular demands or to the professional zeal of specialists. The process is still continuing. Not only each newly-developed branch of useful knowledge, but even every popular social reform (scientific temperance,

[14] Charles DeGarmo, *Herbart and the Herbartians.* New York: Scribner, 1896, pp. 114–116.
[15] *Ibid.,* p. 117.

for instance) demands a representation in the school-room. The result is often a detrimental atomization of the pupil's time and attention. Not having time to digest any subject thoroughly, he soon becomes a mere taster in all learning.[16]

Thus, the doctrine of correlation means that curricula should be so organized that similar or related ideas are presented together or in sequence, for such presentation promotes apperception of their relationships. American colonial history, for example, would be taught in conjunction with the literature of that period. Geography lessons might focus on the topography and ecology of the colonies. In brief, subject matters would be correlated around a "big" central or "core" idea, such as colonial life.

The doctrine of concentration refers to the use of "core" ideas around which various subject matters are correlated, the function of such subject matters being the presentation of ideas that will promote deeper and wider understanding of the core idea. Obviously, then, selection of an idea that will serve as the core is literally of central importance, and only those ideas that are capable of providing points of contact with all or most subject matters being taught are suitable.

For the most part, the Herbartians turned to history and literature as sources for core ideas. According to Ziller, "Every pupil should pass successively through each of the chief epochs of the general mental development of mankind suitable to his stage of development. The materials of instruction, therefore, should be drawn from the thought material of that stage of historical development in culture, which runs parallel with the present mental stage of the pupil."[17] Not only is history to furnish the core ideas, but it also is used as a guide to determine the sequence in which core ideas are to be presented. As may be seen in Ziller's statement, he accepts a culture-epochs interpretation of mental development.

The following sketch of a course of study for elementary school, developed by a Miss Rice in 1903, illustrates the way in which culture epochs were used to determine curriculum organization.

Grade 1. Making and furnishing playhouses; comparison with the life of primitive man.

Grade 2. Weaving and cooking; comparisons with primitive life in the hunter and shepherd stages.

16 *Ibid.,* pp. 117–118.
17 Tuiskon Ziller, quoted in Frank Pierrepont Graves, *A History of Education in Modern Times.* New York: Macmillan, 1914, pp. 213–214.

Grade 3. Cooking, gardening, pottery making; primitive farming and the beginnings of trade and city life.

Grade 4. Wood and metal work; local history and famous explorers.

Grade 5. Weaving and sewing; colonial life, and the colonial history; our struggle for independence and similar struggles in Greece, Switzerland, and Holland; physical culture, games, architecture and sculpture of Greece.

Grade 6. Printing and bookbinding; period of discovery and exploration in American history, development of arts of printing and inventions connected with navigation, study of medieval conditions.

Grade 7. Wood and metal work; home economics, including civic regulations in regard to housing and sanitation; Roman or English history, with emphasis upon the evolution of government; structure of local government.[18]

Here we see the first grade "concentrating" on the life of primitive man. Notice the care given in correlating various subject matters to this core idea, as illustrated in the following unit of study.

Primitive life: hunting and fishing stage, means of securing food, digging and gathering, hunting and fishing.

Manual training: digging stick, clubs, stone axes, slings, rude traps, snares, spears, stone knives, weirs, nets, bows, arrows, quivers, woven grass bags, baskets.

Literature: *Land of Story Books, Story of Mowgli.*

Reading: *Story of Ab.*

Nature Study: study of stones in connection with their use as primitive weapons.

Art: study of pictures, as Lion and Tiger by Dicksee; primitive design studied and applied to bow and arrow.

Arithmetic: Measurements—problems in connection with construction work.

Music: Crooked Ear.

Physical education: dramatizational plays, stories, poems and songs, hunting games; Buffalo, Eagle, Bear, Reindeer Dances, Acorn Dance, Hunt the Wolf.[19]

Although most of the early Herbartian courses of study employed culture epochs as core, concentration and correlation may be achieved without culture epochs. In fact, Herbartians were not long in turning to other core topics. Nevertheless, the idea of organizing subject matters around central topics or themes has been and continues to be an important practice in American education. The "core curriculum" movement, which was popular in the 1930s and

[18] Quoted in Dorothy McMurry, *Herbartian Contributions to History Instruction in American Elementary Schools.* New York: Bureau of Publications, Teachers College, Columbia University, 1946, p. 78.

[19] *Ibid.,* pp. 88–89.

1940s, represented little if any modification of the Herbartian doctrines of concentration and correlation.

Just as Herbartian courses of study reflect the doctrines of concentration and correlation, plans for individual lessons illustrate concern with teaching method and apperception. The following lesson plan is from DeGarmo's *The Essentials of Method.*

WHAT ARE THE ESSENTIAL ELEMENTS OF A SENTENCE?

(A)

(1) Preparation—Why do we talk or write? To convey our thoughts to others. How is our thought expressed? In words. Are the words arranged in any particular way? Yes, in sentences. Do you know, then, what a sentence is? It is the expression of a thought in words. Can one word make a sentence? Can two? Do any sentences require at least three? The words which are necessary to make a sentence might be called its essential elements. Do you suppose the number of essential elements is the same in all sentences? Let us try to find out.

(2) Presentation—How many words are there in the sentence,

Dogs are animals?

There are three. What does the word *dogs* express? The idea of a certain kind of animals. The word *animals?* The idea of a certain class of living things. What does the word *are* express? Not the idea of a thing, but an affirmation, or decision, of the mind with regard to dogs and animals. Could there be a thought which does not think or affirm *something of something else?* No. Could any one of the three words be omitted without destroying the present sense of this sentence? No. What is asserted of *dogs? What* they are.

In the sentence,

Dogs are brave,

what is asserted of *dogs? How* they are. *Bravery* is asserted of them.

Could any of these words be omitted? In the sentence,

Dogs are barking,

what is asserted of *dogs?* The action *barking.* What word makes the assertion? The word *are.* Could any of these words be omitted? No. How many essential elements have we found in each of the three sentences? About what has each assertion been made? *Dogs.* This word is, as you know, called what? The *subject.* What is the second or asserting word in these sentences called? It is called the *copula.* What is the third word called? It is called the attribute, because it shows what has been attributed to the subject.

All of these sentences have had three essential words or elements; can you give me a statement about *dogs* which shall contain but two words?

Dogs bark.

Is this an assertion? Yes. About what is the assertion made? *Dogs.* What is asserted of them? The action *barking.* What word asserts the action *barking* of dogs? (A probable pause.) The word *bark.* How many offices does the word bark appear to perform? Two. What are they? The office of the *copula* and also that of the *attribute.* Can you make another sentence about *dogs* which shall contain but two words? Yes.

Dogs are.

What does this mean? What have you asserted of dogs? I have asserted their existence (dogs exist—are existing). What word asserts this? The word *are.* How many offices does the word *are* appear to fulfill? Two; that of *copula* and that of *attribute.*

(B)

(3) In each of the foregoing sentences we have found three elements. Can you tell what they are? (1) An *assertion* (2) *of something* (3) *about something else.* Must every sentence tell or assert something? Can you assert without asserting something? Can you assert anything without asserting it *of* something? How many elements, then, appear necessary to every sentence?

FORMULATION.—*There are three essential elements in every sentence,* SUBJECT, COPULA, *and* ATTRIBUTE; *but the copula and attribute may be blended into one word when the attribute is verbal.*

(C)

(4) Select the essential elements in each of the sentences of your reading lesson (subject, copula, and attribute; or, if the last two are blended, subject and verb). Remember that subject and attribute may have many modifying words.[20]

The reader may have noticed that this lesson plan does not clearly include a separate step called assimilation or association. However, careful reading of the plan will show that assimilation comes after each presentation of the five example-sentences, and culminates prior to the formulation of the generalization, i.e., of the grammatical rule.

Although the following plan is not clearly divided into the five formal steps, the procedure is obviously the same:

[20] Pp. 110–112.

LESSON PLAN

"SEVEN AT ONE BLOW"

I. Objectives
   A. To know what is make-believe and what is real.
   B. To use facts in deciding what a person's job is.
II. Materials
   A. *American Adventures* (4)
   B. Study Book for *American Adventures*.
III. Procedures
   A. Preparation—Arouse interest in main character and meaning of his vocation.
   B. Silent reading—Stimulate purposeful reading through discussion and interpretation of story.
   C. Re-reading—Re-read passages of story again in order to strengthen the understanding of difference between the real and the make-believe—(Children contribute to list on Chalkboard)
   D. Follow-up
      1. Relate descriptive sentences to children and through word clues, have them guess occupation.
      2. Study book—Obtain from context word-clues which suggest occupations.
      3. Suggest reading during free-reading period the collections of make-believe stories found on classroom library table.
IV. Evaluation
   A. Ability to know the difference between real and make-believe.
   B. Ability to use facts from context to determine what a person's job is.

This lesson plan was not written in the 1890s, nor in the early 1900s. It was written in 1963 by a student in a methods course at the University of Kansas.[21] Perhaps the fact that Herbartian methodology is still being taught, albeit in modified form, is the best indication of the impact Herbart and the Herbartians have had on American educational thought and practice.

At this point, we should call attention to the respective roles of teacher and pupil, as seen from the perspective of Herbartianism. Armed with a correlated and concentrated curriculum, a teacher's task is to reproduce in student minds the same organization of ideas that is set forth in the courses of study and the lesson plans; the "method" being the five formal steps of instruction. In effect, a student's own ideas are important only because they must be utilized in the

21 We wish to thank Professor Vernon E. Troxel for use of this lesson plan.

first of the five steps. Thus, a teacher, if effective, is in complete control of student minds, whereas students, if "good" students, are passive and receptive.

Seen in this light, teaching is educational engineering, and an educational engineer's blueprints are courses of study and lesson plans. Instruction *constructs* pupil minds by starting with and from the ideas that pupils already have, then correcting, refining, supplementing, and organizing those ideas into the apperceptive masses designated by the course of study. In consequence, instruction becomes imposition or indoctrination of pre-established patterns of thought. Some Herbartians even included in their lesson plans the questions that were to be asked by pupils. Thus, Herbartian methodology left little room for creative or reflective thinking on the part of students; none was permitted that could be avoided.

Herbartianism in the United States

Almost as soon as DeGarmo and the McMurrys returned from Jena, new terminology appeared in educational literature—apperception, concentration and correlation, and culture epochs. Illinois State Normal University became the major center for teacher training in Herbartian pedagogy. When the National Education Association met at Saratoga Springs in the summer of 1892, DeGarmo and the McMurrys were instrumental in founding the Herbart Club. Three years later, in 1895, the club became the National Herbart Society for the Scientific Study of Education. The concerns of the society gradually shifted from problems in Herbartianism to those of American education in general. In 1901 the society changed its name to the National Society for the Scientific Study of Education, then, at a later time, eventually dropped "Scientific" from the title. Perhaps the dropping of Herbart's name from the name of the society shows most clearly the demise of Herbartianism as a popular educational movement. But, in education as in other spheres of human activity, although popular movements may pass out of the picture they tend to leave their marks. This seems to be particularly true of Herbartianism.

One of the first tasks American Herbartians had was that of explaining such principles as apperception, interest, concentration, correlation, and culture epochs. At the same time they were actively attacking faculty psychology, which still was dominant in American education. In this attack they were aligning themselves with new psychological theories that were appearing at the time.

Dorothy McMurry, in one of the most comprehensive American studies of the Herbartian movement, writes:

Among the particular Herbartian theories, apperception was commonly accepted. Even W. T. Harris, United States Commissioner of Education, and at the time the outstanding figure in American education, honored the Herbartians in approving this one of their principles, although he was critical of all the rest.

Although apperception implied the child's reaction to the ideas presented to him, and the cultural epoch theory was supposedly based upon the development of the child, an acceptance of Herbart's idea of the way in which the mind is built up through experience led to an emphasis upon subject matter on the part of American Herbartians. They made a series of attempts to work out complete, articulated, detailed courses of study for all of the elementary school subjects; and they stressed the important part played by the teacher in the learning process, in providing the right ideas and directing the way in which the child should assimilate them.[22]

Briefly, we may assess the significance of the Herbartian movement by considering some of the aspirations it inherited from its predecessors and how its treatment of those aspirations provided a starting point for its successors.

According to DeGarmo:

. . . One of the main results of the labors of Comenius, Rousseau, and Pestalozzi [No doubt Locke should be included too.] is the firmly fixed conviction that observation, or the use of the senses, and in general the consideration of simple concrete facts in every field of knowledge, is the sure foundation upon which all right elementary education rests. This truth is now the acknowledged starting-point of all scientific methods of teaching, yet the fact of the importance of observation in instruction does not carry with it any information showing how the knowledge so obtained can be utilized, or what its nature, time, amount, and order of presentation should be. In short, it does not show how mental assimilation can best take place, or how the resulting acquisitions can be made most efficiently to influence the emotional and volitional side of our nature. Perception is, indeed, the first stage in cognition, but its equally important correlative is apperception or mental assimilation. It is Herbart and his successors who have made us distinctly conscious of this fact.[23]

Herbart's hope had been to "systematize instruction" on the basis of the principle of proceeding from the known to the unknown. His psychology of apperception, and the five formal steps of teaching as developed by Ziller and

[22] *Op. cit.*, p. 53.
[23] *Herbart and the Herbartians*, pp. 6–7.

Rein, appeared to many to have solved the problem of finding the method of sound, systematic instruction. Thus, in the view of Herbartians, education had achieved scientific stature; scientific in the sense that teaching procedures were derived from, or were applications of, psychological laws or principles.

As noted earlier, Herbartian influence may still be found in American education. In Chapter 11, the idea of core curriculum, which grew out of the doctrines of correlation and concentration, will be examined. Also, in our discussion of Edward L. Thorndike's psychological connectionism and the specific-objectivist movement in curricula making, we shall see Herbartian lesson plans transformed into the "programs" that recently have become *programmed instruction*.

The Herbartians made important contributions to American education. They were leaders in the fight against faculty psychology, which however continued to have widespread influence on teaching procedures and curriculum content and organization. They made us increasingly sensitive to the significance of interest and its effects on learning. They promoted belief in and development of teacher education. This they did, and much more. But, even though Herbartians made much of pupil activities and pupil interests, the starting point of all instruction in their view is a supposedly passive mind, which simply *receives* sensations or impressions. As John Dewey is reported to have said, this is a schoolmaster's psychology, not the psychology of a growing mind.

Suggested Readings

Adams, John, *The Herbartian Psychology Applied to Education*. Boston: Heath, 1897.

DeGarmo, Charles, *Herbart and the Herbartians*. New York: Scribner, 1896.

DeGarmo, Charles, *The Essentials of Method*. Boston: Heath, 1897.

Graves, Frank P., *A History of Education in Modern Times*. New York: Macmillan, 1914, Chap. 7.

Herbart, J. F., *A Text-Book in Psychology*, translated by Margaret K. Smith. New York: Appleton-Century-Crofts, 1895.

Herbart, J. F., *Herbart's ABC of Sense-Perception and Minor Pedagogical Works*, translated, edited, and with a Preface by William J. Eckoff. New York: Appleton-Century-Crofts, 1896.

Herbart, J. F., *Outlines of Educational Doctrine*, translated by Alexis F. Lange. New York: Macmillan, 1901.

Krug, Edward A., *The Shaping of the American High School*. New York: Harper & Row, 1964, Chap. 5.

Lange, Karl, *Apperception*, DeGarmo edition. Boston: Heath, 1902.

McMurry, Charles A., *The Elements of General Method*. New York: Macmillan, 1903.

McMurry, Charles A., and McMurry, Frank, *The Method of the Recitation.* Bloomington, Ill.: Public School Publishing Company, 1897.

McMurry, Dorothy, *Herbartian Contributions to History Instruction in American Elementary Schools.* New York: Bureau of Publications, Teachers College, Columbia University, 1946.

Sheldon, E. A., "Object Teaching," in *American Journal of Education,* 14:93–102, March, 1864. Reprinted from C. H. Gross and C. C. Chandler (eds.), *The History of American Education Through Readings.* Boston: Heath, 1964, pp. 241–249.

Many of today's educational methods stem directly from Froebel: mobility of children and furniture within the classroom, guided play, singing, dancing, choice of activity and warm teacher-pupil relationship. (Courtesy of Culver Pictures Inc., New York)

9 ?❧ FROEBEL: Play in Education

Play in Early Schooling

In recent years, we in the United States have been devoting considerable attention to preschool education. One aspect of this attention is shown by the development of manufacturing and marketing "educational toys." Educational toys are big business, and one manufacturer stresses his claim that his toys have educational value by labeling his products with the copyrighted "Playskool." We have come a long way in our attitude toward play since the time of our Puritan fathers. Even those among us who frown upon "frivolous" play may salve our consciences by providing children with "educational toys"; play being acceptable as long as a child "gets something out of it." Even some of the cartoon shows for children on television have "educational" segments, which in all likelihood are offered primarily as a sop to parents afraid that their children are not gaining much of value from the show as a whole.

At the same time, nursery schools are being established in many communities throughout the United States. These schools, now private for the most part, typically enroll children three to five years of age. Children attend school half-days only, and their curricula consist mainly in organized play and "creative" activities, such as drawing, painting, and modeling. Of the educational values claimed for nursery school, the following appear to be most prevalent: (1) it enables children to begin the process of learning how to get along with others; (2) it supplements the educational opportunities of a home; (3) it enables children to get a head start in formal learning; and (4) it prepares a child for kindergarten.

Without commenting on the respective educational values of the foregoing, we can say that none of the educational ideas lying behind these practices appears to be new *in principle*. Although we as a people have only recently become aware of the educational importance of the first five years of a child's life, educational theorists have for centuries stressed this importance. As we have seen, if *tabula rasa* psychology means anything in terms of educating a child, it means that one cannot start too soon in supervising the kind of ideas a child acquires from his environment. On the other hand, if one adopts the position of education as unfoldment, one cannot start too soon in protecting a child from those aspects of his environment seen as likely to interfere with his natural development. Either way, education—in its broadest sense—begins at birth. Or, as Colonel Francis W. Parker is said to have replied to a woman who asked when she should begin educating her 6-year-old child, "Madam, hurry home! You are already six years late."

Moreover, both Locke and Rousseau changed the thinking of many about the moral nature of children. Even if one did not agree with Rousseau that children are naturally good, one might at least agree with Locke that neither are they naturally bad. Viewed from either of these perspectives, play takes on new significance. As noted earlier, Locke advocated the use of play to teach the alphabet; play being neither good nor bad in itself, but only in terms of its use. Rousseau saw play as the spontaneous and free expression of a child's nature; hence good. But neither Locke, Rousseau, nor any other theorist that we have studied dealt as much with the importance of the preschool years and with the educational value of play as did Friedrich Froebel.

Froebel

Few educators today discuss Friedrich Froebel other than as founder of the kindergarten movement. They might mention in passing that he was a follower of Pestalozzi and that he had a mystical bent in his ideas on education. No doubt Froebel's reputation for mysticism has been instrumental in keeping some readers away from his works, particularly in an age that places its trust in "operational" concepts and scientific verification of psychological theories.

Another factor that may account for the neglect of Froebel's views is the assumption that he was concerned only with infant education. Of course, the kindergarten stands as his major achievement and most of his writings are on infant education, but it should not be concluded that the education of young children was his sole educational interest. A translator of Froebel's *The Education of Man,* W. N. Hailmann, suggested in his preface "that his [Froebel's] educational principles and methods, like his practical educational activity, were not confined to the earliest years of childhood, but embraced the entire impressionable period of human life."[1] However, Hailmann recognized that Froebel had never given a thorough, systematic statement to his views on education beyond childhood and early youth. In similar vein, Frederick Eby writes that those "who make the effort to pierce beneath a somewhat forbidding exterior will find an insight that illumines the entire field of education."[2] The purpose here is to examine this "illuminating" insight and how it has affected American educational programs.

Friedrich Froebel was born in 1782 in Oberweisbach, located in the Thüringian forest of southern Germany. His father was a pastor, but did not spend much time with Friedrich. Froebel's mother died when he was nine months old and, according to reports, his stepmother exhibited unconcealed hostility and resentment toward him. Moreover, he was not allowed to attend the regular boys' school, but went to a girls' school that his father directed. In short, the first 10 years of his life were not happy.

When he was 10, Froebel moved into the home of his maternal uncle. This uncle, Pastor Hoffman, lived in Stadt-Ilm, and it was at the parish school there that Froebel received perhaps the most systematic instruction of his life. Religion appears to have had the greatest influence on Froebel at this time. He wrote, ". . . I especially enjoyed the hours devoted to religious instruction."[3] Froebel lived with this uncle until he was about 15. Because of his love for the outdoors, in the summer of 1797 he was apprenticed to a forester. Two years later, in 1799, the apprenticeship ended and he returned to his father's house. The forester had not lived up to his part of the contract and had lied to Froebel's father, saying the boy was lazy. However, Froebel had been studying on his own,

[1] W. N. Hailmann, "Translator's Preface," in Friedrich Froebel, *The Education of Man.* New York: Appleton-Century-Crofts, 1887, p. xvii.

[2] Frederick Eby, *The Development of Modern Education.* Englewood Cliffs, N.J.: Prentice-Hall, 1952, p. 496.

[3] F. Froebel, *Autobiography of Friedrich Froebel,* translated by Emilie Michaelis and H. Keatly Moore. Syracuse: C. W. Bardeen, 1889, p. 19.

and demonstrated to his father what he had taught himself. This demonstration satisfied the father, but not the stepmother. Froebel soon left home again; this time to go to the University of Jena, where he was to take a sum of money to his brother who was studying medicine. Froebel wrote:

When I reached Jena I was seized by the stirring intellectual life of the place, and I longed to remain there a little time. Eight weeks of the summer half-year's session of 1799 yet remained. My brother wrote to my father that I could fill that time usefully and profitably in Jena, and in consequence of this letter I was permitted to stay. I took lessons in map and plan-drawing, and I devoted all the time I had to the work. At Michaelmas I went home with my brother, and my step-mother observed that I could now fairly say I had passed through the university.[4]

Froebel then persuaded his father to allow him to return to Jena, where he took a variety of subjects, most of them elementary. He wrote:

My stay in Jena had taught me much; by no means so much as it ought to have taught me, but yet I had won for myself a standpoint, both subjective and objective. I could already perceive unity in diversity, the correlation of forces, the interconnection of all living things, life in matter, and the principles of physics and biology.[5]

In 1801, Froebel left the university and spent the next four years trying to find an occupation that he could enjoy. In 1805, while visiting friends in Frankfurt, he met one Herr Gruner, headmaster of the Frankfurt Model School. Gruner persuaded Froebel to become a teacher in this school.

The watchword of teaching and of education was at this time the name of PESTALOZZI. It soon became evident to me that Pestalozzi was to be the watchword of my life also; for not only Gruner, but also a second teacher at the school, were pupils of Pestalozzi, and the first-named had even written a book on his method of teaching.[6]

Toward the end of August 1805, Froebel went to Yverdon to visit and observe in Pestalozzi's school. This visit lasted until mid-October, when he returned to Frankfurt and his teaching position. Froebel wrote that he left "with a settled

[4] *Ibid.*, p. 28.
[5] *Ibid.*, pp. 31–32.
[6] *Ibid.*, p. 52.

resolution to return thither as soon as possible for a longer stay."[7] In 1807, Froebel left the school to become tutor to three boys. Then, in 1808, he took the boys to Yverdon where most of the next three years was spent at Pestalozzi's school.

To throw myself completely in the very heart of Pestalozzi's work, I wished to live in the main buildings of the institution, that is to say, in the castle itself. We would have cheerfully shared the lot of the ordinary scholars, but our wish could not be granted, some outside jealousies standing in the way. However, I soon found a lodging in immediate proximity to the institution, so that we were able to join the pupils at their dinner, their evening meal, and their supper, and to take part in the whole courses of their instruction, so far as the subjects chosen by us were concerned; indeed, to share in their whole life. I soon saw much that was imperfect; but, notwithstanding, the activity which pressed forth on all sides, the vigorous effort, the spiritual endeavor of the life around me, which carried me away with it as it did all other men who came within its influence, convinced me that here I should presently be able to resolve all my difficulties. As far as regarded myself personally, I had nothing more earnest to do for the time than to watch that my pupils gained the fullest possible profit from this life which was so rich in vigour for both body and soul. Accordingly we shared all lessons together; and I made it my special business to reason out with Pestalozzi each branch of instruction from its first point of connection with the rest, and thus to study it from its very root.[8]

But Froebel goes on to say:

The want of unity of effort, both as to means and aims, I soon felt; I recognized it in the inadequacy, the incompleteness, and the unlikeness of the ways in which the various subjects were taught. Therefore I endeavoured to gain the greatest possible insight into all, and became a scholar in all subjects—arithmetic, form, singing, reading, drawing, language, physical geography, the natural sciences, etc.[9]

Froebel left Yverdon in 1810, and returned to Frankfurt. In 1811, he went to the university at Göttingen where he concentrated on physics, chemistry, mineralogy, and natural history. He also studied history, politics, and political economy. From 1812 to 1813, he studied in Berlin, but his sojourn there was interrupted by renewal of the Napoleonic wars, and he joined the army. In 1814, Froebel was appointed assistant curator of the Berlin mineralogical museum. It is during this period that he

[7] *Ibid.*, p. 57.
[8] *Ibid.*, pp. 78–79.
[9] *Ibid.*, p. 79.

. . . perceived a double truth; first, that man must be early led towards the knowledge of nature and insight into her methods—that is, he must be from the first specially trained with this object in view; and next, I saw that a man, thus led through all the due stages of a life-development should in order to be quite sure to accomplish in all steadiness, clearness, and certainty his aim, his vocation, and his destiny, be guarded from the very beginning against a crowd of misconceptions and blunders. Therefore I determined to devote myself rather to the general subject of the education of man.[10]

In 1816, Froebel started an experimental school at Keilhau. He named the school The Universal German Institute, five of his nephews forming the nucleus of its student body. He originally intended to limit enrollment to 24 students, but that number quickly was surpassed. Assisting were two men, a Herr Middendorff and a Herr Langethal.

The Institute, however, was not prosperous partly perhaps because it was out of favor with the Prussian government. The government believed the school was teaching socialism and atheism. Because of this disfavor, Middendorff and Langethal eventually left the school. Around 1825, a Herr Zech was sent by the government to inspect the school. Zech submitted a highly favorable report to his superiors. According to Hailmann:

The report of Commissioner Zeh [Hailmann's spelling varies, *i.e.*, Zeh and Zech] averted, indeed, the immediate and forcible dissolution of the Keilhau Institute, but it could not undo the indirect evil effects of the Prussian persecution. By this the little colony was reduced to straits that placed book-publishing and even book-writing beyond the power of its members. It is true, in the very next year after Commissioner Zeh's report (1826), the first volume appeared. Yet the institute had not enough popularity left to induce a publisher to assume the risk of the work, although there was still enough substance and faith in the little band to enable it to do this independently.

Immediately after the publication, however, affairs grew worse. In 1829 the number of pupils had been reduced from sixty to five, and in 1831 Froebel was driven from his post, although the enterprise was still kept up in the hands of friends.[11]

Following his departure from Keilhau, Froebel went to Switzerland where he supervised a number of schools. One of these was an orphanage at Burgdorf. In

[10] *Ibid.*, p. 98.
[11] *Op. cit.*, p. xviii. The publication to which Hailmann referred is Froebel's *The Education of Man*.

1836, because of his wife's ill health, he returned to Germany. It was at this point that he began the kindergarten period of his life.

The school at Keilhau was an elementary school for children 7 years of age and older. However, Froebel was convinced that education must take into account every stage of human development. He wrote: *"The child, the boy, man, indeed, should know no other endeavor but to be at every stage of development wholly what this stage calls for."*[12] We have seen this idea—that each stage of human development has its own "perfection"—in Rousseau. But Froebel rejects Rousseau's saltatory or "leaping" theory of human development. According to Froebel:

. . . it is highly pernicious to consider the stages of human development— infant, child, boy or girl, youth or maiden, man or woman, old man or matron— as really distinct, and not, as life shows them, as continuous in themselves, in unbroken transitions; highly pernicious to consider the child or boy as something wholly different from the youth or man, and as something so distinct that the common foundation (*human being*) is seen but vaguely in the idea and word, and scarcely at all considered in life and for life.[13]

Consequently:

The development and formation of the whole future life of each being is contained in the beginning of its existence. The untroubled realization and the undiminished efficiency of the life of each being dependent wholly on the com- prehension and fostering, on the recognition and firm carrying out of this beginning.[14]

The Kindergarten, "Unfoldment," and Educational Permissivism

In 1837, at Blankenburg, only a few miles from Keilhau, Froebel organized a school for children too young to attend elementary school. The ages of the pupils ranged from 3 to 7 years. Because organized play was a prominent feature of this school, it was called a "play school." For Froebel, play is important because it

---

[12] *The Education of Man*, p. 30. Italics in original.
[13] *Ibid.*, p. 27. Italics in original.
[14] F. Froebel, *Pedagogics of the Kindergarten*, translated by Josephine Jarvis. New York: Appleton-Century-Crofts, 1895, pp. 6–7.

. . . is the first means of development of the human mind, its first effort to make acquaintance with the outward world, to collect original experiences from things and facts, and to exercise the powers of body and mind. The child indeed recognizes no purpose in it, and knows nothing, in the beginning, of any end which is to be reached when it imitates the play it sees around it, but it expresses its own nature, and that is human nature in its playful activity.[15]

It is important to note that the child *is not conscious* of the *symbolic meaning* of his play; yet, as we shall see, Froebel bases his kindergarten procedures on the assumption that, through organized, supervised play, children may be brought to recognition of the divine unity that not only permeates the universe but is also enfolded within their souls.

In 1840, Froebel decided on the name "Kindergarten," a garden for children. Here in the protective environment of such a garden the enfolded, divine essence that each child possessed would be allowed untrammeled development. As we have seen previously, the analogy of the child and a young plant is of long standing in the history of educational thought, and its use typically has been by those conceiving education as a process of development, or unfoldment, of a previously enfolded pattern.

In 1844, the Blankenburg Kindergarten was combined with the school at Keilhau. However, again the Prussian government acted, finally forcing discontinuation of the kindergarten, as it previously had forced Froebel out of Keilhau. Although the kindergarten had been in operation only seven years, it had received widespread attention. Large numbers of teachers had come to observe and study Froebel's methods. During this period, Froebel expanded and expounded his ideas in writing. Many of these writings have been collected under the titles *Pedagogics of the Kindergarten* and *Education by Development*. A collection of his songs was published under the title, *Mother Play and Nursery Songs.*[16]

After the kindergarten at Blankenburg closed, Froebel traveled about Germany giving lectures on his teaching theory and methods. His audiences were mostly women teachers and mothers. Then, in 1851, about 10 years after the death of his first wife, Froebel married one of his former student-teachers and settled in Liebenstein, Saxe-Meiningen. Here he soon became acquainted with the Baroness Berthe von Marenholz-Bülow. She did much to help Froebel bring his ideas to the attention of people with educational and political influence, and

---

15 Berthe von Marenholz-Bülow, *Reminiscences of Friedrich Froebel,* translated by Mrs. Horace (Mary) Mann. Boston: Lee and Shepard, 1895, p. 67.

16 The *Pedagogics* and *Education by Development* were composed of Froebel's writings and were collected by Wichard Lange and translated by Josephine Jarvis. New York: Appleton-Century-Crofts, 1895 and 1900. The *Mother Play* also was collected by Lange, and translated and arranged by Susan Blow. New York: Appleton-Century-Crofts, 1896.

secured the use of an estate so that he might continue his educational work. Moreover, the Baroness also travelled throughout Europe lecturing on Froebel's methods, and wrote a book of reminiscences of her acquaintance with him.[17]

Until his death in 1852, Froebel devoted his efforts to promoting the kindergarten movement and training teachers for these schools. The movement spread rapidly, but, shortly before his death, the kindergarten was forbidden by law in any territory under Prussian rule, and other German states followed suit. He was a prophet "not without honor save in his own country."

As previously noted, Froebel believed education to be a process of becoming increasingly conscious of the law of Divine Unity. He believed that this law or principle permeates and inheres in all objects and creatures in the universe. In the following passage, which opens *The Education of Man*, this idea of Divine Unity is developed:

In all things there lives and reigns an eternal law. To him whose mind, through disposition and faith, is filled, penetrated, and quickened with the necessity that this can not possibly be otherwise, as well as to him whose clear, calm mental vision beholds the inner in the outer and through the outer, and sees the outer proceeding with logical necessity from the essence of the inner, this law has been and is enounced with equal clearness and distinctness in nature (the external), in the spirit (the internal), and in life which unites the two. This all-controlling law is necessarily based on an all-pervading, energetic, living, self-conscious, and hence eternal Unity. This fact, as well as the Unity itself, is again vividly recognized, either through faith or through insight, with equal clearness and comprehensiveness; therefore, a quietly observant human mind, a thoughtful, clear human intellect, has never failed, and will never fail, to recognize this Unity.

This Unity is God. All things have come from the Divine Unity, from God, and have their origin in the Divine Unity, in God alone. God is the sole source of all things. In all things there lives and reigns the Divine Unity, God. All things live and have their being in and through the Divine Unity, in and through God. All things are only through the divine effluence that lives in them. The divine effluence that lives in each thing is the essence of each thing.[18]

Thus, Froebel concludes:

By education, then, the divine essence of man should be unfolded, brought out, lifted into consciousness, and man himself raised into free, conscious obedience

[17] Von Marenholz-Bülow, *op. cit.*
[18] *The Education of Man*, pp. 1–2.

to the divine principle that lives in him, and to a free representation of this principle in his life.

Education, in instruction, should lead man to see and know the divine, spiritual, and eternal principle which animates surrounding nature, constitutes the essence of nature, and is permanently manifested in nature. . . .

Education as a whole, by means of instruction and training, should bring to man's consciousness, and render efficient in his life, the fact that man and nature proceed from God and are conditioned by him—that both have their being in God. *Education should lead and guide man to clearness concerning himself and in himself, to peace with nature, and to unity with God;* hence, it should lift him to a knowledge of himself and of mankind, to a knowledge of God and of nature, and to the pure and holy life to which such knowledge leads.[19]

Therefore, education in instruction and training, originally and in its first principles, should necessarily be *passive, following* (only guarding and protecting), *not prescriptive, categorical, interfering.*—Indeed, in its very essence, education should have these characteristics; for the undisturbed operation of the Divine Unity is necessarily good—can not be otherwise than good. This necessity implies that the young human being—as it were, still in the process of creation—would seek, although still unconsciously, as a product of nature, yet decidedly and surely, that which is in itself best; and, moreover, in a form wholly adapted to his condition, as well as to his disposition, his powers, and means.[20]

In these passages we see Froebel's adoption of a Roussellian interpretation of child nature and education. To educate is to promote and foster the unfoldment of the divine essence innately enfolded in a child, and this is best accomplished by guarding and protecting him from any experience that might possibly alter this natural development. To repeat, education should be *"passive, following* (only guarding and protecting), *not prescriptive, categorical, interfering."* The evil acts and thoughts of men are not the consequences of an innately and originally evil nature or the stain of original sin; they are the results of instruction that has warped the child's original nature. Thus, Froebel wrote:

If man could only reach a clear and distinct knowledge of his nature—if, after having attained such knowledge wholly or in part, he were not so paralyzed in strength and will by evil habit and infirmity—he would immediately throw off all shortcomings, and even the manifestation of all evil that is in him and done by him—that clings to him, as it were, and hides him like a disguise. All these

19 *Ibid.,* pp. 4–5. Italics in original.
20 *Ibid.,* pp. 7–8. Italics in original.

shortcomings and wrong-doings have their origin merely in the disturbed relations of these two sides of man: his *nature,* that which he has grown to be; and his *essence,* his innermost being. *Therefore, a suppressed or perverted good quality— a good tendency, only repressed, misunderstood, or misguided—lies originally at the bottom of every shortcoming in man.* [Italics supplied.] Hence the only and infallible remedy for counteracting any shortcoming and even wickedness is to find the originally good side of the human being that has been represssed, disturbed, or misled into the shortcoming, and then to foster, build up, and properly guide this good side. Thus the shortcoming will at last disappear, although it may involve a hard struggle *against habit, but not against original depravity* in man; and this is accomplished so much the more rapidly and surely because man himself prefers right to wrong.[21]

Here we see Froebel's adoption of the Roussellian view that "there is no original sin in the human heart, the how and why of the entrance of every vice can be traced."[22] Obviously, then, great significance is placed on understanding and following the development of children, for only by following the enfolded pattern of development can parents and teachers hope to preserve children from vice and wickedness. What is this pattern of development and how are we to know it? Froebel answers as follows:

Every human being who is attentive to his own development may thus recognize and study in himself the history of the development of the race to the point it may have reached, or to any fixed point. For this purpose he should view his own life and that of others at all its stages as a continuous whole, developing in accordance with divine laws. Only in this way can man reach an understanding of history, of the history of human development as well as of himself, the history and phenomena, the events of his own development, the history of his own heart, of his own feelings and thoughts; only in this way can he learn to understand others; only in this way can parents hope to understand their child.[23]

In light of the foregoing, we see Froebel's adoption of an essentially Roussellian position. Human nature is essentially good and contains within itself certain stages of development—infant, child, boy and girl, youth and maiden, man and woman. For children, play is natural and, since nature is good, play therefore is good. In fact, anything else would warp child nature and beget

[21] *Ibid.,* pp. 121–122. Italics in original except as noted.

[22] J. J. Rousseau, *Emile,* translated by Barbara Foxley. New York: Dutton, 1911; reprinted in Everyman's Library, 1938, p. 56.

[23] *The Education of Man,* p. 41.

warped adulthood. Hence, play must constitute the heart of the curriculum—for children at least—and Froebel was the pioneer in making it so. Moreover, to be "permissive, non-interfering," it must logically be free play—nonsupervised—for adult supervision means adult interference and consequently a warped personality.

However, like Rousseau, Froebel's practice was not wholly consistent with the implications of his permissivist theory. This becomes clear when we look at the famous Gifts and Occupations, and their use in the kindergarten. Froebel's preoccupation with the notion of Divine Unity and his mystical interpretation of child psychology culminated in a systematic series of playthings with directions as to how children should play with them and what insights were to be developed by such play. Today, few persons would deny the educational value of play for small children, but few, if perhaps any, would interpret the educational significance of play as Froebel did. As noted earlier, Froebel saw play as a means of mental development, that through play children express their *good-active* human nature.

But Froebel also tells us that children are not conscious of the symbolic meaning of their play. Hence, it is the task of the mother in particular and of the kindergarten teacher to provide a child with appropriate playthings and modes of play. According to Froebel, the first plaything of a child should be a ball. But why a ball? Why not a string of brightly colored beads, a rubber duck, or a rattle? In the following quotation Froebel gives his reasons, at least in part, for choosing a ball.

Therefore, as soon as the life of the child, its power of spontaneous and voluntary action and its use of limbs and senses are aroused; when it can freely move its little arms and hands, when it can perceive and distinguish tones, and can turn its attention and its gaze in the direction from which these tones come; let us give to the child for its spontaneous and voluntary action an object which expresses stability and yet movability, which in this stability and movability can be grasped and handled by the child; in which, as in its own mind, the unity of all manifoldness is contained; which it perceives in its new existence, in which, therefore, though as yet quite unconsciously, it can see its own self-dependent, stable, and yet movable life, as it were, in a mirror, as well as test and exercise such life by such an object. And this plaything is the *sphere,* or rather the *ball.*[24]

In short, Froebel is attributing to children's minds an unconscious yearning and seeking for Divine Unity which he himself felt so keenly. When he writes,

24 *Pedagogics of the Kindergarten,* p. 31.

There is yet another thing which gives to the ball not only a great charm for the children but likewise deep significance as a plaything, and so as a means of education; this is, that the child, feeling himself a whole, early seeks and must seek in conformity with his human nature and his destiny, even at the stage of unconsciousness, always to contemplate, to grasp, and to possess a whole, but never merely a part of such. He seeks to contemplate, to grasp, and to possess a whole in all things, and in each thing, or at least, by means of and with them. . . . This whole for which the child seeks is also supplied to him by the ball,[25]

we have the feeling that he is telling us more about his own quest for security, his unhappy childhood, and his profound religious beliefs than about the mind of a young child. However, psychoanalysis is beyond our competency, and the personal factors involved in the development of his views are not important for our present purpose. What is important is Froebel's series of Gifts and Occupations.

Roughly speaking, the distinction between a Gift and an Occupation is that a Gift consists of certain geometrical objects, such as ball, cylinder, and cube, whereas an Occupation consists of certain activities performed with certain kinds of materials, such as paper-folding, sewing, and drawing.

Although the first gift is called *the* ball, Froebel and his followers actually used six yarn balls, each having one of the standard colors of the spectrum, and each having a string attached for swinging and pulling. These balls were to be used in specified ways, thus creating in the child the ideas of form, motion, color, direction, and promoting muscular development and coordination.

The second Gift consists of a wooden sphere, a cube, and a cylinder. By means of the sphere, the second gift is related to the first. The cylinder represents a transition from sphere to cube, and the cube foreshadows the next series of Gifts. A child plays with these objects and, in so doing, compares their properties or characteristics.

The third Gift is another wooden cube, but it is divided into eight smaller cubes. The child is to gain the idea of part-whole relationships and to use the cubes as building blocks. Gifts four through six are variations of the third Gift, each being a division of a cube into various geometrical figures. These Gifts also were to be used as building blocks and as materials for creating geometrical designs. There are other Gifts that we shall not mention here,[26] for their inclusion seemingly would serve little purpose.

[25] *Ibid.*, p. 33.
[26] Those interested in pursuing this topic further should find Froebel's *Pedagogics of the Kindergarten,* cited earlier, of particular interest; also Kate Douglas Wiggin and Nora Archibald Smith, *Froebel's Gifts.* Boston: Houghton Mifflin, 1899.

As previously noted, Froebel's Occupations are activities with materials such as paper, yarn, and clay. These materials were to be used in specified ways and only after the complete series of Gifts had been finished. Again, the emphasis was upon eliciting from the child certain ideas and upon providing opportunity for the child to express himself through activities with these materials.[27] Thus, we see in Froebel's Gifts and Occupations a continuation of the Pestalozzian doctrine of sense impressionism and its attending methodology of proceeding *from known to unknown*. Each gift, with the exception of the first, contains some element similar to the preceding gift and each prepares the way for the subsequent one. The ball is chosen to be the first because it, of all sensible objects, satisfies the child's unconscious seeking for unity or wholeness. Thus, instruction is systematized. Moreover, instruction is psychologized, to use Pestalozzi's term, in that each gift serves to render the child increasingly conscious of his enfolded nature.

But, if one starts with the assumption that children are naturally good and have active minds, why the emphasis on supervised, controlled play? Why not let children play with whatever they wish and however they wish? Froebel tells us that *"God created man in his own image; therefore, man should create and bring forth like God."*[28] We have been told that education should be permissive and follow the naturally unfolding development of the child; it should not be prescriptive, categorical, interfering. In short, education should be negative. But, in practice Froebel, like Rousseau, does not follow this principle to its logical conclusion. Froebel prescribes what the child is to learn and do. In one place he writes that "all prescription should be adapted to the pupil's nature and needs, and secure his co-operation."[29] By securing the child's cooperation, despotism or educational authoritarianism is thought to be avoided.

But "securing the child's cooperation" does not reconcile permissivism with authoritarianism. The fact remains that, once one has adopted a "hands-off" educational program, one is logically committed to the policy of never interfering with a child's wants, wishes, and desires. And this further means that a teacher following this policy must be permissive, passive, following. The child is aways right.

On the other hand, even the most malevolent despot would seek cooperation and would try to have his subjects wish to do what they must do, simply because this makes it easier to maintain the position. As Talleyrand is supposed to have remarked to Napoleon, "You can do anything with bayonets but sit on them,"

---

[27] See Kate Douglas Wiggin and Nora Archibald Smith, *Froebel's Occupations*. Boston: Houghton Mifflin, 1898.
[28] *The Education of Man*, p. 31. Italics in original.
[29] *Ibid.*, p. 14.

though reference to Napoleon at this point is meant to impute to him neither malevolence nor beneficence.

From the foregoing, it is obvious that Froebel was in no sense an educational permissivist. But it seems equally obvious that the doctrine of education as unfoldment does logically entail educational permissivism. Therefore, to invoke unfoldment *in theory* and deny it *in practice* is to be guilty of gross self-contradiction, avoidance of which would seemingly mean either to go the whole way or to formulate a theory based on something other than unfoldment. We have seen Rousseau's difficulty in this regard, and Pestalozzi's as well, and we shall see it again in twentieth-century Progressive Education. Has there ever been either an able teacher or an able educational theorist who was basically convinced that in school he could let children do entirely as they want to do? We think not. Therefore, to make theory consistent with necessary practice means adoption of theory that embodies clear rejection of the doctrine of education as unfoldment.

The Kindergarten Movement in the United States

Finally, let us look at development of the kindergarten in the United States. As pointed out earlier, Froebel's ideas about the education of young children rapidly spread across Europe, but kindergartens soon were banned in Prussia and in the lesser German states. This ban on kindergartens, however, did not weaken the influence of Froebel's ideas, for the kindergarten was first introduced in the United States by German immigrants during the 1850s and 1860s. Many of these immigrants, forming "little Germanies" in farming areas as well as in cities, set up their own German-speaking schools and many of these had kindergartens. Credit for establishing the first kindergarten in the United States usually is given to Mrs. Carl Schurz, who had studied under Froebel. Her kindergarten, which was German- speaking, was established in Watertown, Wisconsin, in 1855. According to Cubberley, 10 more kindergartens were organized in German-speaking communities during the next 15 years.[30]

Credit for the first English-speaking kindergarten in the United States goes to Horace Mann's sister-in-law, Elizabeth P. Peabody. In 1860, she and others—probably including her sister, Mary Peabody Mann—became interested in Mrs. Schurz's accounts of Froebel's theory and opened a private kindergarten

[30] Ellwood P. Cubberley, *The History of Education.* Boston: Houghton Mifflin, 1920, p. 766.

in Boston. The school was successful, but Miss Peabody is said to have felt that she did not fully understand Froebel's principles. Consequently, in 1867, she went to Hamburg, Germany, to study with Froebel's widow. In 1868, largely due to Miss Peabody's efforts, the first training school for kindergarten teachers was established in Boston. Miss Peabody also wrote and lectured on kindergarten principles and practices. Graves compares her work in spreading the kindergarten movement in the United States with that of Baroness von Bülow in Europe.[31] The reader may have noticed that the Baroness' *Reminiscences of Froebel* which was cited earlier in this chapter was translated by Mary Peabody Mann.

In 1872, Maria Bölte opened a training school for kindergarten teachers in New York City. She, too, had studied under Froebel's widow. One of Miss Bölte's students was Susan E. Blow. In 1873, William T. Harris, city superintendent of schools at St. Louis, invited Miss Blow to establish kindergartens in the public schools there. Initially, 12 kindergartens were opened, but as soon as Miss Blow had trained enough teachers the number of kindergartens increased to more than 50. Thus, St. Louis led the way in introducing the kindergarten into public education.

William T. Harris (1835–1909) ranks with Barnard and Mann as one of the influential leaders in development of the public-school system in the United States. Like Barnard, he served as United States Commissioner of Education, from 1889 until 1906. He established *The Journal of Speculative Philosophy* and through this periodical was instrumental in acquainting Americans with German and Greek philosophy. It was in this journal that John Dewey published his first philosophical articles, and it was Harris who encouraged Dewey to continue his philosophical studies. But our concern here is with Harris as superintendent of the St. Louis schools—a position he held from 1868 to 1880—and with the kindergarten movement. Of Harris' concern for the kindergarten, Curti writes:

Although he prized highly the function of the capitalist class, Harris, as an educator, was greatly concerned over the dangers involved in the typical rearing given the offspring of the wealthy. He lamented that well-to-do mothers, eager to play a prominent role in "society," turned over their children to low-bred servants, who frequently spoiled them and thus deprived civilization of the directive ability which he thought such children inherited from their parents. Believing that the kindergarten could salvage these pampered children of the rich, a function he considered of at least equal importance with its power to

[31] Frank Pierrepont Graves, *A History of Education in Modern Times*. New York: Macmillan, 1914, p. 248.

redeem moral weaklings from homes of poverty and squalor, Harris was a pioneer in its behalf.[32]

Thus Harris saw the kindergarten as a device for protecting and promoting the development of young children. Those marked for leadership by virtue of their birth into an economically successful home would be "protected" from its excesses. Those unfortunate enough to be born into homes of economic poverty, also a sign of moral degradation, would be provided opportunity to mitigate the effects of their surroundings.

Harris and Miss Blow worked together in spreading Froebelianism and the kindergarten idea. He was general editor of D. Appleton and Company's International Education Series, and Miss Blow wrote and edited a number of books on Froebel and the kindergarten, which were published in this series. Also in the series was W. N. Hailmann's translation of Froebel's *Education of Man.* Hailmann, superintendent of schools at La Porte, Indiana, was recognized in 1884 for his efforts on behalf of the kindergarten movement, when he was made first president of the newly formed kindergarten section of the National Educational Association.

Between 1880 and 1900, such cities as San Francisco, New York, Boston, Philadelphia, Buffalo, Pittsburgh, Rochester, Providence, Milwaukee, and Minneapolis incorporated kindergartens in their public school systems. In some states, the incorporation of kindergartens in public schools was delayed because of state laws forbidding school attendance of children under six years of age. This obstacle soon was overcome, however, and kindergartens shortly became the first rung of the educational ladder in many if not most public-school systems.

Another leader in introducing Froebelianism into American educational thought and practice was Colonel Francis W. Parker (1837–1902). Parker began his career in education at the age of 16, serving as a country schoolmaster. He left teaching in 1862 to serve in the Union army where he earned his colonelcy, but returned to it after the war, teaching for a time in Dayton, Ohio. Dissatisfied with the state of educational theory and practice in the United States, at least as he knew it, he went to Europe to study. He was impressed with the schools that he saw in Germany, Holland, France, Switzerland, and Italy, and returned to the United States with the view of putting into practice what he had seen and learned.

Cremin tells us:

[32] Merle Curti, *The Social Ideas of American Educators.* Paperback edition published by Littlefield, Adams: Paterson, N.J., 1961, pp. 323–324. Reprinted by permission from Cooper Square Publishers, Inc., New York.

His opportunity was not long in coming. In 1873 the school board of Quincy, Massachusetts, sensing that all was not right with the system, decided to conduct the annual school examinations in person. The results were disastrous. While the youngsters knew their rules of grammar thoroughly, they could not write an ordinary English letter. While they could read with facility from their textbooks, they were utterly confused by similar material from unfamiliar sources. And while they spelled speedily through the required word lists, the orthography of their letters was atrocious. The board left determined to make some changes, and after a canvass of likely candidates, elected Parker to the Quincy superintendency of schools.

Things soon began to happen. The set curriculum was abandoned, and with it the speller, the reader, the grammar, and the copybook. Children were started on simple words and sentences, rather than the alphabet learned by rote. In place of time-honored texts, magazines, newspapers, and materials devised by the teachers themselves were introduced into the classroom. Arithmetic was approached inductively, through objects rather than rules, while geography began with a series of trips over the local country-side. Drawing was added to encourage manual dexterity and individual expression. The emphasis throughout was on observing, describing, and understanding, and only when these abilities had begun to manifest themselves—among the faculty as well as the students —were more conventional studies introduced.[33]

Thus, the "Quincy System" of teaching was born, and one may see the influences of Pestalozzi and his followers at work in shaping curriculum and instructional procedures.

Parker left Quincy to become a supervisor in the Boston schools. He served in this capacity from 1880 to 1883. Then, in 1883, he became principal of the Cook County Normal School at Chicago, a position he held until 1899. While at Chicago, Parker became one of the leading advocates for Froebelian principles in education. In 1882, he wrote:

Froebel said that the principles he discovered and advocated, when thoroughly applied, would revolutionize the world; and he was right. In the kindergarten is the seed corn and germination of the new education and the new life. . . . One and all the true principles of education are applied in the kindergarten; these principles should be applied (simply changing the application to adapt it to different stages of growth) through all education. . . .[34]

[33] Lawrence A. Cremin, *The Transformation of the School.* New York: Knopf, 1961, pp. 129–130.
[34] Francis W. Parker, *Talks on Pedagogics,* quoted in Samuel Chester Parker, *A Textbook in the History of Modern Elementary Education.* Boston: Ginn, 1913, p. 471.

One of the principles that Parker particularly had in mind was Froebel's idea of "creative self-expression." According to Parker, thought is necessary for expression and expression helps clarify the thought that lies behind it. In this connection Parker wrote:

Expression may be generally defined as the manifestation of thought and emotion through the body by means of physical agents. The modes of expression are:

1. Gesture,	4. Music,	7. Painting,
2. Voice,	5. Making,	8. Drawing,
3. Speech,	6. Modeling,	9. Writing.

All works of man's hand and brain are the products of these forms of expression. . . . Language is by far the greatest outcome of thought and expression. . . . Next to language may be placed the tools and instruments which man has used through all the ages in manifesting his needs and his aspirations to others. Art products . . . may be placed next, followed by construction or building.

We must conclude that the use of all the modes of expression is an imperative necessity in all-sided growth, in the realization of the highest possibilities of manhood and character.

The pedagogical value of training in all modes of expression may be briefly stated:

1. The child's individual concepts are very simple and crude; it has no complex concepts.

2. The fundamental use of exercise in all the modes of expression is to intensify those individual concepts upon which analysis, comparison, classification, original inferences, and generalization depend.

3. Concepts are developed very slowly. The demand for expression should be adapted to the growth of concepts. Any attempt beyond this limit cripples mental action.

4. *The difficulties of technique or skill are very much overestimated.* The reasons for this overrating is that attempts are commonly made to make forms of expression without adequate motive and unimpelled by thought, forms that have no thought correspondence.

5. If, in the studies of the central subjects [content subjects], all the modes of expression are continually and skillfully used to intensify thought, every child would acquire proficiency in modeling, painting, and drawing.[35]

In light of the foregoing, we see that Froebelianism, albeit in many cases misunderstood or modified in form, was one of the significant movements in the development of American educational thought and practice. Significant as the

[35] *Ibid.*, pp. 472-473. Italics in original.

kindergarten as an institution may be, however, the idea that children should be allowed and encouraged to express *their* ideas no doubt ranks among the great educational ideas of modern times. But, as in the case of many other educational ideas, it may be and has been carried to excess, as it later was in the Progressive Education movement. The idea that children should be free to "express" themselves has been used as justification for educational license. If one assumes that children are by nature actively good and that to guide or to thwart their activities is bad, then one is committed to a program of negative education: self-expression becomes an end in itself. Its educational consequences are taken for granted and not given critical attention, because of the assumption that, with such a program, the natural goodness of a child will unfold and all will be well.

Suggested Readings

Cremin, Lawrence A., *The Transformation of the School*. New York: Knopf, 1961, Chap. 5.

Cubberley, Ellwood P., *The History of Education*. Boston: Houghton Mifflin, 1920, pp. 764–769.

Curti, Merle, *The Social Ideas of American Educators*. Paterson, N.J.: Littlefield, Adams, 1961, Chaps. 9, 11, 13.

Eby, Frederick, *The Development of Modern Education*, 2nd ed. Englewood Cliffs, N.J.: Prentice-Hall, 1952, Chap. 19.

Eby, Frederick, and Arrowood, Charles F., *The Development of Modern Education*. Englewood Cliffs, N.J.: Prentice-Hall, 1934, Chap. 21.

Froebel, F., *The Education of Man*, translated and with a Preface by W. N. Hailmann. New York: Appleton-Century-Crofts, 1887.

Froebel, F., *Autobiography of Friedrich Froebel*, translated by Emilie Michaelis and H. Keatly Moore. Syracuse: C. W. Bardeen, 1889.

Froebel, F., *Pedagogics of the Kindergarten*, translated by Josephine Jarvis. New York: Appleton-Century-Crofts, 1895.

Froebel, F., *Mother Play and Nursery Songs*, translated by Josephine Jarvis. New York: Appleton-Century-Crofts, 1896.

Froebel, F., *Education by Development*, translated by Josephine Jarvis. New York: Appleton-Century-Crofts, 1900.

Graves, Frank P., *A History of Education in Modern Times*. New York: Macmillan, 1914, pp. 220–251.

Parker, Samuel C., *A Textbook in the History of Modern Elementary Education*. Boston: Ginn, 1913, Chap. 18.

von Marenholz-Bülow, Berthe, *Reminiscences of Friedrich Froebel*, translated by Mrs. Horace (Mary) Mann. Boston: Lee and Shepard, 1895.

Wiggin, Kate D., and Smith, Nora A., *Froebel's Occupations*. Boston: Houghton Mifflin, 1898.

Wiggin, Kate D., and Smith, Nora A., *Froebel's Gifts*. Boston: Houghton Mifflin, 1899.

A Language Laboratory at Indiana University. Here we see students learning a foreign language by having it "talked into them" much as John Locke recommended nearly three centuries ago. We also may see the idea of individualized, programmed instruction at work. Lockean psychology, as later developed and refined by Thorndike and others, has provided one of the major theoretical foundations for development and use of the new educational technology. (Courtesy of the Ford Foundation, William Simmons)

10 ❧ *THORNDIKE* and the

Specific-Objectivist Movement

By the turn of the century, the Herbartian dream of a science of education based upon psychological laws or principles had worked its way into the mainstream of American educational thought, even though Herbart's psychology of apperception had failed to achieve widespread acceptance. One might be Herbartian (as many were) in the sense of adopting the five formal steps of teaching without committing oneself to the principle of self-active ideas or of culture epochs. However, education could become a science only in the degree that it was, in fact, based upon *scientfic* psychology.

Psychology in Herbart's time was largely speculative and introspective, with little or no emphasis on experimentation. Indeed, although Herbart insisted that his psychology was scientific, at the same time he was convinced that psychology could not be treated experimentally.[1] Later, other psychologists, seeing the advances in such sciences as physics, chemistry, and physiology, became convinced that psychology should forego speculation and introspection in favor

[1] See R. S. Peters, (ed.), *Brett's History of Psychology*. London: Allen & Unwin, 1962, Chap. 13.

of experimentation. As this conviction took hold, the methods of psychology shifted to observation of behavior, of lower animals as well as human.

We have examined Locke's view of mind as *tabula rasa,* gaining ideas via sense impressions. Environment thus is seen as the prime mover in human behavior because it "creates motions in our nerves," which are carried to the brain and thus produce, in some unknown way, ideas in the mind, which in turn lead to action.[2] Herbart's psychology, although different from Locke's in many significant aspects, adopts a sensationist, *tabula rasa* view of mind and of learning. In either case, ideas are *ultimately* derived from sensation, and in both schemes ideas lead to actions, actions to habits, and habits constitute character.

Modern behavioristic or stimulus-response psychology takes up where Locke, Herbart, and others such as Edward B. Titchener left off. It, too, assumes that environment is the prime mover, but it adopts the method of observation of behavior as its investigative technique. Such terms as "mind," "consciousness," "thinking," "ideas," and "purpose" are either rejected as referring to superstitious "entities" or are redefined. The old scheme, "ideas →actions →habits →character," became translated into "stimuli →responses →habits →character." With this change, psychology—particularly *educational* psychology—entered a new phase.

The Herbartians had convinced us that teaching procedures should be based upon scientific psychology. The behaviorists announced that they had succeeded in making psychology truly scientific. Thus, it was claimed that at last a science of education was possible.

With this new approach to psychology, it is little wonder that, although the kindergarten gained wide acceptance in American education, its advocates, particularly the orthodox Froebelians, met stiff resistance to their views concerning the psychological nature of children and the value of "symbolic" play. One of these critics wrote:

And what shall I say of those who by a most extraordinary intellectual perversity attribute to children the habit of using common things as symbols of abstractions which have never in any way entered their heads; who tell us that the girl likes to play with her doll because the play symbolizes to her motherhood; that the boy likes to be out of doors because the sunlight symbolizes to him cheerfulness? . . .

If we live in houses because they symbolize protection, if we like to see Sherlock Holmes on the stage because he symbolizes to us craft, or Uncle Tom because he symbolizes to us slavery, or a clown from the circus because he

[2] See any unabridged edition of John Locke, *An Essay Concerning Human Understanding,* Book II, Chap. 8, paragraph 12.

symbolizes to us folly; if we eat apples because they symbolize to us the fall of man, or strawberries because they symbolize to us the scarlet woman, then perhaps the children play with the ball because it symbolizes "infinite development and absolute limitation."

No one has ever given a particle of valid evidence to show any such preposterous associations in children's minds between plain things and these far-away abstractions.[3]

This critic, Edward Lee Thorndike, has been and perhaps still is the most famous educational psychologist the United States has produced. His system of psychology, which he called "connectionism," may be said to have completely dominated educational psychology in this country for 30 years, roughly between 1900 and 1930. Even though connectionism and stimulus-response psychology have undergone modifications, their influence on teaching method and curriculum organization continues today.

Thorndike

Edward Lee Thorndike was born in 1874 and died in 1949. Apparently, little has been written about his youth; in his autobiography[4] Thorndike himself makes no mention of it. While a student at Wesleyan University, he became acquainted with William James' *The Principles of Psychology*. This book so impressed him that in 1896, although his primary interest had been literature, he went to Harvard to study psychology with James. Thorndike wrote that "by the fall of 1897, I though of myself as a student of psychology and a candidate for the Ph.D. degree."[5] While at Harvard, Thorndike became interested in animal learning. His earliest experiments, which were with chickens, were conducted first in his rooms, then, after his landlady complained, in the basement of William James' home.

Thorndike studied at Harvard for two years, but upon receiving a fellowship from Columbia University went there to study with James McKeen Cattell, who like James had studied under Wundt. He took to Columbia two of his

---

[3] Edward L. Thorndike, *Notes on Child Study*, quoted in Samuel Chester Parker, *A Textbook in the History of Modern Elementary Education*. Boston: Ginn, 1913, pp. 459–460.

[4] Edward L. Thorndike, *Autobiography*, in *Psychology and the Science of Education: Selected Writings of Edward L. Thorndike*, Geraldine M. Joncich (ed.). New York: Teachers College. Columbia University, 1962.

[5] *Ibid.*, p. 28.

"most educated" chickens and there continued his research in animal learning and behavior. In 1898, he received the doctorate and published his dissertation, *Animal Intelligence,* a work acknowledged as a landmark in the history of psychology.[6]

Upon graduation, Thorndike took a position in education at the College for Women of Western Reserve University. To prepare for this position, he spent the summer reading about educational theories and methodology. The following year, he was invited to teach psychology and child study at Teachers College, Columbia University, where he stayed for the remainder of his career.

The Reflex-Arc Theory and Psychological Connectionism

In his *Educational Psychology* of 1913, Thorndike discusses human behavior and learning in these words:

A man's nature and the changes that take place in it may be described in terms of the responses—of thought, feeling, action and attitude—which he makes, and of the bonds by which these are connected with the situations which life offers. Any fact of intellect, character or skill means a tendency to respond in a certain way to a certain situation—involves a *situation* or state of affairs influencing the man, a *response* or state of affairs in the man, and a *connection* or bond whereby the latter is the result of the former.[7]

A man's intellect, character and skill is the sum of his tendencies to respond to situations and elements of situations. This number of different situation-response connections that make up this sum would, in an educated adult, run well up into the millions.[8]

Apparently, then, *all* of human behavior is explainable in terms of the formula S →R. The S of the formula represents a stimulus or a stimulating element of a situation. It causes excitation in the nervous system, after which the system transmits the excitation (or impulse) to a muscle or a gland, both excitation and transmission being represented by the arrow. Discharge of the impulse

---

[6] Edward L. Thorndike, *Animal Intelligence.* New York: Macmillan, 1911.

[7] Edward L. Thorndike, *Educational Psychology,* 3 vols. New York: Teachers College, Columbia University, 1913, Vol. 1, p. 1. Italics in original.

[8] *Ibid.,* Vol. 2, p. 4.

into muscle or gland causes it to respond (the R of the formula). Let us look at this more closely.

Since the eighteenth century, the concept of a "reflex arc" has received considerable attention in physiology. A reflex typically is defined as an unlearned, immediate response to a stimulus. In 1924, Herrick outlined the process of a reflex arc as follows:

1. The *stimulus,* a physical agent of some sort which impinges upon excitable protoplasm.

2. The *excitation,* or the direct effect of the stimulus upon the specific protoplasm which is affected. A special receptive apparatus is usually provided for each kind of stimulus to which the body is sensitive, namely, the sense organ or receptor. The sense organ is usually regarded as part of the nervous system, though it may contain a very complex assortment of non-nervous accessory tissues.

3. The *afferent transmission.* The apparatus is a sensory nervous pathway which transmits the excitation from the receptor to a centre of correlation.

4. The *central adjustment.* The adjuster is a nerve centre in which the afferent impulse is transferred to the efferent pathway, with or without more or less complex modification of the excitation in the centre itself.

5. The *efferent transmission.* The apparatus is a motor nervous pathway which transmits the excitation to the peripheral organ of response.

6. The *response.* The specific apparatus of response is termed the effector, which is usually not a part of the nervous system—muscles, gland, electric-organ, etc.[9]

A human nervous system is composed of millions of individual cells called neurons, and there appear to be no structural connections from one to another. They are separated from each other by tissue gaps, called *synapses.* The nature of synapses has been the subject of much speculation, but Thorndike assumed that across them develop some kind of connection between sensory and motor neurons, forming chains or discharge paths. That is, synapses are the points across which connections are made between receptors and effectors—stimuli and responses. According to Thorndike, "Even the most complicated nervous systems are variations of this general arrangement of shorter or longer series of neurons making circuits from sensitive surfaces to organs of response.[10] And earlier, in 1898,

[9] C. J. Herrick, *Neurological Foundations of Animal Behavior.* New York: Holt, Rinehart and Winston, 1924, p. 121.

[10] Edward L. Thorndike, *The Elements of Psychology.* New York: A. G. Seiler, 1917, p. 151.

The connections formed between situation and response are represented by connections between neurones and neurones whereby the disturbance, or neural current, arising in the former is conducted to the latter across their synapses. The strength or weakness of a connection means the greater or less likelihood that the same current will be conducted from the former to the latter rather than to some other place. The strength or weakness of the connection is a condition of the synapses.[11]

Thus, synaptic resistance to the passage of neural impulses was seen as the key to understanding behavior.

Thorndike believed that men come into this world equipped with certain "original tendencies," which he assumed to be inborn connections between stimuli and responses. He wrote:

An original bond between a situation and response in human behavior has as its physiological basis an original ease of conduction of the physiological action aroused in certain neurones toward a certain final path rather than toward any other. The original arrangement of the neurones . . . is the main determinant of what responses of sensation and movement the given situation will provoke.[12]

Hence, all unlearned behavior is explainable in terms of inherited physiological relationships between sensory and motor neurons. This coterie of original connections or bonds constitutes original human nature and is the raw material or starting point for all learning and education. But, before we look at Thorndike's interpretation of learning, we should pay particular attention to his use of the term "situation."

As a general rule, Thorndike used the phrase "situation-response" to describe animal and human behavior. The word "situation" has a much wider connotation than does "stimulus." As noted previously, the word "stimulus" typically refers to a physical agent such as a light ray or a sound wave. On the other hand, the word "situation" connotes not only physical agents but nonphysical as well, such as number. However, Thorndike apparently used the word "situation" as a working synonym for "stimulus." He wrote:

Save in early infancy and amongst the feeble-minded, however, any situation will most probably act unevenly. Some of its elements will produce only the response of neglect; others will be bound to only a mild awareness of them;

---

[11] *Animal Intelligence*, pp. 246–247.
[12] *Educational Psychology*, Vol. 1, p. 221.

others will connect with some energetic response of thought, feeling or action, and become positive determiners of the man's future.[13]

In this quotation we see Thorndike saying that not only is the environment active and man passive, but also that the environment is composed of "prepotent" elements capable of shaking themselves free from the rest of the environment and thereby determining the responses made in that "situation." Although Thorndike did not consistently use the "active environment–passive man" form of expression in his writings, his assumption that all human behavior is the result of stimuli *external to* whatever "conduction unit" (or reflex-arc series) may be involved cannot logically be taken to mean anything else. Prepotent elements—stimuli—impinge upon receptors, causing an excitation in a neuron chain that eventuates in a physiological movement, a response.[14]

In his book *Education,* Thorndike wrote: [Synapses] are modified in the course of education so that it becomes easier or harder for neurone number one to discharge into the receiving end of neurone number two. *The physiological basis for education is the modifiability of synapses between neurones.*[15] Earlier, he had written:

The connections formed between situation and response are represented by connections between neurones and neurones whereby the disturbance, or neural current, arising in the former is conducted to the latter across their synapses. The strength or weakness of a connection means the greater or less likelihood that the same current will be conducted from the former to the latter rather than to some other place. The strength or weakness of the connection is a condition of the synapses.[16]

He characterized the preceding as "the essence of my account of the physiological mechanism of learning."[17] "Learning is connecting, and man is the great learner primarily because he forms so many connections."[18] Let us look now at the ways in which connections may be formed.

Throughout his career, Thorndike formulated a number of psychological "laws," but our concern here will be with those of exercise, readiness, and effect. In our view, these constitute the heart of Thorndike's theory of learning.

The law of exercise is subdivided into the law of use and the law of disuse.

[13] *Ibid.,* Vol. 2, p. 27.

[14] It is important to note that so-called "internal" stimuli are always *external* to the conduction unit transmitting the neurological impulse to an effector.

[15] Edward L. Thorndike, *Education.* New York: Macmillan, 1912, p. 64. Italics in original.

[16] *Animal Intelligence,* pp. 246–247.

[17] *Educational Psychology,* Vol. 1, p. 227.

[18] *Ibid.,* Vol. 2, p. 54.

The law of use is that "When a modifiable connection is made between a situation and a response, that connection's strength is, other things being equal, increased."[19] Thorndike also stated this law as follows: ". . . *When any neurone or neurone group is stimulated and transmits to or discharges into or connects with a second neurone or neurone group, it will, when later stimulated again in the same way, have an increased tedency to transmit to the same neurone group as before. . . .*"[20] Thus, the law of use is a statement to the effect that repetition is an indispensable, causal factor in learning. Moreover, the repetition of an S-R connection must not admit of any variation; otherwise, neuron A will not discharge into neuron B, and this means that the resistance of the synapse lying between A and B will not be worn down or reduced. Learning is a process of creating preferred paths of neurological discharge, through lowered synaptic resistance, so that S_1 will invariably lead to R_1.[21]

On the other hand, the law of disuse states: "When a modifiable connection is *not* made between a situation [stimulus] and a response during a length of time, that connection's strength is decreased."[22] One might say that the law of disuse is not a law of learning, but, instead, a law of forgetting. However, if learning is seen as *any* modification in neural connections, then weakening a connection (or forgetting) is a form of learning. Disuse of a connection apparently makes possible the restoration of synaptic resistance, which in turn disrupts the connection between stimulus and response.

The law of effect, which as we shall see was a forerunner of the contemporary doctrine of reinforcement, is that

When a modifiable connection between a situation [stimulus] and a response is made and is accompanied or followed by a satisfying state of affairs, that connection's strength is increased: When made and accompanied or followed by an annoying state of affairs; its strength is decreased."[23]

By "satisfaction" or "a satifying state of affairs," Thorndike meant that an individual does nothing to avoid a situation and its response, or that he tries to prolong or to undergo a situation and its response. By "annoyance" or "an annoying state of affairs," he meant that an individual does nothing to prolong

19 *Ibid.*, Vol. 2, p. 2.

20 *The Elements of Psychology*, p. 165. Italics in original.

21 Thorndike modified his position on the efficacy of repetition in learning in his *Fundamentals of Learning* of 1932 (New York: Teachers College, Columbia University). However, as noted at the beginning of this chapter, our concern is with the position that Thorndike was taking when his influence was a major determinant in educational theory.

22 *Educational Psychology*, Vol. 2, p. 4.

23 *Ibid.*

a situation and a response, or tries to avoid or to put an end to a situation and its response.[24] However, this description of satisfaction and of annoyance does not tell us much, and Thorndike himself must have been aware of its vagueness because in 1916 he returned to his doctrine of neurological connections for what appears to be his ultimate explanation.

I believe that the original [as well as learned] tendencies of man to be satisfied and to be annoyed—to welcome and reject—are described by these three laws of readiness and unreadiness: (1) that *when a conduction unit is ready to conduct, conduction by it is satisfying, nothing being done to alter its action;* (2) that *for a conduction unit ready to conduct not to conduct is annoying, and provokes whatever responses nature provides in connection with that particular annoying lack;* (3) that *when a conduction unit unready for conduction is forced to conduct, conduction by it is annoying.*[25]

In the preceding pages, we have seen that Thorndike assumed that man, as well as other animals, is a passive (reactive) creature whose behavior is determined by the stimulus-response connections obtaining in his nervous system. Moreover, not only is environment the prime mover (active), but certain elements of a given environmental situation are more active (prepotent) than others. The upshot of all of this is that human beings are seen as acting without purpose or without ends-in-view. Man simply *reacts*.

But, if human beings do not act with foresight or anticipation of consequences, how are we to explain problem-solving behavior? Thorndike's answer to this question is that problem-solving is, fundamentally, random trial and error. In his *Briefer Course* he wrote:

If we take a box twenty by fifteen by twelve inches, replace its cover and front side by bars an inch apart, and make in this front side a door arranged so as to fall open when a wooden button inside is turned from a vertical to a horizontal position, we shall have means to observe such. A kitten, three to six months old, if put in this box when hungry, a bit of fish being left outside, reacts as follows: It tries to squeeze through between the bars, claws at the bars and at loose things in and out of the box, stretches its paw out between the bars, and bites at its confining walls. Some one of all these promiscuous clawings, squeezings, and bitings turns round the wooden button, and the kitten gains freedom and food. By repeating the experience again and again, the animal gradually comes to omit all the useless clawings, and the like, and to manifest only

24 *Ibid.*, p. 2.
25 *Educational Psychology: Briefer Course.* New York: Teachers College, Columbia University, 1916, p. 55. Italics in original.

the particular impulse (e.g., to claw hard at the top of the button with the paw, or to push against one side of it with the nose) which has resulted successfully. It turns the button around without delay whenever put in the box. It has formed an association between the situation, *confinement in a box of a certain appearance,* and the response of *clawing at a certain part of that box in a certain way.*[26]

Close reading of the above, of course, shows that the kitten "tries to," "claws at," "stretches," and "bites at," all expressions that clearly depict the kitten's attempts to get out of the cage, using whatever means it "saw" as even remotely possible. Sooner or later, it "hits" upon the correct means, albeit a very uncatlike one. Moreover, the expression "trial and error"—"if at first you don't succeed, try, try again"—clearly implies repeated attempts to achieve a given end-in-view. Hence, unsuspecting readers have been eased into the assumption that S-R connectionism, based on the reflex-arc theory, is at one with what may be called *goal-insight* theory or purposive, field-theoretical psychology.

However, though we cannot here present the evidence that supports our saying so, Thorndike did not assume behavior to be purposive and had no intention of doing so. For him, "trial and error" was a case of the "laws of association" at work—frequency, recency, intensity, contiguity, etc. To the various S's in the situation the kitten evinced seriatim the various R's connected thereto, the last and most recent one terminating the situation. Since the last one—turning the button—had to be common to all trials, it had to be one of the most frequent. It had also to be in each case the most recent, as well as the most contiguous temporally and perhaps spatially. Intensity might even be at work in its behalf. Therefore, after a number of practice runs, the incorrect responses tended to fall away and only the correct one remain.
Moreover:

There are certain states of affairs which the animal welcomes and does nothing to avoid—its satisfiers. There are others which it is intolerant of and rejects, doing one thing or another until relieved from them. Of the bonds which the animal's behavior makes between a situation and responses those grow stronger which are accompanied by satisfying states of affairs, while those accompanied by annoyance weaken and disappear. Exercise strengthens and disuse weakens bonds. Such is the sum and substance of the bulk of animal learning.[27]

Hence, for Thorndike, trial-and-error learning demonstrated "the laws of readiness, exercise, and effect, uncomplicated by any pseudo-aid from imitation,

[26] *Educational Psychology: Briefer Course,* p. 129. Italics in original.
[27] *Ibid.,* pp. 131–132.

ideomotor action, or superior faculties of inference."[28] Not only is trial-and-error learning "the sum and substance" of animal learning, it is fundamental in human learning as well. As Thorndike wrote, "similarly a person whose general aim is to solve a mechanical puzzle may hit upon the solution, or some part of it, in the course of *random fumbling,* may hit upon it sooner in the next trial, and so progress in the learning—all with little help from ideas about the puzzle or his own movements."[29]

Although Thorndike did not deny the efficacy of ideas, his interpretation of the nature of ideas as "inner, concealed responses in the neurones themselves"[30] does not shed light on the function of ideas in problem-solving or in thinking. He suggested:

In studying mental functions one might begin at the real beginning—man's original nature—and trace each formation of each bond, getting eventually the entire history of each function in terms of original tendencies and environmental circumstances cooperating under the laws of exercise, effect, and readiness. Such a thoroughgoing genetic method would be admirable in intention, but its execution is impossible in our present state of ignorance.[31]

Thus, we return to the starting point of our discussion: "Any fact of intellect, character or skill means a tendency to respond in a certain way to a certain situation."

We have seen that Thorndike considered learning to be connecting responses to stimuli. Therefore, "teaching is the arrangement of situations which will lead to desirable bonds and make them satisfying."[32]

A volume could well be written showing in detail just what bonds certain exercises in arithmetic, spelling, German, philosophy, and the like, certain customs and laws, certain moral and religious teachings, and certain occupations and amusements, tend to form in men of given original natures; or how certain desired bonds could economically be formed. Such would be one useful portion of an Applied Psychology of Learning or Science of Education.[33]

Again, in his *Principles of Teaching,* he wrote:

Using psychological terms, the art of teaching may be defined as the art of giving and withholding stimuli with the result of producing or preventing cer-

28 *Ibid.,* p. 131.
29 *Ibid.,* p. 139. Italics ours.
30 *Ibid.,* p. 173.
31 *Ibid.,* p. 177.
32 *Ibid.,* p. 174.
33 *Ibid.,* p. 174.

tain responses. . . . The aim of the teacher is to produce desirable and prevent undesirable changes in human beings by producing and preventing certain responses.[34]

In light of the foregoing, we see the way in which Thorndike represents, and how he developed, the tradition of education as formation from without. Like Locke and Herbart, Thorndike assumed a passive, plastic human nature that may be molded, within limitations, by a teacher. By controlling the ideas or the S-R bonds that a child develops, a teacher controls his actions. By controlling a child's actions, a teacher controls his habits, which in turn constitute his intellect, character, and skills. According to Thorndike, the reason we have been unable to gain absolute control over the behavior and characters of men is that our knowledge of human nature is incomplete.[35] Nevertheless, by using what we do know of human nature, teaching may be made efficient and effective.

Curriculum "Research": Activity Analysis and Specific-Objectivism

Although Thorndike was interested in curriculum matters, his influence on American education was confined primarily to psychology, methodology, and measurement. Let us look now at some of the curriculum proposals that seemingly grew out of acceptance of connectionistic psychology.

If teaching is concerned with changing human behavior, that is, with producing desired responses, the question for curriculum makers is, "What responses do we desire to have learned?" In 1924, Franklin Bobbitt, professor of education at the University of Chicago, answered this question as follows:

It is helpful to begin with the simple assumption, to be accepted literally, that education is to prepare men and women for the activities of every kind which make up, or which ought to make up, well-rounded adult life; that it has no other purpose; that everything should be done with a view to this purpose; and that nothing should be included which does not serve this purpose.

Education is primarily for adult life, not for child life. Its fundamental responsibility is to prepare for the fifty years of adulthood, not for the twenty years of childhood and youth.

When we know what men and women ought to do along the many lines and

---

[34] In Joncich, *op. cit.*, pp. 60–61.
[35] *Ibid.*, p. 62.

levels of human experience, then we shall have before us the things for which they should be trained. The first task is to discover the activities which ought to make up the lives of men and women; and along with these, the abilities and personal qualities necessary for proper performance. These are the educational objectives.[36]

As formulated by Bobbitt and afterwards slightly improved by Briggs, the statement of educational purpose was, "Teach the child to do better what he is going to do anyway." (Briggs' "improvement" was to insert the word "better.") Hence, it was first necessary to find what people do; to observe people and record their activities. Although in *How to Make a Curriculum* Bobbitt neglected specifically to say so, this indeed was his first step—in both the Los Angeles and the Denver studies. And it opened a whole field of "educational research," one of the outstanding products being Thorndike's *The Teacher's Word Book,* a compendium of the ten, twenty, or thirty thousand (or more) words most commonly used in the United States,[37] as shown by tallying the words appearing in newspapers, popular magazines, business letters, personal letters, widely read books, and whatever else represented what people read. The items thereby collected were then arranged in order of frequency, with the most frequent at the top. Hence, since in a given period of time pupils could cover only so much territory or so many items, it was simply a matter of counting down the list that many items and cutting off those below. There were all manner of refinements of this procedure, but they were merely variations on this as the basic theme.

Bobbitt then needed to separate his master list into categories, and he hit upon 10, as follows:

1. Language activities; social intercommunication.
2. Health activities.
3. Citizenship activities.
4. General social activities—meeting and mingling with others.
5. Spare-time activities, amusements, recreations.
6. Keeping one's self mentally fit—analogous to the health activities of keeping one's self physically fit.
7. Religious activities.
8. Parental activities, the upbringing of children, the maintenance of a proper home life.

---

[36] Franklin Bobbitt, *How to Make a Curriculum*. Boston: Houghton Mifflin, 1924, pp. 7–8.

[37] New York: Teachers College, Columbia University, 1921.

9. Unspecialized or non-vocational practical activities.
10. The labors of one's calling.[38]

However, such categories tended to define subject matter or curriculum *areas;* not specific objectives. Moreover, the activities themselves were not to be taken as educational objectives, but rather the *abilities* necessary to perform these activities. With both these considerations in mind, therefore,

General unanalyzed objectives are to be avoided. For the ten major divisions of human action, it would be possible to state ten corresponding abilities. These would be so general as to be practically useless for curriculum-making. "Ability to care for one's health," for example, is too general to be useful. It must be reduced to particularity: ability to manage the ventilation of one's sleeping-room, ability to protect one's self against micro-organisms, ability to care for the teeth, and so on.[39]

But "ability to care for the teeth" is itself comprised of such specific activities as brushing after meals, brushing "up and down" rather than "across," seeing the dentist twice a year, and so on. These specific activities, in Thorndikean terms, represent desirable responses to specific situations or stimuli. A child learns these desirable responses in accordance with the laws of exercise and effect, which is to say that he must perform, must make, these responses. Or, as Bobbitt put it: "Whether we appeal to science or to common sense, the dominant principle of educational method appears to be this: *The mind grows as it is exercised.* Ability to function is developed through normal exercise of function. One learns to do a thing through doing it."[40]

Thus, the task of education is to determine what specific activities or functions a person will perform in life, designate the abilities to perform these activities as the specific objectives of education, and teach children and youth these abilities. This, of course, is why we have chosen to call the movement "specific objectivism." Viewed in this light, education is directed toward "life adjustment," which simply means preservation of the *status quo.* For, in Bobbitt's view, "There are more ways of going wrong than of going right. The *status quo* is usually better than changes in the wrong directions."[41] Hence, his emphasis on the

[38] Bobbitt, *op. cit.,* pp. 8–9.
[39] *Ibid.,* p. 32.
[40] *Ibid.,* p. 51. Italics in original.
[41] *Ibid.,* p. 7.

present or actual activities of mankind, and by this he meant the activities of Americans in the 1920s, when he was conducting his researches.

Method: The Washburne Plan

The fact that children learn at different rates has always been a problem, particularly when classes are large. Individualized instruction, with each child learning at his own rate, long has been considered ideal, but how is it to be done in a class of 30 to 40 children? The problem becomes particularly pressing when one considers the objectives of education to be specific abilities or activities. It was this problem that concerned Carleton W. Washburne, and his answer to it was a forerunner of modern programmed instruction.

In 1919, Washburne was appointed superintendent of the Winnetka public schools. Winnetka, a suburb of Chicago, was a community of prosperous citizens, greatly interested in the educational ideas of Washburne and of his mentor, Frederic Burk. As superintendent, Washburne divided the faculty into instructional-level groups, meeting with first-grade teachers on certain days, and so on with the rest of the faculty. He writes:

At the beginning I asked the teachers in each group what their objectives were—what they hoped to teach their children during the year and what problems they were finding. Very soon arithmetic became a major subject of inquiry; above the first grade, arithmetic caused more failures among the children than did any other subject, in spite of more time being given to it than to any other study.

What knowledge of arithmetic and what skill did each successive grade seek to give to the children? The answers at first were general—addition, multiplication, fractions, and so on. "But specifically what do you expect every child to know at the end of the year?" I would ask. The teachers tried to specify—and they always specified more than every child could possibly master.

"But can *every* child know all that, well, by the end of the year?"

"No, but this is what we should try to teach them. We must keep our standards high."

"But is a standard which a child cannot reach, even with every effort, a useful standard? Have we a right to tell a child he must do what he cannot do and that failure to do it will be punished by low marks or by repeating the grade the next year? Have we a right to deceive parents into thinking we will teach their children things we know many of the children cannot learn at this stage of their development?"

Through such questions, pursued with the rigor I had learned from Burk, the teachers gradually became more clear thinking and realistic. In time they agreed with Burk's maxim: "A YEAR'S WORK IN A SUBJECT IS WHAT THE *slowest, normal, diligent,* CHILD CAN ACCOMPLISH IN A YEAR." Children below normal intelligence should not be pushed beyond their ability—let them successfully complete as much of the year's work as comes within their ability. Children above normal intelligence should not be held back, but encouraged to do as much more than a year's work as they can. Children who were not diligent would be penalized by slower progress, but their interest, and consequent effort, should be stimulated by the teacher.[42]

Thus, there was a twofold problem: (1) to analyze course content into specific objectives, and (2) to devise a plan of instruction so that each child would be allowed to master each of the objectives at his own rate. Washburne set the faculty to work on the first phase of this problem, and he supplied the device by which each child would be allowed to learn at his own rate. This device came to be known as the "Winnetka Plan."

Before looking at the instructional technique of the Winnetka Plan, let us examine the ways in which Washburne determined what the content of the curriculum should be. He describes his procedure as follows:

It is a comparatively simple matter to determine what knowledges and skills are commonly needed. Scientific investigations of the demands of society in this field are well under way. It is becoming possible to build the knowledge-and-skill part of the curriculum upon research. The Winnetka schools have contributed their share to such research.

We, in Winnetka, have made an exhaustive study of the common allusions to persons and places in periodical literature, recognizing that in order to read intelligently a person must have familiarity with these persons and places. We have made comparative analyses of the vocabulary studies of others, to determine what words children are most likely to need to spell. We have made statistical studies of primary reading books to find what phonograms are most useful to children learning to read, and have analyzed the 10,000 commonest words in the English language to discover the syllables which occur so commonly as to demand instant recognition. With others, we have measured the speed and accuracy possessed by successful, intelligent men and women in various arithmetical processes, as a guide to the degree of skill children are likely to need.

[42] From the book *Winnetka: The History and Significance of an Educational Experiment,* by Carleton W. Washburne and Sidney P. Marland. © 1963 by Prentice-Hall, Inc., Englewood Cliffs, N.J. Pp. 22–23. Italics in original.

As a result of such studies of our own, and of studies of the same general type made by others, we have, as far as possible, built the knowledge-and-skill part of our curriculum on the known needs of society.[43]

Thus, curriculum content is determined by obtaining through statistical techniques those knowledges and skills that are most frequently used or alluded to in American life.[44]

Essentially, the central idea of the Winnetka Plan was that children should use self-instruction materials prepared by the teachers. These materials presented the subject matter step-by-step—objective by objective. An example of the step-by-step (or programmed) organization in arithmetic is as follows:[45]

. . . let us consider the first steps in simple multiplication taken *after* a child had mastered all the basic multiplication facts (2 × 3, 4 × 8, 3 × 6, etc.). The process was broken down into three steps as follows:

Step 1—No zeros, no carrying, e.g.   41
                                                                        ×2

Step 2—Zero, at end of multiplicand, e.g.   20
                                                                        ×4

Step 3—Carrying introduced, e.g.   13
                                                                        ×5

Each of these three steps had three exercises—A, B, and C—that were to be correctly completed before a child started on the next step. At the end of a series of steps, a child could ask for a practice test. Washburne describes the procedure this way:[46]

[The test] was made up of one example of each step and usually an example combining all steps. It was made in five forms, all of the same difficulty and all constructed in the same way. Three of these forms were in the child's book, with an answer sheet for self-correction, like this:

    1. If Bill wanted to make 3 notebooks, each with 26 sheets, how many sheets of paper would he need?

[43] Carleton W. Washburne, "The Philosophy of the Winnetka Curriculum," *Twenty-Sixth Yearbook of the National Society for the Study of Education*, 1927, Part I, pp. 219–220.
[44] Also see the following: Carleton W. Washburne, "*A Program of Individualization,*" *24th Yearbook of the National Society for the Study of Education*, 1925, Part II, pp. 77–83, 257–272; Carleton W. Washburne, "*Basic Facts Needed in History and Geography,*" *22nd Yearbook of the National Society for the Study of Education*, 1923, Part II, pp. 216–233.
[45] Washburne and Marland, *op. cit.*, p. 26.
[46] *Ibid.*, pp. 26–27.

2. Susan was making cookies for a large party. The recipe made 32 cookies. If she made the recipe 3 times, how many cookies would she have?
3. Carolyn said she could save 20 cents a week to buy a new record. In 4 weeks how much could she save?

The answer sheet looked like this:

1.   26 sheets
    ×3
    ――――
    78 sheets—Step 3

2.   32 cookies
    ×3
    ――――
    96 cookies—Step 1

3.   20 cents
    ×4
    ――――
    80 cents—Step 2

If a child made a mistake on the practice test, the answer sheet showed him the nature of his mistake. Once a child had completed one of the three practice tests *without mistakes,* he was allowed to take a "real test" over each unit before proceeding to the next series of steps. Moreover, a "real test" had to be passed 100 percent.

After a child had passed a "real" or performance test, this information was recorded in the teacher's "goal record book" and on the child's "goal card." Washburne and Marland write:

When a child passed a test he took his goal card to the teacher who entered the date. The rising column of dates showed his progress. Every six weeks the teacher drew a red line across the top of the highest date in the column, thereby showing the rate of progress. There were no report cards with marks "excellent," "good," "poor," etc.—every child was 100 percent in all that he had done. But some had done more than others.[47]

With each child using his own workbook,[48] teachers were free to circulate through the class, giving individualized instruction, criticism, and encouragement. However, the programmed part of instruction was concerned only with

――――――――

[47] *Ibid.,* p. 28.
[48] According to Washburne and Marland, these self-instructional materials "were the model on which the first published 'work books' were made by a commercial publisher." *Ibid.,* p. 25.

"tool subjects," or those knowledges and skills "that everyone needs to know." As Washburne and Marland put it:

For the skill subjects of arithmetic, reading and the mechanics of the language arts there were certain minimal requirements where, sooner or later, children had to achieve uniformity. One does not want originality in spelling or in the basic conventions of punctuation or in the knowledge that $6 \times 9 = 54$ or in the essential meaning of a printed page. Therefore, for these aspects of learning, adaptation to individual differences involves, primarily, variation in *time* to fit each child—when he shall begin a unit of work, in accordance with his own maturity and experience, and how rapidly he shall accomplish it.[49]

On the other hand, there are subjects in which creativity can be allowed, and there are activities that children working in groups can perform with profit. However, we shall not consider this "afternoon" aspect of the Winnetka Plan here, for it represents the permissive, Progressive, side of Washburne's position. Progressivism will be considered in our next chapter.

The significance of the Winnetka Plan lay in its attempt to provide for individual differences in learning and, at the same time, teach for specific, clearly identifiable objectives. In a real sense, it was a return to the method of re-citation; the child "recited" to his workbook, and the answer sheet "corrected" his recitation. The widespread use of workbooks in American education today attests to the pervasive and continuing influence Winnetka (and, shortly afterwards, Morrison) had on curriculum and methods. Despite the *claims* that teaching machines and programmed instruction are a "major breakthrough," those who know their educational history see this, not as a breakthrough, but as a variation of the Winnetka Plan in new technological dress. Moreover, the psychology that is used to support programmed instruction today appears to be little more than slightly modified connectionism.[50]

One of the leading proponents of teaching machines and programmed instruction, B. F. Skinner, writes:

The Law of Effect has been taken seriously; we have made sure that effects *do* occur and that they occur under conditions which are optimal for producing the changes called learning. Once we have arranged the particular type of con-

[49] *Ibid.*, pp. 87–88. Italics in original.
[50] See Morris L. Bigge, *Learning Theories for Teachers*. New York: Harper & Row, 1964, Chaps. 3–6.

sequence called a reinforcement, our techniques permit us to shape up the behavior of an organism almost at will.[51]

However, Skinner does not make clear, at least in this article, what he means by "reinforcement." He writes that "The sheer control of nature is itself reinforcing."[52] And again, in terms of teaching, "If the natural reinforcement inherent in the subject matter is not enough, other reinforcers must be employed."[53] Nevertheless, "The simple fact is that, as a mere reinforcing mechanism, the teacher is out of date. This would be true even if a single teacher devoted all her time to a single child."[54]

With regard to the process of instruction, Skinner takes the position that "The whole process of becoming competent in any field must be divided into a very large number of very small steps, and reinforcement must be contingent upon the accomplishment of each step."[55] The reason for this procedure is that "by making each successive step as small as possible, the frequency of reinforcement can be raised to a maximum, while the possibly aversive consequences of being wrong are reduced to a minimum."[56] Thus, the curriculum is broken down into specific objectives, and instruction is mechanized as follows:

The technical problem of providing the necessary instrumental aid is not particularly difficult. There are many ways in which the necessary contingencies may be arranged, either mechanically or electrically. An inexpensive device which solves most of the principal problems has already been constructed. It is still in the experimental stage, but a description will suggest the kind of instrument which seems to be required. The device consists of a small box about the size of a small record player. On the top surface is a window through which a question or problem printed on a paper tape may be seen. The child answers the question by moving one or more sliders upon which the digits 0 through 9 are printed. The answer appears in square holes punched in the paper upon which the question is printed. When the answer has been set, the child turns a knob. The operation is as simple as adjusting a television set. If the answer is right, the knob turns freely and can be made to ring a bell or provide some other conditioned reinforcement. If the answer is wrong, the knob will not turn. A counter may be added to tally wrong answers. The knob must then be reversed

[51] B. F. Skinner, "The Science of Learning and the Art of Teaching," in Wendell I. Smith and J. William Moore, *Programmed Learning: Theory and Research.* Princeton: Van Nostrand, 1962, p. 19.
[52] *Ibid.*, p. 28.
[53] *Ibid.*
[54] *Ibid.*, pp. 29–30.
[55] *Ibid.*, p. 29.
[56] *Ibid.*

slightly and a second attempt at a right answer made. (Unlike the flash-card, the device reports a wrong answer without giving the right answer.) When the answer is right, a further turn of the knob engages a clutch which moves the next problem into place in the window. This movement cannot be completed, however, until the sliders have been returned to zero.

The important features of the device are these: Reinforcement for the right answer is immediate. The mere manipulation of the device will probably be reinforcing enough to keep the average pupil at work for a suitable period each day, provided traces of earlier aversive control can be wiped out. A teacher may supervise an entire class at work on such devices at the same time, yet each child may progress at his own rate, completing as many problems as possible within the class period. If forced to be away from school, he may return to pick up where he left off. The gifted child will advance rapidly, but can be kept from getting too far ahead either by being excused from arithmetic for a time or by being given special sets of problems which take him into some of the interesting bypaths of mathematics.

The device makes it possible to present carefully designed material in which one problem can depend upon the answer to the preceding and where, therefore, the most efficient progress to an eventually complex repertoire can be made.[57]

Here we see a thoroughly mechanized "Winnetka Plan" based upon "trial-and-error" learning and the law of effect. In our judgment, such an approach can hardly be considered a breakthrough; in principle, it is Winnetka revisited.

At this point it seems worthwhile to note that the meaning of the phrase "science of education" was expanded by Bobbitt, Washburne, and others (such as Charters and Snedden) to mean not only basing methodology upon scientific principles but also determining curriculum content by statistical analysis of the kinds of activities people most frequently perform, the vocabulary most frequently used in newspapers, magazines, and books, and the kinds of information or facts most frequently used or alluded to in American life. Roughly speaking, those activities, words, and facts found to be used or alluded to most frequently in American life are taken to be of most educational value. Thus, frequency of use is the criterion for curriculum content.

However, the frequency of an event does not of itself tell us much about its value. To paraphrase Bode: Suppose that we scientifically determine that a community has a certain burglary rate. What does this rate indicate for that community? Does it mean that the community needs more burglars or more policemen? Those who would determine curriculum content "scientifically" and consequently would "teach them to do better what they are going to do any-

---

[57] *Ibid.,* pp. 30–31.

way" seemingly subscribe to the view that whatever *is* is *right*. This view inevitably leads to an uncompromising, unapologetic attempt to indoctrinate students in current beliefs and attitudes.

Method: The Morrison Plan

Washburne's "Winnetka Plan" has been of interest to us both because it illustrates the specific-objectivist method of determining subject-matter content for elementary school and because it illustrates a methodology that is specific-objectivist as well as being designed to "break the lockstep" and care for individual differences. Another methodological proposal, highly influential from about 1925 to 1935, was that of Henry Clinton Morrison,[58] important for us because it illustrates the specific-objectivist method for secondary schools.

Although both McMurry and Washburne employed the term "unit" prior to Morrison, it was the latter who seemingly inaugurated its widespread usage. For a decade and more after the original publication of Morrison's book, when one encountered the term "unit plan" one could be fairly certain that an approximation of Morrison's idea was involved. High-school textbooks, especially in natural sciences and social studies, were recast from chapters into units, though in many cases not much more was done than could be reflected in the "Table of Contents" wherein several chapters would be grouped together under unit headings. Nowadays, the term "unit" is such a standard one that it tends to be only the "old-timers" who realize how recent is its origin. Moreover, its present-day use is far from being distinctly Morrisonian; it now refers mainly to long-term assignments, of 2–3 weeks or more, in contrast with the old, page-by-page, daily-lesson assignments from a single textbook, to be recited verbatim.

Morrison's proposal necessitated little change from conventional curriculum content; not nearly as much as did Bobbitt's, Washburne's, or Thorndike's. It was *reorganization* of content that concerned Morrison. His proposal focused upon his idea of "mastery," and this idea seems to furnish the key to (1) course reorganization, (2) teaching method, and (3) testing. We shall take these in order.

Morrison's idea of "mastery" did not at all carry the conventional meaning of high-level capacity or expertness. Instead, it meant for him only the achievement of a fundamental grasp of a matter under study. For example, in learning

[58] Henry Clinton Morrison, *The Practice of Teaching in the Secondary School*, 2nd ed. Chicago: University of Chicago Press, 1931.

to ride a bicycle, one struggles for a time to achieve equilibrium, then all of a sudden it comes! Previously, the contraption would not behave; afterwards, it is docile and cooperative—balance can be maintained indefinitely. It is this achievement that Morrison called *mastery;* a "personality adaptation" has occurred.[59] This kind of adaptation, once mastered, was classed as a "special ability," to be contrasted with the various and varying degrees of "skill" that later may or may not be developed. Morrison wrote as follows:

> *Performance and learning distinguished.*   As we have repeatedly seen, these learning products which contribute to and constitute the education of the individual originate in experience. Now the manifestation of experience which is involved in the learning process constitutes *performance.* Further, the application of a learning product, after mastery, in its appropriate use, is performance. In neither case, however, is performance itself a learning product, any more than is the experience out of which learning arises. The relationship can perhaps graphically be represented in the following diagram.

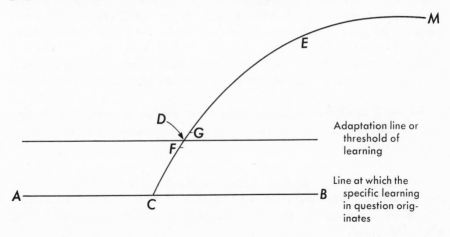

AB may be thought of as the level at which the new learning begins to differentiate from the general *apperceptive mass,* that is, the ideational and experiential background. CDEM is the performance line. From point C the pupil is practicing. The practice may be in the form of reflective thinking, or of contemplation of material and instruction intended to lead to a product in appreciation, or of language, and so on. As he continues to practice, his performance becomes better and better up to point E at which the level of diminishing returns begins, and finally he reaches some point like M at which further practice ceases to yield results. Now at point D he crosses the adaptation line, or the line at which the

[59] *Ibid.,* pp. 16–23.

true learning product appears. His performance is not different *in kind*, objectively, from D onward from what it is in the interval CD; but between F and G a momentous change has taken place. At F, learning has not registered; at G it has registered. Beyond D, *skill* in the use of the learning product is developing. Below D it is a misuse of terms to say that there is any skill at all. Performance can be measured but the learning product cannot be measured: its presence can be revealed only through characteristic symptoms.[60]

An "adaptation," once "mastered," possesses two basic qualities: *unity* and *permanence*.

The adaptation is a unitary thing, and the pupil either has attained it or he has not. Individuals may differ greatly in the length of time and the ease with which they take on the change which a given adaptation implies, they may differ in the convincing character of the evidence touching the presence of the adapatations which their behavior reveals; but, if two pupils have attained a given adaptation, they cannot differ with respect to the fact of their attainment. Skill, on the other hand, is essentially a variable. Any individual can be at different points on the curve of skill development at different times, and it can truthfully be said that at each point he has some skill. Two individuals can differ widely in skill and yet each possess skill. It is often critically important in pedagogical analysis to determine whether we are dealing with an adaptation or a skill.[61]

Not only is an adaptation *unitary* in the sense of either having it or not having it—all or none, no halfway possibility—but it is also *permanent*, it never simply fades out.

The ultimate test of a product of learning which has involved a genuine adaptation is that it is not lost, otherwise than through its transformation into new adaptations or through the rise of pathological inhibitions. It is never lost by simply fading out.[62]

Whether or not the reader agrees with Morrison is not the issue for the moment. One must first get these points clear before one can "get the run" of his thinking. This is "mastery," the achievement of a "personality adaptation." And, according to him, secondary education should be concerned only with what Morrison found to be the fundamental adaptations needed by a person for his general living, but not required for vocation or profession or to "become capable

[60] *Ibid.*, pp. 39–40. Italics in original. All of Chapters 2, 3, and 4 should be read.
[61] *Ibid.*, p. 21.
[62] *Ibid.*, pp. 21–22.

of pursuing self-dependent study and in which he utilizes the instructor in the same sense in which he utilizes the library, the laboratory, the occasional public lecturer, the office consultant."[63] Hence, secondary education for him included approximately grades 4 through 14.[64]

"The Learning Unit" Morrison defined as ". . . a comprehensive and significant aspect of the environment, of an organized science, of an art, or of conduct, which being learned results in an adaptation in personality." [65] Translated, this means that a course unit is a body of subject matter, the study of which results in mastery of the adaptation that is involved. For him, there are three different kinds of adaptations: special abilities, such as the bicycle-riding adaptation as we have described it; understandings, which he calls "attitudes of understanding"; and appreciations, which he calls "attitudes of appreciation." The corresponding types of "learning units" are: "pure-practice" for special abilities (Chapter 26); "science-type" for understandings (Chapters 11–16); and "appreciation-type" for appreciations and "right attitudes" (Chapters 17–20). He indeed includes two other types of units, but these are combinations (Chapters 21–25). Since our present purpose will not be served by detailed study of the Morrison idea, we shall limit our treatment to science-type units, and deal with those only briefly.

"Science-type" units are those that achieve understandings. Herein is illustrated what may well be considered Morrison's major contribution to educational theory.

> . . . the subject matter used in the school is not valuable in education for its own sake but only as it is serviceable in generating intelligent and useful inclinations and abilities in the pupil. . . . *while we all learn from experience we do not learn experience.*[66]

In other words, it is not the separate items—"the facts"—included in a unit that are to be "learned" (in the sense of being remembered) and to be tested for in a subsequent examination; it is, instead, the *understanding*, often called the *generalization* or the *principle*. Hence, the test marking completion of a science-type unit must be for understanding, not for memory.[67] Herein is a vital difference between Morrison's "unit plan" and Washburne's "Winnetka Plan," for Wash-

---

[63] *Ibid.*, p. 7.
[64] *Ibid.*, Chap. 1.
[65] *Ibid.*, pp. 24–25. All italicized in original.
[66] *Ibid.*, p. 20. Italics ours.
[67] *Ibid.*, pp. 313–321. Therein Morrison explains his idea of "the final mastery test," an idea which, though not new, was given a big and needed boost.

burne was content with testing for memorized items whereas Morrison insisted upon a student demonstrating that he could *use* or *apply* what he knew rather than merely repeat it.

It was, moreover, on this point that Charles Hubbard Judd waged his long-time polemic against Thorndike's theory of transfer by "identical elements."[68] Judd insisted that we transfer or use what we know only when our knowledge is in the form of generalizations; when it represents "generalized experience." Otherwise, it is not transfer; it is mere repetition. And that, he maintained, was a point not included—at least, not made clear—in the "identical-elements theory," which was part of Thorndike's connectionism. Morrison's plan represented emphatic rejection of teaching for item-by-item memorization; "we learn from experience we do not learn experience." Memory-type or *memoriter* learning he characterized as "lesson learning,"[69] and thought of it as a "perversion" of education.

Morrison's teaching method is summed up in his "mastery formula": "Pretest, teach, test the result, [diagnose difficulties,] adapt procedure, teach and test again to the point of actual learning."[70] This is reminiscent of General Grant's formula, "Fight it out on this line if it takes all summer." And that is essentially what it was, for the unitary quality of an adaptation—you either have it or you don't have it, there is no half-way stage—makes this a logical necessity. For science-type units—those ending in an understanding—Morrison's was a five-step procedure: exploration, presentation, assimilation, organization, recitation. Because Herbart's (as it came to us) was also a five-step plan, Morrison's plan has frequently been taken as Herbartian, which it definitely was *not*, as we shall note in a moment.

Exploration was solely a test, to determine how much each student already knew of the unit—how familiar he was with the "assimilative" content and whether he possessed the understanding. If at that point understanding were satisfactorily demonstrated, the student was excused from working on the unit, for Morrison's was a form of individualized instruction and in that way similar to Washburne's. *Presentation* was a lecture, telling "the story of the unit" as it was characterized in two of the leading textbooks of the period.[71] Other names

[68] Charles Hubbard Judd, *Psychology of High School Subjects.* Boston: Ginn, 1915, pp. 412–435.

[69] *Ibid.*, Chap 4.

[70] Morrison, *op. cit.*, p. 81. See the whole of Chapter 6. The addition, "diagnose difficulties," is ours. It was recognized by Morrison as essential, but was inadvertently omitted in this statement of his formula.

[71] The Pieper-Beauchamp *General Science* and the Pieper-Beauchamp-Frank *Biology*, both published by Scott and Foresman, Chicago, were two distinctly Morrisonian textbooks for high school, prepared while the three authors were working with Morrison in the University of Chicago High School, of which Morrison was head.

given to the presentation were "preview" and "overview," for a while widely used, even in some college textbooks—notably in educational psychology. It represented a short sketch of the unit as a whole, indicating salient data and explaining the principle that was to be learned.[72]

Assimilation represented the heart of unit study, for during it and by means of it *mastery* was to be achieved. After presentation, a student presumably could regurgitate (recite); he had the words. But assimilation (a biological term) meant incorporation into the cell-tissue structure of the learner; it had become a part of him and could not be regurgitated; the principle had become a part of the very self, an "adaptation in personality." The student had what anyone and everyone had who understood (had "mastered") the principle:

Hence, the process of training pupils to think is nothing else than . . . establishing the adaptations which are implied in the study of the sciences. The student who has actually acquired the true products in the learning of physics has by the very fact learned to think as the physicist thinks.[73]

This point is important, for throughout Morrison's discussions of the process of "assimilation" he repeatedly uses the terms "thinking" and "reflection." He therefore can easily be taken as going along with Dewey in the latter's emphasis on reflective thinking as vital for democratic teaching. But such is a thoroughgoing *mis*interpretation of Morrison.

The reader is reminded that all such assimilative problems should be devised for the purpose of developing the unit understanding intended and not for the purpose of training pupils in "problem solving."[74]

Wrong Emphasis on Problems.   The emphasis placed upon problem-solving in many mathematical texts sometimes tends to throw assimilative material completely out of focus. At bottom, the difficulty arises from confusion in the objectives. The proper objective, for instance, may be the application of the mathematical process known as the equation to the interpretation of certain concrete situations. The textbook-maker hopes to develop in conjunction therewith an abstract power which he calls "problem-solving ability." The two objectives cannot be developed in unison unless one is a function of the other, and this is not often the case.[75]

Morrison's was *understanding-level* teaching; not reflective teaching as will be discussed in our Chapter 12. Morrison's third step, assimilation, was focused

[72] Morrison, *op. cit.* For these steps see Chapter 14.
[73] *Ibid.*, p. 34.
[74] *Ibid.*, pp. 247–248.
[75] *Ibid.*, p. 250.

solely on developing the particular understanding sought. No alternative under-standings—hypotheses, principles, ideas, or what will you—were to be considered, or even mentioned. In this way, Morrison was distinctly Thorndikean; always practice "right" responses, never let "wrong" responses occur.[76]

Since Morrison's was a plan for individualized instruction, like Washburne he had to provide opportunity for each student to work by himself so he could progress at his own rate. But, unlike Washburne, each class began and ended each unit together. In fact, the class would be together on steps one, two, four, and five; only during step three, assimilation, was each student "on his own." Hence, in order that each student be informed as to what was expected of him, as in the "Winnetka Plan", a "guide sheet" or *worksheet* was necessary.[77] Prior to Washburne and Morrison, student worksheets and workbooks had no place in American education; after them, particularly after Morrison, such equipment has become so widely used as to be almost universal.

For Morrison, however, completion of what the guide sheet called for was not an absolute requirement; it was no end in itself. As a student worked, the teacher would be keeping track—reading the student's notebook, talking with him per-sonally, holding occasional group discussions either with large groups or small, and otherwise knowing when help was needed and filling the need. This Mor-rison called "rapport testing," and through it the teacher could obtain a fairly accurate notion of how far each student had progressed toward "mastery." Then, whenever a student appeared to have reached mastery, regardless of how far he had progressed through the guide sheet, he would be given an opportunity to take the formal "mastery test." Passage of the test meant completion of "assimilation."

For this book, we cannot go into further detail on the Morrison idea. The reader is advised to do considerable reading in Morrison's book because in it is to be found much of the origin of schoolroom practice over the past 30 years or more. "Mastery testing," as we have previously noted, occupies about the latter third of the chapter on assimilation. The next chapter (16) deals with the last two steps—organization and recitation. However, if the reader will recall Morrison's definition of a unit, he will probably see that, by definition, the unit ends with completion of step three—assimilation. A unit is designed to achieve mastery, and mastery is supposedly demonstrated by passage of the mastery test. As a result, the profession has not been much impressed by Organi-zation (writing from memory an outline of the unit) and Recitation ("floor talks" on various phases of the unit), so these steps have been little used.

[76] Morrison's chapter on assimilation was number 15.
[77] Morrison, *op. cit.*, pp. 304–312.

As for Morrison being Herbartian in his five-step teaching procedure for science-type units, similarity seems to be limited to Morrison's second and third steps. Herbart's first step—preparation—was an interest-raising one; Morrison's was exclusively to find what a student knew or did not know. Morrison's pages 107–115 make pretty clear that he was not concerned with "working up" interest; interest or motivation was expected, demanded if necessary, and that was that! For both Morrison and Herbart, the second step—presentation—was essentially the same. But Morrison's third step—assimilation—essentially included Herbart's last three: comparison or assimilation, generalization, and application. Thus, Morrison's last two steps were not Herbartian; nor were they a logical part of what Morrison defined as a unit, hence not even logically Morrisonian.

It is true, however, that in general outlook Herbart and Morrison are highly compatible; they both belong to the Locke-Herbart-Thorndike thought pattern. Learning is taken to be inductive, proceeding from the particular to the general; sensations ⟶ ideas ⟶ actions ⟶ character. A passive, or reactive, learner is assumed; *tabula rasa*. Teacher is always right, regardless of how placatory he may try to be.

Analysis

To summarize the connectionist, specific-objectivist program for American education during the first half of the twentieth century, it was no polyglot. It was a highly coordinated and essentially consistent or harmonious line of thinking, if a *neutral-reactive* learner be posited; *tabula rasa*. It represented the Aristotelian defection from Plato and reached us by way of Francis Bacon (*Novum Organum*) on the one hand and Thomas Aquinas (Thomism) on the other, all endorsing the inductive method of truth-getting. Included were the deism of Thomas Paine, Thomas Jefferson, and Benjamin Franklin, if not of Abraham Lincoln, and the agnosticism of Thomas Henry Huxley.

Being inductive, specific-objectivism represented educational design that proceeded from parts (or elements) to whole; it was elementistic, often called atomistic. Educational objectives were expressed in itemized lists, whether long or short, of knowledges, skills, and attitudes to be achieved. In terms of S-R psychology, these were the "bonds" to be established; it didn't greatly matter how, just as long as establishment was achieved. Therefore, theorists of this ilk could, and often did, claim "no brief for any particular method." Curriculum (content) was important; not method or teaching theory.

It is for this reason that our last representative, Morrison, seemingly must be classified as specific-objectivist. His idea of the unitariness of each "personality adaptation"—you either have it or you don't have it—makes each unit a curricular element that, once achieved, can be counted seriatim, like marbles. "The whole will equal the sum of its parts." Moreover, once established each "personality adaptation" is permanent—it never disappears by simply fading out. Therefore, once a teacher is satisfied that a given unit objective has been achieved, he can check it off in his record book and forget about it. And in further consequence, Morrison can logically say that "a valid method" in the "appraisal of pupil progress" rests on a *count of the true learning products* which the pupil has attained and in which his mastery has been verified by the best evidential means at our command."[78] This is elementistic-atomistic theory in curriculum construction as well as in teaching method, and for this reason we feel obliged to classify Morrison as a specific-objectivist.

On the other hand, there is a vital aspect of Morrison's theory that tends to negate at least the connectionist aspect of specific-objectivism—"S-R bonds." The idea that for science-type units understanding is the "personality adaptation" to be achieved and none else, is one that ill fits the concept of $S \longrightarrow R$. For example, Morrison's idea of mastery-testing is to examine a student's capacity to *use* an idea; not merely to *repeat* the words in which the idea was originally expressed. To do this, a test item must present a situation the student has never before experienced, at least not in the exact form appearing in the test. The item must be *novel*, else memory alone can handle it. This was Judd's point in insisting that the identical-elements theory could not account for transfer of training. If a presumed repetition of a given bond does not follow the pre-established "path of lowered synaptic resistance," then the S-R bond idea is stretched beyond the elastic limit and is unable thereafter to recover. Judd's idea of "generalization" as the vehicle for transfer means that a "sense of relationship or pattern" has been established—one that has wide applicability so that it can transfer—and this, as we shall see in Chapter 12, is the *insight* theory of learning and transfer; a theory basically opposed to psychological connectionism.

Although at times Morrison wrote in connectionist terms and at others in terms of Herbartian "apperception," his idea of *understanding* as a personality adaptation and as *the* objective in science-type units was highly compatible with the insight theory of learning, opposed to connectionistic "conditioning." There was only one "fly" in this ointment; Morrison's idea—that a given understanding is the same for all who have it, so that "The student who has actually acquired the true products in the learning of physics has by the very fact learned to think

[78] Morrison, *op. cit.*, p. 72. Italics in original.

as the physicist thinks"[79]—fails to fit. If, as in relativistic (Dewey) theory, a generalized insight is a given person's interpretation *of the experiences that he has had,* then an understanding is *not* a fixed entity—the same for all who have it. It is not even the same, from one time to another, for a given person; every time he experiences a new case in which he finds that a previous understanding is truly applicable, the understanding has to that extent increased in size or scope. This is one of the incompatibilities with which Morrison's writings are replete.

There are many analyses of the writings of the various representatives of specific-objectivism in American education, including even some by Thorndike himself, that pinpoint self-contradictions or failure to square with available evidence. And proponents of the view, including Thorndike himself, have over the years since the turn of the century progressively given ground on point after point, so that nowadays few responsible writers are willing to stand firm on the principle of learning as a repetitional or "drill" process, based on the presumed mechanism of differential synaptic resistance that is progressively lowered by repeated use. Some even go so far as to claim that the idea no longer exists, and that those who speak of it at all are simply "resurrecting dead cats," perhaps for the sake of promoting an argument.

But, for the first third and more of the present century, Thorndike's influence on actual practice in this country overshadowed that of all others—including Dewey and the Progressives. And practices that are more in keeping with the Locke-Herbart-Thorndike thought-pattern than with any other (unless it be Puritan re-citation) still seem to dominate American education. In the next two chapters, we shall deal with two other points of view that have been actively at work and have made their mark during the twentieth century. But seemingly neither, or perhaps both combined, has effaced connectionistic specific-objectivism.

Suggested Readings

Bobbitt, Franklin, *The Curriculum.* Boston: Houghton Mifflin, 1918.
Bobbitt, Franklin, *How To Make A Curriculum.* Boston: Houghton Mifflin, 1924.
Bobbitt, Franklin *et al., Curriculum Investigations.* Chicago: The University of Chicago Press, 1926.
Buckingham, B. R., *Spelling Ability: Its Measurement and Distribution.* New York: Teachers College, Columbia University, 1913.

[79] *Ibid.,* p. 34.

Finley, Charles W., and Caldwell, Otis W., *Biology in the Public Press*. New York: The Lincoln School of Teachers College, Columbia University, 1923.

Herrick, C. J., *Neurological Foundations of Animal Behavior*. Holt, Rinehart and Winston, 1924.

Judd, Charles Hubbard, *Psychology of High School Subjects*. Boston: Ginn, 1915.

Morrison, Henry Clinton, *The Practice of Teaching in the Secondary School*, 2nd ed. Chicago: University of Chicago Press, 1931. First published in 1926.

Parker, Samuel C., *A Textbook in the History of Modern Elementary Education*. Boston: Ginn, 1913, Chap. 18.

Persing, Ellis C., "Present Objectives in Biology," *Science Education*, Vol. 17, No. 1, February, 1933, pp. 24–34.

Skinner, B. F., "The Science of Learning and the Art of Teaching," in Wendell I. Smith and J. William Moore, *Programmed Learning: Theory and Research*. Princeton: Van Nostrand, 1962.

Thorndike, Edward L., *Notes on Child Study*. New York: Macmillan, 1903.

Thorndike, Edward L., *Animal Intelligence*. New York: Macmillan, 1911.

Thorndike, Edward L., *Education*, New York: Macmillan, 1912.

Thorndike, Edward L., *Educational Psychology*, 3 vols. New York: Teachers College, Columbia University, 1913.

Thorndike, Edward L., *Educational Psychology: Briefer Course*. New York: Teachers College, Columbia University, 1916.

Thorndike, Edward L., *The Elements of Psychology*. New York: A. G. Seiler, 1917.

Thorndike, Edward L., *The New Methods in Arithmetic*. Chicago: Rand McNally, 1921.

Thorndike, Edward L., *The Teacher's Word Book*. New York: Teachers College, Columbia University, 1921.

Thorndike, Edward L., *Human Learning*. New York: Appleton-Century-Crofts, 1931.

Thorndike, Edward L., *Human Nature and the Social Order*. New York: Macmillan, 1940.

Thorndike, Edward L., *Psychology and the Science of Education: Selected Writings of Edward L. Thorndike*, Geraldine M. Joncich (ed.). New York: Teachers College, Columbia University, 1962.

Washburne, Carleton W., "Basic Facts Needed in History and Geography," *Twenty-Second Yearbook of the National Society for the Study of Education*, 1923, Part II, pp. 216–233.

Washburne, Carleton W., "A Program of Individualization," *Twenty-Fourth Yearbook of the National Society for the Study of Education*, 1925, Part II, pp. 77–83; 257–272.

Washburne, Carleton W., "The Philosophy of the Winnetka Curriculum," *Twenty-Sixth Yearbook of the National Society for the Study of Education*, 1927, Part I, pp. 219–228.

Washburne, Carleton W., *Adjusting the School to the Child*. New York: Harcourt, Brace & World, 1932.

Washburne, Carleton W., and Marland, Sidney P., *Winnetka: The History and Significance of an Educational Experiment*. Englewood Cliffs, N.J.: Prentice-Hall, 1963.

About 1921, in one of the schools of New York City, an experimental project named the Little Red Schoolhouse was begun. It was supervised by a young teacher, Elisabeth Irwin. The project's goal was a more spontaneous, richer education experience for children. In 1931, the Great Depression ended the project, but deeply interested parents, by subscription, made possible the continuance of the school in its own building. Social studies here become an experience in living: reading, special reports, and neighborhood visits culminate in the pleasure of recording the study in painting. (Courtesy of Little Red School House, New York City)

11 ?~ "*Progressive Education*"

With the advent of the twentieth century, two significant and distinctive educational movements stood almost, if not quite, prepared and ready to spring into action. Both descended from British and Western European forebears, but both were basically American, in birth as well as in upbringing. In the preceding chapter, we have dealt with the connectionistic, specific-objectivist movement, spearheaded by Edward L. Thorndike, and have followed it into the recent development of programmed learning. This may be characterized as the Locke-Herbart-Thorndike line of thought development, although in it were the *tabula rasa* aspect of Comenius, the "practice" of Rousseau as we noted in *Emile,* and the developmental or inductive aspect of Pestalozzi's methodology.

"*Progressivism*" *Delineated*

Now we turn to the second movement, which carried the name *Progressive Education.* Right away, let us call attention to the capital P and the capital E. It is important that we distinguish between Progressive Education and progressive education, the former a proper and the latter a common name. The major importance is that the movement designated by the proper name has long been a center of major confusion and controversy for both laymen and professionals, and possibly a major part of both the confusion and the controversy has grown out of failure to make this simple distinction.

There has been much progressive thinking (note the lower-case p) in this country regarding education during the past half-century and more, on the part of Thorndikeans, of Progressives, and of many others. And progressive (forward-looking) thinking does and should evoke controversy. Properly conceived and practiced, it is the lifeblood of both science and democracy. However, without early and continuing agreement on criteria and the meanings of terms, confusion becomes more and more compounded as controversy continues. Few writers on this matter, either professional or lay, clearly distinguish between progressive education and Progressive Education. Hence, few of those whose ideas go more than even a trifle beyond the traditional, verbalistic re-citationism of Puritan educational theory are able to avoid, sooner or later, being dubbed Progressive, which for many (even of those who should know better) has been and is a mark of opprobrium.

Twentieth-century treatises on Progressive Education—both written and oral—have been so loose in terms of what they are dealing with that nothing but confused thinking can be the result. Typical is a so-called "Landmark" publication, "the first history ever published of the progressive movement" (if we can believe claims on the cover), in the Preface of which the author says, "The reader will search these pages in vain for any capsule definition of progressive education. None exists, and none ever will; . . ."[1] He then goes on to lump together a staggering array of names, dates, places, and events, which, for any but a most sophisticated reader, entirely obliterates any likelihood of getting educational theory out in the open, so that *it* (theory) can be examined. The present writers hope that they appreciate and respect scholarliness, but we have a conviction that a plethora of details can discourage if not preclude scholarly thought; one cannot see the forest because of the trees. Specifically, to lump together a set of eminent educational theorists, such as Dewey, Kilpatrick, Bode, Rugg, Counts, and Childs, and a host of practitioners, together with sociologists, psychologists, anthropologists, economists, historians, and what will you, and call them all Progressives, is to confuse and not to clarify.

We might say that the name Progressive Education should be confined strictly to whatever it was that the Progressive Education Association stood for. This, however, would make it still a decidedly ill-defined term, because Association representatives, though repeatedly quizzed as to what this was, seldom gave

[1] Lawrence A. Cremin, *The Transformation of the School*. New York: Knopf, 1961, p. x.

definitive answers. Moreover, since different representatives gave different answers and since we cannot analyse them all, we shall focus upon the pronouncements of the one who may be said to have invented Progressive Education and who, though never in a narrowly official capacity, was the generally recognized leader of the movement, William Heard Kilpatrick.[2] Much of this chapter, then, will deal with Kilpatrick and will do so in about the same way and for about the same reason that the previous chapter deals with Thorndike. Moreover, it must be emphasized that this chapter does not involve Dewey—the next one does that—for, however much may have been written to the contrary, Kilpatrick and Dewey do not stand for the same set of educational principles. And, for reasons that we hope will presently become clear, we consider that this chapter deals with the twentieth-century culmination of the Rousseau-Froebel line of thought development, paralleling the Thorndike culmination of the Locke-Herbart line depicted in the preceding chapter.

Early "Progressive" Schools

The John Dewey School, connected with the University of Chicago, has been popularly, though we think erroneously, credited as being the first "Progressive" school in the United States. Established in 1896 through the efforts of Dewey, it was originally designed to fulfil a twofold purpose: to serve as a place where children could obtain an elementary education along the lines of Dewey's thinking, and to give the faculty an opportunity to experiment along the lines of increased flexibility of curriculum content in order that children's own interests might play a larger role in choice and treatment of subject matter.

That Dewey never had the idea of turning children loose to do as they please is seemingly well attested by the following excerpt from a talk he gave in the spring of 1899 to an assembly of parents of children in the school: ". . . This is the difference, upon which I wish to insist, between exciting or indulging an interest and realizing it through its direction."[3] In the next paragraph he continued:

[2] See Samuel Tenebaum, *William Heard Kilpatrick: Trail Blazer in Education*. New York: Harper & Row, 1951. On the other hand, for critical, analytical discussion, see the following: John Dewey, "The Way Out of Educational Confusion," in R. D. Archambault (ed.), *John Dewey on Education*. New York: Modern Library, 1964. *Dewey's Experience and Education*. New York: Collier Books, 1963. Boyd H. Bode, *Progressive Education at the Crossroads*. New York: Newson, 1938. Bode's *Modern Educational Theories*. New York: Macmillan, 1927, Chap. 7, also in paperback.

[3] John Dewey, *The School and Society*. Chicago: University of Chicago Press, 1900, p. 41.

. . . All children like to express themselves through the medium of form and color. If you simply indulge this interest by letting the child go on indefinitely, there is no growth that is more than accidental. But let the child first express his impulse, and then through criticism, question, and suggestion bring him to consciousness of what he has done, and what he needs to do, and the result is quite different.[4]

On the next page, he follows by giving an example of "the work of a seven-year-old child":

. . . They had been talking about the primitive conditions of social life when people lived in caves. The child's idea of that found expression in this way: the cave is neatly set up on the hillside in an impossible way. You see the conventional tree of childhood—a vertical line with horizontal branches on each side. If the child had been allowed to go on repeating this sort of thing day by day, he would be indulging his instinct rather than exercising it. But the child was now asked to look closely at trees, to compare those seen with the one drawn, to examine more closely and consciously into the conditions of his work. Then he drew trees from observation.

Finally he drew again from combined observation, memory, and imagination. He made again a free illustration, expressing his own imaginative thought, but controlled by detailed study of actual trees. The result was a scene representing a bit of forest; so far as it goes, it seems to me to have as much poetic feeling as the work of an adult, while at the same time its trees are, in their proportions, possible ones, not mere symbols.[5]

After the first years of the Dewey school, Dewey himself had little time to keep in personal touch with the teaching; hence, possibly more permissivism developed than he would have approved. And in 1904 he left Chicago to join the Columbia University faculty. In 1909, Charles Hubbard Judd acceded to the headship of Education at the University of Chicago, including the elementary school (the Dewey school). During the midtwenties, in a class attended by one of the present writers, Judd remarked that even then the school had not recovered from the influence of John Dewey, the remark intended to imply that there was still too much pupil freedom. A few years later, however, one of the present writers happened to be visiting with an older couple (the husband a retired Denver businessman) whose son was a pupil in the school when Judd took over. Both parents emphatically denied the existence of wide-open permissivism in the school. But they did feel that *in Judd's opinion* there was too much

[4] *Ibid.*
[5] *Ibid.*, p. 42.

pupil freedom, adding that, although he assured all teachers in the school that they were welcome to remain, within a very few years practically all had found occasion to obtain employment elsewhere.

Seemingly, the reason for the Dewey school's reputation as Progressive (permissivist) was that, in comparison with the run of elementary schools of the time, there was a large degree of pupil freedom. The story is told of Dewey, in setting up the school originally, trudging the streets of Chicago looking for a school-furniture store that would supply a set of pupil desks or chairs that were not to be screwed down to the floor, chairs that could be moved about as occasion demanded. Not only were such items not immediately to be found, but the dealers were surprised that anyone would be so foolish as to think a school could be run with such furniture.

Possibly enough of a step beyond Parker's schools at Quincy[6] to be called our first Progressive school (albeit only mildly permissivist, at that) was Dr. Felix Adler's Ethical Culture School of New York City, established about 1883, originally called the Workingman's School, and still in existence. If John Dewey's school should be called the second, then possibly the Francis W. Parker School of Chicago would be third, and fourth would be Dr. Junius L. Meriam's laboratory school at the University of Missouri.

Founded in 1901 by Miss Flora J. Cooke and named in honor of Colonel Parker, the 16-teacher faculty of the Parker school sought to cut across the strict, subject-matter boundary lines of conventional elementary-school courses and work out something akin to what later under Kilpatrick came to be known as the "project method." The school has long maintained its forward-looking point of view; in the Eight-Year Study by the Progressive Education Association during the nineteen thirties, it was chosen as one of the six most experimental of the thirty schools participating.

But it was the Meriam school, founded in 1904, that among these early innovators perhaps was most deserving of the name "Progressive." Though after a time Meriam gradually came to a degree of organization of a school day into regular periods (though not conventional subjects), in its earlier years each day's activities were organized solely on the basis of current concerns of the pupils. What the children wanted, they did, even following the fire engine down the street on occasion. Many years later, a seasoned teacher who had done his practice teaching in the Meriam school jokingly commented that, even though Dr. Meriam was insistent that his practice teachers let their pupils do as they pleased, there was no chance for Meriam's own students (the practice teachers) to do as they pleased.

[6] See ante, p. 180.

During the second decade of the twentieth century, there was a rapid increase in the number of schools (mostly private) that were considered by their founders as distinctly nonconventional. Since these are listed and described in many of the references cited at the close of this chapter, we shall not name them here. Suffice it to say that, in 1919, a group of innovation-minded persons, mostly directors of many of these schools, came together and organized the Progressive Education Association.[7] From its beginning, the Association was a vibrant force in American education, and doubtless deserves credit for being the greatest single agent in promoting the changes that came to pass in American elementary schools during the first half of the twentieth century, to say nothing of what it did for secondary and higher education. It had a life-span of 36 years, its end being announced in 1955 by its president, H. Gordon Hullfish.

From its inception, the leaders of the P.E.A. were insistent that the Association should not adopt or become identified with any particular credo. It was essentially, as Cremin phrases it, an "Organization of Dissent." Anyone who was unhappy with the traditionalism of Puritanic *re-citation* or even with the domination by teachers or other curriculum specialists that connectionistic specific-objectivism represented, was welcomed. And this, paradoxically, included the "Winnetka-Plan" Carleton Washburne, who for two terms was president of the Association, assuming the stance of a "Progressive" because he devoted half of each school day to pupil-adopted projects, though his accession to educational eminence was not as a sponsor of projects but (as we indicated in the preceding chapter) as the designer of the other half of each school day—the "Winnetka Plan."

Not so paradoxically, this also included the Harold Rugg of the Rugg-Shumaker *The Child-Centered School*,[8] for, as Rugg once publicly said to Washburne (at least, in approximation), "There is only one basic difference between you and me; whereas you are willing to devote only one-half of a pupil's time to self-directed activities, I am willing to let them have three-fourths or more of their time for such."[9] Rugg's Progressivism was to be confined to the esthetic—"man feeling."[10] It was in the arts—music, painting, sculpture, poetry, the dance, etc.—that children were to be encouraged in creative self-expression, child-centering. The other side for Rugg—the intellectual, "man thinking"—was to be dis-

---

[7] The story of the Association is told in detail by Cremin, *op. cit.*, Chap. 7.

[8] Harold Rugg and Ann Shumaker, *The Child-Centered School*. New York: Harcourt, Brace & World, 1928.

[9] This was, as I recall, at the annual meeting of the National Society for the Study of Education, in connection with its official public presentation of the 26th Yearbook, on *Curricula and Curriculum Making*.

[10] See Rugg and Shumaker, *op. cit.*; also, Harold Rugg, *Culture and Education in America*, New York: Harcourt, Brace & World, 1931.

tinctly teacher-controlled, well programmed ahead of time. Herein was the domain of his series of social-studies textbooks that caused such a furor on the part of conservative organizations during the midthirties (see pp. 275–276).

Thus, although the founders of the P.E.A. of whom Stanwood Cobb was typical, were highly desirous of being identified with no particular credo, from its very beginnings the Association became identified on the negative side with opposition to teacher domination and on the positive side with adherence to Kilpatrick's "project method"; the identification with the Rugg-Shumaker "child-centered school" came later. Correlatively, it was the "interests" of children upon which school curricula were to be based; not the activities of adult life, for which school children were to be "prepared." This identification with children's *interests* was further crystallized in the midtwenties by Kilpatrick's "pupil-purposing, pupil-planning, pupil-executing, pupil-judging,"[11] in which he was enthusiastically supported by his early doctoral student, Ellsworth Collings.[12] Thus it is that we come to the writings of Kilpatrick, writings that expressed his thinking at the time when, as "the million dollar professor," he was exercising large influence on the thinking of thousands of American teachers and other school personnel.[13]

Analysis of Kilpatrick-Collings Thinking

We have found, even back to Comenius and further, that educational theorists have been wrestling with the problem of curricular balance between the wants, wishes, desires, or propensities of children and the requirements desired, or laid down by adults. As expressed in *Emile,* Rousseau's *theory* was that unspoiled child-nature should reign, but his *practice,* as shown by his examples, was that enlightened adult-standards (Rousseau's ideas, of course) should be the final determinant. And our findings have been that, as with Rousseau, educational theorists have been unable to do better than jump back and forth from one extreme to the other—child domination on the one hand and adult fiat on the other. We have previously noted Froebel's difficulty with the matter. A century

[11] William H. Kilpatrick, *Foundations of Method.* New York: Macmillan, 1926.

[12] Ellsworth Collings, *Experiment with a Project Curriculum.* New York: Macmillan, 1923. Based on Collings' doctoral dissertation, under Kilpatrick's direction.

[13] The following analysis of Kilpatrick will be as brief as present purposes will permit. For a more extensive treatment, or perhaps we should say a somewhat different one, see Ernest E. Bayles, *Democratic Educational Theory.* New York: Harper & Row, 1960, Chap. 15.

later, Kilpatrick appeared to be having the same difficulty. After a question as to whether he really means that the children in class shall do the purposing (thereby determining curriculum), Kilpatrick answers:

"As I see it, the word purpose is used in two somewhat different senses, and we must distinguish them to get the right idea. Your question uses the word 'select' as if child purposing means primarily that the child, and the child alone, shall select and determine what shall be done; and you seem further to imply that we expect the teacher to accept the child's selection."

"Well, what else could you mean?"

"I said there were two senses in which the word purposing is used. Do you see any difference between a child's doing what he wishes and a child's wishing what he does?"

"I think I see what you mean."

"Well, our plan is primarily that a child shall wish what he does, that he have and put soul and purpose into what he does. If this is his attitude toward what he does, then are set and readiness and satisfaction and annoyance best utilized for his learning, as we have many times said."

"Then the suggestion might come from the teacher, and the child still purpose the matter in the sense you most wish?"

"Quite so. We have, so far, not based any argument on the child's originating or even selecting (in the sense of his deciding) what shall be done. So far, all that we have claimed will be met if the child whole-heartedly accepts and adopts the teacher's suggestion."

"And is this whole-hearted acceptance the other, the second, sense of purposing?"

"Yes."

"And you don't care whether the child purposes in the first sense or not—that is, you don't care whether he does or does not originate the idea, or whether he does or does not choose (that is, decide and determine) what he is to do?"

"I didn't say I didn't care. I do care; I care both positively and negatively, care to encourage it sometimes, care to discourage or rather educate it at other times."

"Now I am completely lost. What do you mean, care positively and negatively? Please explain."

"Go back to my distinction between doing as he wishes and wishing what he does. Take the first, 'do as he wishes.' Suppose a child wishes to do wrong; then I wish him stopped, caught, redirected, educated in some way, so that (a) he shall learn that what he had proposed was wrong, (b) he shall learn why it was wrong, (c) he shall so regret wishing this particular wrong that hereafter he will less probably wish it again. In a word when he wishes to do wrong, I wish him to learn the error of his way and so to repent of his wrong inclination that he will hereafter not so wish again. Is this wishing him to do as he pleases?"

"No, it is not. At least it is not so when he pleases to do wrong."

"But who is to say whether he is wrong? That's the rub."

"The teacher. That's one thing the teacher is there for."[14]

This excerpt is from Kilpatrick's major publication during the time of his greatest influence on American educational thought. No later pronouncement was of equal significance until his postretirement book, *Philosophy of Education*.[15] In this quotation, Kilpatrick would permit a pupil to do as he pleases, *as long as he pleases to do what the teacher deems to be right*. But the moment the pupil pleases ("wants") to do wrong—obviously to "think wrong"—he is to be educated "so to repent of his wrong inclination that he will hereafter not so wish again." This, of course, is unqualified authoritarianism; no dictator would do more.

But Kilpatrick immediately softened the blow by temporizing that, "if the child purposes to do wrong, it will not usually suffice for the teacher merely to forbid, still less merely to punish."[16] In the pages that follow, the thought is that children must be given "freedom enough to practice choosing. . . . As much as they can use wisely." And how much is that? "Growing is the test. If they learn how to make better moral distinctions and if they better act accordingly, they are growing, and then they are using their freedom wisely. If not, they are not so using it."[17] But a reader will look in vain for definitions of key words such as "wisely," "growing," "wise teacher guidance," "better moral distinctions," and the like. Though Kilpatrick says that "Growth is always our criterion"[18] for the amount of freedom children may be given for purposing, selecting, deciding, or originating, the reader should keep in mind that "growth" may be in bad directions as well as good. For example, the very viciousness of cancer is "growth," even growth that leads to more growth.

Seemingly, central in Kilpatrick's theory was the formula *pupil purposing, pupil planning, pupil executing, pupil judging*.[19] These are his four steps of purposeful activity, coupled with insistence that the *pupil* must do each. This represented the heart of the Progressive protest against conventional teaching; that the latter represented *teacher* purposing, planning, and judging, with pupils doing only the executing. This was the point of *project method*; that the project

14 William H. Kilpatrick, *Foundations of Method*. New York: Macmillan, 1926, pp. 207–208.

15 William H. Kilpatrick, *Philosophy of Education*. New York: Macmillan, 1951. To the claim that *The Educational Frontier* came between these two books, the present writers would reply that the latter was a joint effort of seven writers sponsored by the National Society for College Teachers of Education, in which Bode and Dewey doubtless exerted the dominant influence, Kilpatrick merely serving as chairman and "going along" with the rest.

16 *Foundations of Method*, p. 208.

17 *Ibid.*, p. 210.

18 *Ibid.*, p. 211.

19 *Ibid.*, pp. 204–206.

was to be *pupil* chosen, so that what was to be learned—curriculum—would be necessitated by pupil choice because such learnings would be *instrumental* to completion of the project; hence, "instrumental learning." Prior even to *Foundations of Method,* Kilpatrick was insistent that the project method should not be used "to put over prior-chosen subject matter." It was pupil purposes (not teacher purposes)—hence, pupil "interests"—that were to determine curriculum content. This was what he meant by "intrinsic subject matter," as opposed to "extrinsic," the basis for his figure,

$$E \underline{\hspace{6cm}} I$$

as presented in *Foundations,* page 286. The *E* end of the spectrum, for extrinsic, represented conventional teaching; the *I* end, for intrinsic, represented what was for him the ideal, toward which, according to him, "our most progressive schools" had for a century been tending and at which "Dr. Collings's school was run approximately."[20]

From the foregoing, it is evident that, between pages 208 and 286 of *Foundations of Method,* Kilpatrick gradually swings back, from a statement that is as dogmatic and dictatorial as anyone with that leaning could want, to a statement of position that we had come to expect from him—in ideality, educational permissivism. Hence, Dewey could say, as he did in his Introduction to the Tenenbaum biography,

In the best sense of the words, progressive education and the work of Dr. Kilpatrick are virtually synonymous. I say in the best sense because the phrase "progressive education" has been and is frequently used to signify almost any kind of school theory and practice that departs from previously established scholastic methods. Many of these procedures, when they are examined, are found to be innovations, but there seems to be no sound basis for regarding them as progressive. For progress is not identical with mere change, even when the changes may incidentally here and there involve some casual improvement over what previously existed. Still less is it identical with a happy-go-lucky process or flashy, spur-of-the-moment improvisations. "Progressive education" in the sense in which it properly applies to the work of Dr. Kilpatrick implies direction; and direction implies foresight and planning. And planning—as is surely obvious—implies taking thought; the quality and depth of thought depending upon how large and significant a field is taken for the exercise of direction, foresight, and planning.

These remarks are, I believe, pertinent because what has often been criticised as constituting progressive education has taken progressive education to mean

[20] *Ibid.*

methods on the part of the teacher which are marked chiefly by following the immediate and spontaneous activities of children in the schoolroom.[21]

In similar vein, Wynne could remark that Rousseau never did mean to let children do as they please, and could write,

> Since Rousseau also called for a return to nature, many thought he meant that the elaboration, expansion, or unfoldment of primitive tendencies was the ultimate end of education and the good life. With the exception of Kant, most critics down to our own time have thus interpreted Rousseau. Such a belief is an important aspect of what may be called the Rousseau tradition.

· · ·

> But the recent Rousseau scholars whose interpretation lends support to our account of the natural-perfection theory deny the validity of the foregoing Rousseau tradition. While they admit the possibility of such an interpretation, they reject as inadequate the method of study that has been responsible for it. It is, they think, the direct result of taking the part for the whole. There are, they admit, many passages in Rousseau's works, especially in *Emile*, which, if taken in isolation, suggest just such an interpretation of the return to nature and such laissez-faire implications as those described. But they insist that these statements are a consequence of Rousseau's rhetoric and his informal style of writing in which ideas are presented just as they come rather than in a formal statement of principles. They may regret his failure to provide any single complete formulation of his philosophy and its implications, but are convinced that they are all aspects of a single conception.[22]

Strange though it may at first seem to a reader, the present writers agree with both Dewey and Wynne as expressed in the foregoing excerpts. We do not believe that either Kilpatrick or Rousseau meant to turn children loose; only partial reading of either writer would seemingly justify interpreting him as completely permissivist. But the point that we feel is essential—and the one not made by Dewey or Wynne—is the one we keep reiterating; that with Rousseau, Froebel, and Kilpatrick *theory was one thing and recommended "practice" was another*. *Emile* was Rousseau's influential book on education, *Education of Man* was Froebel's (at least for general theory), and *Foundations of Method* was Kilpatrick's. We have, we hope, documented all three with fairness, and we

[21] Samuel Tenenbaum, *William Heard Kilpatrick: Trail Blazer in Education*. New York: Harper & Row, 1951, p. vii.
[22] John P. Wynne, *Theories of Education*. New York: Harper & Row, 1963, pp. 57–58.

feel it small wonder that serious and thoughtful readers, both contemporary with these writers and subsequent to them, have been left wondering what they really did mean. Some educational philosophers today even seem to go so far in their consequent pessimism as to take the position that, between educational theory and educational practice, there *can* be no logical connection. Such pessimism we deplore. We feel that there is no need for such disparagement or despair; that Dewey has already supplied us with theory that we can "take seriously," in that from it practical teaching procedures can be logically deduced and theory and practice can become thoroughly at peace with one another. This we shall consider in the following chapter.

Meanwhile, pursuant to Kilpatrick's reference to "Dr. Collings's school," let us take a look at the position taken by this "follower" of Kilpatrick, one of his early doctoral students.[23] The pronouncement, however, upon which we shall draw is not the widely known one, but another of a later date.[24]

These shifts that we have been noting—between permissivism on the one hand and authoritarian domination on the other—are basically between theory and practice. They are not, fundamentally, between practice at one time and practice at another. When, in practice, one permits a pupil to choose, plan, etc. only as long as he does so in terms of what is "right," one is not being permissive in any genuine sense. The rein may be held loosely so that there is no appreciable pull on the bit, *but the rein is held;* the moment the purposing and planning go wrong, the rein tightens and the bit pulls in no uncertain terms. Use of a whip may not be needed, but the pull of the bit is indication enough that the whip is close at hand and will be used if necessary. (We hope the reader knows enough about riding a horse to make this metaphor intelligible.) Permission to do as one chooses *only* as long as one chooses to do what the teacher has in mind *is not permissivism*.

Moreover, as Dewey noted at one time, the pendulum metaphor as used to denote back-and-forth swings between extremes is faulty because it implies that the ideal is a midposition wherein there is no movement at all. He said that it is a change of direction that is needed, which the pendulum does not exemplify. Seemingly, the "on the fence" metaphor is a much better one, but the common attitude toward being on the fence must be changed. To be "on the fence" is really an accomplishment because it requires a fine sense of equilibrium—of balance between the pull toward one side and the pull toward the other. Assuming the "progress" line to be *along* the fence, it represents high competence

[23] Collings, *op. cit.*
[24] Ellsworth Collings and Milbourne O. Wilson, *Psychology for Teachers.* New York: Scribner, 1930.

to move on that line and maintain balance—it is a case of walking a tightrope. A writer who is permissivist in theory and dogmatic in practice is never "on the fence." Instead, he is first on one side and then on the other. That mythical bird, the mugwump, who sits on the fence with his mug on one side and his wump on the other is not one to be sneered at; he displays a fine sense of balance, even though he is merely sitting.

Were Collings' pronouncements, even on theory, any less equivocal than were Kilpatrick's?[25] The present writers feel that, to a degree, they were; and on the side of permissivism. In Collings' fourteenth chapter, "Guidance of Purposive Behavior," he does indeed seem to say that the teacher must "guide." He says "guidance is fundamental"[26] but he goes on to say that "The teacher enables boys and girls to respond successfully along their drive in the face of difficulties," and "She sees, in other words, that success attends the response of boys and girls along their drive. . . ."[27] Finally, "direction is along each and all the traits of purposive behavior [purposing, planning, executing, judging] for each and every boy and girl. And this is guidance through direction of purposive behavior."[28] In other words, "direction of purposive behavior" is seeing to it that *pupils'* "drive" lines are *followed*.

In the next four chapters, Collings deals successively with the four "traits of purposive behavior." Following is the first full paragraph and part of the second paragraph of the chapter on "purposing":

1. *Pupil Purposing. Purposive behavior contemplates pupil purposing in every instance.* It does so for at least two reasons. First, purposive behavior involves, as we have seen, the functioning of a series of interrelated stimulus-response mechanisms along a particular line. Purposing is the functioning of one of these series of stimulus-response mechanisms and, as such, involves the response of boys and girls along their drive in this particular, for stimulus-response mechanisms function in this fashion. Pupil purposing is, in this sense, one of the earmarks of purposive behavior. Second, purposing is one of the lines of growth. Growth of boys and girls in this particular involves, as we have seen, change in drive and response and it takes place through boys and girls responding along their drive in purposing. It is in this manner that boys and girls grow in pur-

---

[25] Though we shall not go into it, it should be noted that, in the books under scrutiny, Kilpatrick and Collings both employ Thorndike's connectionist psychology and rely on it heavily. Moreover, though during the thirties Kilpatrick ostensibly turned to configurational theory, in his postretirement book, *Philosophy of Education,* he appeared to be back in the Thorndike fold.

[26] Collings and Wilson, *op. cit.,* p. 263.

[27] *Ibid.,* pp. 265–266.

[28] *Ibid.,* p. 268.

posing—in choosing more wisely. *Pupil purposing is, in this sense, the key to growth in this particular of conduct.* Such growth is desirable for the success of an individual in a democracy depends very largely upon wise purposing. *If the teacher does the purposing growth in this particular is thwarted. The resultant change is in the teacher's drive and response since it is her stimulus-response mechanisms that function.* Teacher purposing blocks, in this sense, the functioning of the stimulus-response mechanisms of boys and girls along this line and, in so doing, prohibits growth in purposing. *Pupil purposing thus is fundamental in purposive behavior and growth. Without it purposive behavior, on the one hand, is thwarted, and, on the other hand, growth of boys and girls in purposing is blocked.*

2. *Procedure in Pupil Purposing.* Purposing includes, as we have seen, three interrelated steps. First, *it involves initiation of goal.* This includes boys and girls *suggesting* goals to pursue.[29]

The opening paragraphs of the three chapters that follow are almost verbatim reproductions of the foregoing, except that, where "purposing" appears above, "planning" appears in chapter 16, "execution" in chapter 17, and "judging" in chapter 18. Hence, if we can believe words at all, it seems clear that the formula, "pupil purposing, pupil planning, pupil executing, and pupil judging," is to be taken literally. It is the pupils who decide; no exception is registered, not even when they decide "wrongly." This is permissivist *theory*.

As to *practice*, Collings' chapter 13 (pp. 193–261) is devoted mainly to what he says are "stenographic reports [that] typically illustrate each of the four lines of purposive behavior"[30] in what he called "children's activities"—presumably what Kilpatrick called projects. Five such "activities" are reported, the second on "How Billy Made His Wagon." Lack of space precludes inclusion of more than the following excerpt, but it seems sufficient to typify what Collings considers ideal (or at least satisfactory) practice:

II.   How BILLY MADE HIS WAGON (*Construction Activity*)

1. Purposing.

"Gee, I wish I had a wagon like Carl's," remarked Billy at one of the hand periods. "I'd like to have one to play with."

"Why don't you make one?" asked Carl. "I made mine."

"Shucks, I can't make the wheels," responded Billy. "I can't saw a circle."

"Oh, that's easy," added Carl. "Miss Jones will show you how."

29 *Ibid.*, pp. 271–272. Italics ours.
30 *Ibid.*, p. 203.

"I'll see," remarked Billy. "I'd sure like to have one."

"Sure, I'll help you," replied Miss Jones to Billy's inquiry. "Can you get the materials?"

"I think so," answered Billy. "Mamma has a pine box at home that I'm sure she'll give me."

"All right, bring your material to-morrow, and I'll help you plan your wagon," added Miss Jones. "I think the pine box will do."

"I'll get it," remarked Billy joyfully. "Carl'll let me have his wagon to make mine by, I'm sure."

"Be thinking over how you'll want to make your wagon," advised Miss Jones. "We'll discuss the materials, tools, and processes in making the wagon at the next conference."

"I'll find out all I can from Carl," added Billy as the gong sounded.

2. Planning.

"Billy, let's discuss the materials needed in making your wagon first, before you begin your work," suggested Miss Jones at the next meeting.

"I'd like to do so," agreed Billy. "I ruined my sled because I couldn't saw straight."

"Do you have your materials?" inquired Miss Jones. "Seems to me we ought to consider them first."

"There's my box my mamma gave me," replied Billy. "Do I need any more?" He thought he could make the wagon box and wheels from the box.

"What about the tongue?" remarked Miss Jones. "I think your box is all right."

"Oh, I'd forgotten that," answered Billy, rather puzzled. "Carl made his out of heavy wire. I can get some at home just like it."

"I'm sure the wire will do," suggested Miss Jones, "I can think of nothing better."

"I'll make a loop in the end of the wire to pull the wagon by," explained Billy. "I can fasten the other end to the front axle."

"That's a good idea, Billy," approved Miss Jones. "I hadn't thought of the loop in the end."

"Carl's hasn't a loop, but I saw one in the store with one," continued Billy, "I want the loop just big enough for my hand."

"How big are you going to make your wagon, Billy?" inquired Miss Jones at this point. "You'll have to know in order to find out the length of the different pieces of lumber, won't you?"

"Just the same size as Carl's," replied Billy rather quickly. "I'd like to have the wagon box and wheels just the same size."

"Then you can measure Carl's wagon to find out how to cut your lumber," suggested Miss Jones.

"Sure, I hadn't thought of that," agreed Billy. "I'd had the lumber sawed if I'd known how long to cut it. Oh, I don't know how to saw the wheels either."

"The wheels are sawed out with the coping saw," explained Miss Jones. She pointed out that the wheels are first marked off with a pair of compasses.

"But how do you mark them off?" persisted Billy. "I don't see yet."

Miss Jones explained that the size of the wheel is determined by placing one point of the compass on the spindle of the wheel and moving the other point out to the outer edge of the wheel.

"Oh, I think I know now," interrupted Billy. "I'll get the compasses and try." Billy got a pair of compasses, placed one point on the axle of Carl's wagon, and moved the other point out to the edge of the wheel as Miss Jones had explained. He then set the compasses on a plank and marked off a wheel.

"That's it," approved Miss Jones. "You know now how to make a wagon wheel, don't you?"

"Well, I think so," responded Billy proudly. "I'll bore a little hole in the center of the wheel for the nail. That will keep it from bursting the wheel," he explained.

"That's a good idea, Billy," agreed Miss Jones.[31]

Close reading of the foregoing seemingly reveals that in no case does Miss Jones say Bobby nay; but it also reveals that in no case does Bobby say Miss Jones nay. True, Bobby learns a number of things because they ostensibly are needed by him to complete his project. This is the principle of *instrumental learning,* learning supposedly because the pupil sees it as needful rather than because teacher requires it.[32] But Miss Jones thinks everything that Bobby suggests is just fine and Bobby thinks the same of everything Miss Jones suggests. In no case is there even incipient disagreement, if we can believe the report. A case of disagreement is indeed exemplified in the third project that is reported, playing Roly Poly, but it is a disagreement among the pupils and is settled by a vote, preceded by little if any discussion.

Our feeling about the case of Bobby building his wagon is that it is too good to be true. Pupil and teacher just don't see eye to eye so completely, unless both have agreed, tacitly or otherwise, not to disagree with each other. In such case, if there is not to be complete docility on the part of both, the one who really wants something has merely to get in his word first. This may be practice, say, in choosing, but it is practice only in the sense of going through the motions. It is not practice that is guided in such a way that the pupil makes dependable headway in learning to choose more wisely than he would without the practice. Wise choosing means taking a look at the various possibilities, anticipating what

[31] *Ibid.,* pp. 214–217.

[32] Though this is what Kilpatrick characterizes as "intrinsic subject matter" and puts it at the *I* end of the spectrum (see ante p. 228), it is no less "extrinsic" than is learning for the sake of satisfying teacher. We fear that Kilpatrick's *E* and *I* are *both E's.*

will come of each, and choosing the one that best satisfies the criteria that have been agreed upon.

Miss Jones missed many opportunities for such practice during Bobby's wagon building. For example, why should Bobby want to build a wagon? What does he want to do with it? Will one "just like Carl's" serve the purpose Bobby has in mind? Is Carl's a good coaster? Or a good one to haul groceries? How about that tongue? How does Bobby plan to fasten it to the wagon? Will that hold the front wheels steady enough either to coast well or to haul groceries satisfactorily? Bobby needs to have some resistance from Miss Jones, whether she senses his first choice as good or bad, simply to help him learn what it takes to make good choices rather than poor ones. This isn't having Miss Jones' "stimulus-response mechanisms . . . function" rather than Bobby's (if one must use such stilted terminology); it is Miss Jones helping Bobby gain insight into what must go into choosing, if it is to become *wise* choosing.

Our analysis of both the Collings books leads us to conclude that his descriptions of practice fail to cover crucial points. His theory, if we can take it at face value (and, if we can't, what shall we take?), is complete permissivism on the part of the teacher. But his practice is that, if a teacher can get a word in first, the teacher's word holds. How else, in *Experiment with a Project Curriculum,* would a bunch of southwest-Missouri kids be euchred into wanting to study why Mr. _____'s family had so much typhoid fever? Theory or no theory, every teacher knows he *has* to keep his hand on the steering wheel. Let us have theory that justifies this; not theory that makes a conscientious teacher feel guilty when he does what he knows he must do.

Kilpatrick's "Project Method" and Instrumental Learning

In the final chapter of Kilpatrick's *Foundations of Method,* he comes to the term, *project,* and recognizes four types: (1) producer; (2) consumer; (3) problem; and (4) drill. Bobby building his wagon was obviously a producer project. What is learned—what teacher is supposedly concerned with—is needed in order to complete the project; it is an instrument, hence, *instrumental learning.* Educational literature carries the name, *incidental* learning, but what is incidental may be merely accidental; hence "instrumental" is a term seemingly better fitted to express the idea. What is accidental is, of course, to be used, but education requires something more than such hit or miss; mostly miss. What a pupil is concerned with is, of course, the object to be produced (or maybe an event, such as putting on a play for parents' day). But, since what is instrumental is dependent on the end-in-view and since that end is supposedly decided by pupils, *it is pupil choices that determine curriculum*. This is the rationale that underlies "pupil purposing."

This was the rationale that underlay the introduction and earlier use of the term, *project;* by Franklin Ernest Heald (1870–1943), specialist in agricultural education (1914–1918) in the U.S. Department of Agriculture, who first organized vocational agriculture education at the national level in the early days of Smith-Hughes and Smith-Lever Acts. The future farmers of America were to learn how to grow wheat or corn by growing it, or how to raise pigs by raising them. The learnings were indeed instrumental and, for vocational education, the plan has proven to be very useful. But choice of projects (hence, of curriculum) was by no means wholly in the hands of pupils; if they were to learn farming, there were certain things they would have to learn and, what those were, teacher would perhaps know best.

When, however, the idea of project method was later introduced into *general* education, albeit on the elementary level, a difficulty in theory arose. The over-all purpose or end for *general* education is nowhere near as clear to all concerned (if to any) as it is for any case of vocational or professional education. To complicate the matter further, Kilpatrick was insistent that projects were not to be chosen for the purpose of "putting over prior chosen subject matter." This reflected the original protest basic to Progressivism, that domination by teachers should be greatly reduced and pupil "interests" given a play; hence, the term afterwards popularized by Rugg and Shumaker, *the child-centered school*. In consequence, pupil choices were left "on their own," without benefit of a universally recognized over-all purpose by which to guide them. Small wonder that teachers were mystified and that caricaturists had a field day. All wanted to know whether the Progressives were serious about "pupil purposing."

Kilpatrick's Type I (producer) project may, or may not, have been his favorite. It was, in any case, one that fitted eminently into his scheme of thinking, as presented in *Foundations of Method,* either instrumental or incidental learning assuming a logical place therein. In passing but returned to in the next chapter, the Type III (problem) project is also of this kind. Much information— many learnings—is needed in order to solve an intellectual problem, as Kilpatrick notes;[33] hence, instrumental learning has a logical place in Type III. Since the name, problem project, is merely another one for Dewey's "complete act of thought," as introduced in *How We Think* (1910), it is obvious that the *reflective teaching* of John Dewey was admissible under the cover of the project method.

[33] *Foundations of Method,* p. 348.

The Type II (consumer) project, however, seems to be "a different breed of cat." When a class is studying New England colonial life, the children of Holland, Indian life, the city water-supply system, or how a local dairy is run, it is neither seeking to produce something nor to solve an intellectual problem. It is studying what someone else has done; sitting on the sidelines, as it were, and for that reason characterized once by Bode as "sideline education." It is studying a project, albeit one that is being or has been performed by someone else, and for that reason may be included under project method. But the class members are not at work on the project; they are merely observing (consuming) it. They are the "sidewalk superintendents" or the "downtown quarterbacks." Hence, what *they* learn is not necessary for the performance of the project and we therefore do not have *instrumental* learning. Since the educational backwash of Kilpatrick's admission of consumer projects into his educational scheme known as the project method is one of many facets, we shall have to give it considerable attention.

McMurry's Consumer-Type "Projects" and the Absence of Instrumental Learning

Inclusion of consumer-type projects under the general category of the project method can seemingly be laid to Dr. Charles A. McMurry, "the grand old man of Peabody." (See ante, p. 143.) This grew out of his book, *Teaching by Projects*,[34] published in 1920, and a series of leaflets under his editorship, published and distributed around 1920–1925 by the George Peabody College for Teachers,[35] under the general name of "Type Studies and Lesson Plans."

Our previous treatment of McMurry was in connection with the Herbartianism of the 1890s, in which the five-step teaching procedure received most attention. During the early teens, McMurry was stressing what he called "type studies," in which the Herbartian principles of correlation and concentration played a large role. The correlational core, for example, might be the great deserts of the world, in which case one such desert—say, the Sahara—would be taken as typical, or the "type," and subjected to highly detailed study. Location with relation to climatic zones and prevailing winds, topographical features, the manner of life of the people, the nature of the oases, animal and plant wildlife, domesticated animals, transportation and the caravan routes, trade, mode of

[34] C. A. McMurry, *Teaching by Projects*. New York: Macmillan, 1920.
[35] There were at least four volumes, with 4–6 issues per volume. An outstanding one was "Methods in Handling Types as Large Units of Study," Vol. 3, No. 1.

government—all these matters, and more, would receive detailed and realistic treatment until the Sahara Desert was very well known. Then, in turn, other great deserts would receive attention, first in the northern hemisphere then in the southern, comparing all the while with the Sahara as the type but going into less and less detail as the study progressed. The final windup would be a summary of the salient characteristics of world deserts as a whole, the culmination of an inductive study that started in a multiplicity of particulars and then moved progressively to the general.

Thus, with the popularization of the project method in the late teens and the early twenties, McMurry needed to make only one small change to become a participant in the movement. Since a project is generally thought of as something that is devised, planned, and performed by persons, and since deserts and mountain systems and the like would perhaps be considered "acts of God" rather than of man, McMurry merely turned to great projects of man for his centers of correlation and concentration— "The Panama Canal and Ocean Transportation Routes," "The Salt River Project and Irrigation," "Glasgow and Ship Building," "The Virginia Plantation," "New York City as a Center for Commerce and Business," "The Trek of the Turner Boys and the California Gold Rush," "The Rebuilding of Vienna, Hamburg, and Paris." These and many other titles were included in the leaflet series produced and distributed by Dr. McMurry. Hence, with Kilpatrick's endorsement by inclusion of consumer projects as Type II, McMurry's type-study program became part of Progressive Education.

From "Interests" to "Needs"

Since (as previously noted) McMurry's projects were essentially teacher-planned, the Kilpatrick-Collings stress on *pupil* purposing, planning, etc. was greatly mitigated. Here was promise of relief for Progressives from the pain of being continually accused of complete reliance on pupil "interests." McMurry also made the point that, in his opinion, producer projects had only limited curricular use, mainly confined to the lower grades, whereas his consumer projects could be widely used, even far into the upper grades. And inclusion of a visit to a local postoffice in connection with a study of the United States postal system had built into it a quality of grown-up realism that could not be matched by a play postoffice set up in a first-grade classroom.

Moreover, with the assistance of educational psychologists, the concept of pupil "needs" began to gain gradual acceptance, so that by 1938 Bode could write, "Any discussion among 'progressive' educators is likely to bring in an early reference to the 'needs' of pupils."[36] And, since pupil needs could be ascertained without waiting until pupils voluntarily divulged them—the pupils might not even know of their existence—the degree of teacher planning legitimized by consumer projects became for them a great asset. So, by shifting emphasis from "interests" to "needs" and by authorizing extensive use of consumer projects, Progressive Educators gradually got themselves off the hook of continuous confrontation by the question, "Do you *really* mean that we should always let children do what they want to do?"

The shift of emphasis, however, had other entailments. First, it probably played a real part in the rather rapid demise of the term, project method. Besides inclusion of the first three types of projects, which we have already discussed, Kilpatrick also gave a ticket of admission to Type IV, the Drill Project. Although perhaps not so intended by him, a drill project could easily be deemed as covering and including almost any kind of re-citational schoolroom activity that the most conventional or traditional teacher might want, including Winnetka-plan units and, by little stretch of imagination, Morrison units. Thus, by becoming so inclusive as to encompass almost everything that might be done in classrooms, the term project-method became meaningless. Whether this was the cause, we do not presume to know, but the fact remains that with the advent of the thirties the term had pretty well ceased being used. To take its place the term *unit* became popular and has continued so until the present writing. It has, however, lost its original Winnetka or Morrisonian connotations, and now seems commonly to mean no more than a long-term assignment in contrast with the traditional, page-by-page assignments of yesteryear.

Second, the interests-to-needs shift made legitimate and highly desirable the employment of any presumably tenable list of specific objectives, whether of the Bobbitt-Thorndike-Washburne type or some other; for such lists were waiting and ready. Thus, the ranks of the Progressive Education Association could become invitingly open to specific-objectivist-minded school personnel, and a Carleton Washburne could twice become president of the Association. But such a turn could also alienate many hard-core members of the early years of the Association who could hardly forget that originally the Thorndikeans were as much subject to their protestations as were followers of the Puritan tradition. Thus when, in 1944, the name of the Association was changed to The American Education Fellowship, even a long-standing critic such as William Chandler

[36] *Progressive Education at the Crossroads,* p. 62. In this connection, both Chapters 3 and 4 should be read.

Bagley could regret the demise of an organization that had done so much to improve American education.[37]

Third, though not accounting for it, the interests-to-needs shift could justify sponsorship by Progressives of the core-curriculum movement that experienced a rapid rise to popularity during the late thirties.[38] Whether Hollis L. Caswell did, or did not, consciously follow the pattern of Herbart's principles of correlation and concentration is not important here. The fact remains, however, that those principles and the core-curriculum idea in its early forms were virtually identical concepts and that, while a member of the George Peabody College faculty, Caswell could hardly have been unaware of McMurry's ideas on the project method in education and the consumer-type units (or projects) that McMurry had worked out.[39] Whether a "resource unit" was based on a producer-type or on a consumer-type project, hence whether the principle of instrumental (or incidental) learning was or was not used, the core-curriculum movement did receive Progressive support and its rationale was fully in accord with Kilpatrick's *Foundations of Method*.

Progressivism and Rousseau's Theory

We see in the Progressive Education movement of the first half of the twentieth century that the Roussellian theory of education as unfoldment played a considerable role. That such a role was not consciously intended by those responsible for the movement should doubtless be granted. Few indeed were the writers who explicitly advocated unalloyed permissivism, and few were the schools that practiced it. The recent and not-so-recent critics of American education who bewail the passing of good old Puritanic discipline should realize that they are barking up the wrong tree when they blame Progressivism for supposedly turning schools into nurseries or playgrounds where children are coddled into adulthood. Such schools are, and have been, virtually nonexistent; certainly few and far between. Schools, particularly elementary, may be much different from what they were at the turn of the century, but they are far from

[37] Bagley, William Chandler, "The PEA Becomes the American Education Fellowship," *School and Society*, vol. 59, no. 1525, March 18, 1944, p. 198.

[38] See Progressive Education Association Commission on the Relation of School and College, *Adventure in American Education*. 5 vols. New York: Harper & Row, 1942. Much of the innovating done by the 30 schools during this "Eight-Year Study" was along the line of core curricula.

[39] Hollis L. Caswell and Doak S. Campbell, *Principles of Curricuulm Development*. New York: American Book, 1935.

being permissivist. If things are wrong with the schools, it would seem that specific-objectivism should be blamed rather than Progressivism; for it is specific-objectivist principles that have been, and still are, the dominating factors in twentieth-century American education. Even the remnants of Progressivism, as evinced in the core-curriculum movement, are as thoroughly specific-objectivist as can be found anywhere.

As to core curricula, its proponents opine that not many schools have gone core, and those that have avowedly done so have mainly adopted the diluted form of a double-period, homeroom, social studies-language arts, common-learnings arrangement, taking only part of a school day. In this form, the core idea does not really represent the Herbartian correlation-concentration idea that either producer- or consumer-type projects would exemplify. Instead, the word "core" carries more the implication of general education; the core portion of a school day tends to include the topics that all pupils are expected to cover—what used to be called the "constants." The other subjects in which a given student is enrolled tend to be "electives"—regularly organized courses that the student chooses to suit his own personal plans or interests.

As to the actual role played by the Roussellian *theory* of education as unfoldment, the fact of its presence in professional literature has tended to sensitize teachers to the necessity of treating pupils as *people*—as human beings who have personalities that are different from those of adults, even of the adults they will become, and each of whom has a unique, distinctive personality of his own so must be understood and treated accordingly. This would seem to be the message of the "pupil purposing, etc." formula, and the shock value of its overstatement could well have been the very challenge needed to produce this sensitivity in the minds and hearts of practicing teachers today. When people are moved to ask, "Do you really mean that?" they are stopping and taking notice; some sort of message is getting through. And the subsequent thinking that is evoked, even if merely to refute, makes a mark that is not readily eradicated. Even the comprehensive American high school, which has established a pattern for secondary education that the other nations of the world are striving to imitate, may owe much of its development during the past half-century to the overstatements that we thought the Progressives were making.

In the long run, however, educational theory cannot operate on shock effect. Sooner or later, the shock wears off, the tune goes stale, and the matter is written off as a parcel of foolishness or is made a whipping boy on which to pin the blame for any real or imagined ill that may arise. When a theorist has in effect to say, "Well, that's my theory but don't take it too seriously," the reply should seemingly be, "If we can't take it seriously, then why take it at all?" That has been the trouble with the "pupil-purposing, etc." formula; even Kilpatrick himself, as we have shown, did not take it seriously. Nor, as we have also shown, did Rousseau himself take seriously his own principle of "negative education." That is, we think, the chief reason that recent apologists for Rousseau keep reiterating that down through the years we have not fully understood him.

The search on the part of twentieth-century educational theorists, especially in the United States, has been for a theory that can be taken seriously; taken into all of the ramifications that educational practice must pursue. In other words, the search is for a theory that fully and harmoniously covers the educational enterprise—at least as far as it has gone to date as well as, hopefully, carrying it into the future.

Suggested Readings

Bayles, Ernest E., *Democratic Educational Theory*. New York: Harper & Row, 1960, Chap. 15.

Bode, Boyd H., *Modern Educational Theories*. New York: Macmillan, 1927, Chap. 7. (Now in paperback.)

Bode, Boyd H., *Progressive Education at the Crossroads*. New York: Newson and Company, 1938.

Caswell, Hollis L., and Campbell, Doak S., *Principles of Curriculum Development*. New York: American Book, 1935.

Collings, Ellsworth, *Experiment with a Project Curriculum*. New York: Macmillan, 1923.

Collings, Ellsworth, and Wilson, Milbourne O., *Psychology for Teachers*. New York: Scribner, 1930.

Cremin, Lawrence A., *The Transformation of the School*. New York: Knopf, 1961. (Now in paperback.)

Dewey, John, *Experience and Education*. New York: Collier, 1963. Original copyright 1938.

Dewey, John, *The School and Society*. Chicago: University of Chicago Press, 1900.

Dewey, John, "The Way Out of Educational Confusion," in Reginald D. Archambault (ed.), *John Dewey on Education*. New York: Modern Library, 1964, pp. 422–426.

Kilpatrick, William H., *Foundations of Method*. New York: Macmillan, 1926.

Kilpatrick, William H., *Philosophy of Education*. New York: Macmillan, 1951.

McMurry, Charles A., *Teaching by Projects*. New York: Macmillan, 1920.

National Society for the Study of Education, *Twenty-Sixth Yearbook, Part I, Curriculum-Making: Past and Present*, Guy M. Whipple (ed.) Bloomington: Public School Publishing Company, 1926.

Progressive Education Association Commission on the Relation of School and College, *Adventure in American Education*. 5 vols. New York: Harper & Row, 1942.

Rugg, Harold, and Shumaker, Ann, *The Child-Centered School*. New York: Harcourt, Brace & World, 1928.

Rugg, Harold, *Culture and Education in America*. New York: Harcourt, Brace & World, 1931.

Tenebaum, Samuel, *William Heard Kilpatrick: Trail Blazer in Education*. New York: Harper & Row, 1951.

Wynne, John P., *Theories of Education*. New York: Harper & Row, 1963, Chap. 7.

City school-children genuinely absorbed and challenged by a classroom atmosphere that grows out of concern with a matter deemed important by the members of the class. Dewey's idea that sustained effort is a sequential outcome of genuine pupil interest is well depicted here. (Courtesy of the Seattle School District)

12 ‏⮾ Education as Progressive

Reconstruction of Experience

It is possible that future historians of education will mark 1930 as a turning point for education in the United States. If the reader will take a backward look at the organization of this book, he will probably be aware of our recognition, so far, of three distinctive periods in the American educational experience. First was the colonial period, which seems to have been one of *transplantation* wherein forms and institutions were lifted by the settlers from the soil of their native lands, brought in toto with them, and set out in the soil of the new world.

This continued until about 1750, when the colonists began to chafe under Old World domination, nation-building began, and Franklin's Academy became a harbinger of things to come—a distinctly American set (if not a "system") of educational institutions and practices. Through the Revolutionary War and up to our Civil War (1750–1860) we recognize educationally as a period of nation-building, *nationalization*; development of practically all the basic characteristics of our educational system, even as it exists today.

After a temporary setback due to the Civil War, the educational enterprise began to grow rapidly, doubtless due in large measure to the great boost to the principle of *public* education given by Mann and Barnard. Secondary education furnishes a striking example of such growth. Although the first *public* high school was established in Boston in 1821, it was not until after the "Kalamazoo Case" of 1874,[1] which essentially settled the legality of a high-school district levying a tax for a public high school, that enrollments in secondary education really began to expand. The following statistics, reported by the U.S. Office of Education, are in terms of percentages of youngsters of high-school age (14–17) actually in high school (grades 9–12): 1890, 6.7; 1900, 11.4; 1910, 15.4; 1920, 32.3; 1930, 51.4; 1940, 73.3; 1952, 77.4; 1961, 90.0;[2] and this during a period when the total population trebled.

We recognize the post-Civil-War period, therefore, as one of *expansion;* of rapid, often phenomenal, growth of what in terms of precedent had already been established. And, although as the above figures show, such expansion has continued to the present, we figure 1930 as a rather significant point of change. This was the time after the stock-market crash of October, 1929, and before the great depression of the thirties. Prior to 1930, the total annual expenditure for education in the United States, both public and private, was $3 billion; afterwards, it dropped precipitously to $2 billion and remained there for a while. Now, however, it has gone beyond $32 billion; but much has transpired since 1930, as witnessed by the expansion of "Gross National Product, GNP," from $60 billion annually in 1935 or 1936 to more than $600 billion in 1964.

With such a drop in financial support, school personnel had to do some serious thinking as to (to quote Herbert Spencer) what knowledge is of the most worth. This led to soul-searching. And, whereas prior to 1930 Dewey and Bode were almost alone in considering *democracy* an important factor in determining educational objectives, afterwards the *word* democracy began to appear in educational treatises with growing frequency. The question was, "After all, just how much education does *democracy* require?" And, although in most cases the word was either ill defined or not defined at all, its inclusion began to be recognized as needful.

This soul-searching had other consequences as well. From roughly 1905 to 1925, the wave of specific-objectivism was taken by many educators as grounds for hope that education could and would become "scientific," emancipated from dependence upon philosophy and history. For this reason, what we have chosen to call specific-objectivism has by some been known as the "science-of-education

[1] For one of the best of many discussions of this case and its consequences, see H. G. Good, *A History of American Education,* 2nd ed. New York: Macmillan, 1962, pp. 251–254.
[2] U.S. Office of Education, *Digest of Educational Statistics,* 1963 ed. Washington, D.C.: Government Printing Office.

movement." Prior to 1900, education courses ran heavily to general method (the art of teaching), educational philosophy of the armchair variety, and history of education that began with the primitives and followed down through Egypt, Greece, Rome, Western Europe of the Middle Ages, Renaissance, Reformation, and maybe through the seventeenth century.

With courses as cloistered as these, it is small wonder that philosophy and history of education fell by the wayside, to be replaced by courses that presumably were scientifically based: Bobbitt-type courses on curriculum; courses on educational measurement, concentrating on objective tests and the statistical methods needed in making and handling them; courses in educational psychology, essentially taking Thorndike connectionism for granted and assuming that this represented the *science* of psychology; courses in "special methods," representing the various subject-matter fields taught, and to a degree replacing "general methods" courses; and a scattering of other subjects, including the newly developing field of educational sociology.

After 1930, however, there began a resurgence of attention to courses that had been dropped, but with different orientation on teaching in its broader, theoretical aspects, particularly as it was influenced by our national democratic commitment; on educational philosophy, but in terms of what differences the various philosophies would make in the various and sundry phases of an educational enterprise; on educational history, but with major focus upon more recent developments and less upon those of earlier times, so that the influence of the past upon the present became less important in determining time allotments and emphasis. Educational psychology, too, though grudgingly, began to give bits of ground before the impact of configurational (relativistic) psychological thought, though it is hard even today to find offerings in educational psychology that are completely configurational. And not to be ignored is the recent assault by Banesh Hoffman on objective testing,[3] which, though only beginning, may grow sizably.

What we have been noting so far in this chapter has led us, whether rightly or wrongly, to think of the post-1930 period in American education as one of *reappraisal*. Of course, expansion has gone on, as our figures on secondary education show and as corresponding figures on higher education would also show. Elementary education, on the other hand, has seemingly reached a saturation point and secondary education will probably do so soon; hence, hereafter we should expect enrollments in grades 1–12 to rise or fall as the total population rises or falls. And, since the early thirties, total annual expenditures for all forms of education in the United States have grown from the $2 billion previously

[3] See Banesh Hoffman, *The Tyranny of Testing*. New York: Crowell-Collier, 1962.

noted to practically $32 billion for the year 1962–1963.[4] But with all the expansion, rethinking has continued, aided by rapidly improving research techniques by which such rethinking can be tested.

And, in this rethinking or reappraisal, we should include that done by persons and groups outside of collegiate education faculties, and students who are doing work toward advanced degrees in education: collegiate faculty members other than in education, and the Rickovers and the Conants, to say nothing of the multifarious "attackers," many of whom are described by Dr. Raywid in her book, *The Ax-Grinders.*[5]

Authors as Critics as Well as Reporters

In the present book, the authors have been serving primarily as reporters— interpretational, of course, for no human report can be absolutely objective— but we have also, to a degree, been serving as critics. The reader also will assume, and is invited to assume, the role of critic and, in order to do so discerningly, needs not only to employ carefully worked-out criteria of his own but also to know what criteria the authors have been using. It would seem tautological to say that no human being makes or passes a judgment without having some basis for doing so—some criterion or criteria that he employs. However, it is probably safe to say that it is an exceptional person who is particularly aware at any given time of exactly what criteria he is using.

The ideas, points of view, or theories that have been presented up to now seem to the authors to fall short of ideal. We come now to one that, as far as American educational thought has progressed, appears to supply the corrective that has long been sought. On what basis do we arrive at this judgment? What are the criteria that we have been employing? Our first question has been one of coverage. Does the point of view take into account *all* of the educational aspects or considerations that it seemingly should? This is the criterion of *adequacy*. Is the educational outlook adequate, in terms of the world of which student and teacher are a part and with which they must cope? Does it cover all aspects that need to be covered?

Our second question has been one of *harmony,* or *consistency.* Does the view "hang together"? Does it avoid self-contradiction? This is the criterion that we have found to be continually violated in the views so far considered. Theory and

---

[4] U.S. Office of Education, *op. cit.,* p. 103.
[5] Mary Anne Raywid, *The Ax-Grinders.* New York: Macmillan, 1962.

practice, we have found, were not compatible with each other. We have had to be satisfied with the rejoinder, "Well, that's my theory, but don't take it too seriously."

Our third question has been one of *clarity*. Does the view indicate with clearness the line or lines of action that should be taken if the view were adopted, as well as what lines of action should *not* be taken? Finally, a fourth question that seemingly should be asked is that of *pertinence*. Is the view pertinent to matters that are or should be involved in the enterprise under consideration? In our case, does it relate directly and precisely to education, or is its major focus on matters other than that? Does it adhere to the adage, "Keep your eye on the ball!" or does it, to change the metaphor, "expend its substance on that which is not bread"? Thus, as we come to the thinking of John Dewey with regard to what American education should seek to accomplish and how it should go about it, we shall, as we have previously been doing, apply the criteria of *adequacy, harmony, clarity,* and *pertinence* to his proposals and judge them on these bases.

Dewey's Introduction of "Interaction"

With reference to assumptions as to man's original nature, we have noted the *bad-active* of the Puritans, the *neutral-reactive* of Locke, the *good-active* of Rousseau, and the unsuccessful attempts of Comenius and Pestalozzi at establishing a position that would avoid theoretical pitfalls leading to inconsistencies. Seemingly, it is a middle position that is needed; one that avoids both extremes, of authoritarian dictation on the one hand and absolute permissivism on the other. Locke took the midposition on the *good-bad* issue but failed to do so on the *active-reactive* one.

Dewey went with Locke on the *good-bad* aspect, assuming that inherently or innately man is neither good nor bad but is *neutral*. As a child comes into the world, he is neither good nor bad; he just *is*. He comes equipped with a psycho-physiological structure that has growth potential and, as time goes on, he becomes what he becomes—good, bad, or whatever combination of in-between it may be. What is "natural" to children, therefore, is neither to be condemned nor revered. Play, being natural to childhood, is therefore to be permitted or employed, or to be prohibited, as purposes and occasions require.

Dewey, however, broke new ground on the *active-reactive* choice. Here also he took a midposition; "mid-", at least, in a way, though it may be better to characterize it as *inclusive* rather than "between." This distinction is important, for thereupon hinges the question of whether the characterizing term should be *inter*active or *trans*active. When, seemingly in the later twenties, Dewey finally assigned the position a name,[6] he used "interaction." However, in the Dewey-Bentley book, *Knowing and the Known,*[7] the word "transaction" is adopted and considerable explanation is given as to the reason for the preference. To try making a long explanation short, the basic idea is not to tie together two mutually exclusive entities but to envision both as different aspects of an over-all, inclusive whole, of which the two are the ingredients. Take, for example, the self-nonself antithesis; the assumption is *not* that the two are separate, mutually exclusive absolutes, brought together only by some form of hyphen that serves as an "inter," a betweener. The assumption is, rather, that the two are integral, but distinguishable, parts or aspects of a single configuration. In like manner, one should not consider a water-pressure system in terms of the standtower as the pressure producer, the faucet as the object of pressure, and the connecting pipes as the in-between hyphen. Instead, it should be considered a single J-tube of water, the longer side being subjected to larger gravitational pull than the shorter, with the resultant (or faucet) pressure as the difference between the two; the connecting pipes, therefore, are not "inter" but "trans."

The Dewey-Bentley trinity of terms turns out to be *self-active, interactive,* and *transactive.* The present writers' trinity, covering what we are confident is the same set of concepts, is *active, reactive* (or passive), and *interactive.* With the reader's indulgence, we shall hold to our own terminology; we feel that "reactive" better represents the strategically passive role of a pupil than does "interactive," and this is the point stressed by Locke, the philosophical counterpart of Newton, the scientist. Both make learning (or scientific investigation) an inductive process; "gather the facts and let the facts speak for themselves," "render them general by induction." As for "interactive" *versus* "transactive," we feel that there is no *inherent* advantage of one term over the other and we feel it was Bentley, rather than Dewey, of the Bentley-Dewey team who was really interested in changing from "inter-" to "trans-." Dewey, though always meticulous in precise definition and use of terms, was not one who felt any inherence in them. In fact, he was distinctly Lockean in that regard, taking words as humanly (not cosmically) assigned to carry given meanings. We therefore adhere to Dewey's original usage, and depend mainly on the term, *inter*active, using it as

[6] Probably in *Experience and Nature.* New York: Dover, 1958. (Originally published in 1929). The term interaction is used frequently in *The Quest for Certainty,* New York: Minton, 1929.

[7] John Dewey and Arthur F. Bentley, *Knowing and the Known.* Boston: Beacon, 1949. See especially Chapters 4 and 5.

synonymous or interchangeable with *trans*active; *not* as an alternative for *re*active.

Although Dewey's first systematic use of the term interaction may not have been until the later twenties, we have long felt that from 1896 on he was definitely employing the concept. And, in this conviction, we have Dewey-Bentley support from a footnote in *Knowing and the Known* (p. 116): "The beginnings of this attitude [there labeled the transactive] may be found in his [Dewey's] paper 'The Reflex Arc Concept in Psychology' (1896)."[8] In that article—published 16 years prior to Wertheimer's introduction of the key concept of what is now known as Gestalt psychology—Dewey first says,

Instead of interpreting the character of sensation, idea and action from their place and function in the sensori-motor *circuit,* we [most writers] still incline to interpret the latter from our preconceived and preformulated ideas of rigid distinctions between sensations, thoughts and acts. The sensory stimulus is one thing, the central activity, standing for the idea, is another thing, and the motor discharge, standing for the act proper, is a third. As a result, the reflex arc is not a comprehensive, or organic unity, but a patchwork of disjointed parts, a mechanical conjunction of unallied processes.[9]

In this article, published long before Thorndike and Watson came into the picture, Dewey was in fact talking with reference to William James, the latter even five years later[10] presenting and supporting an unalloyed reflex-arc theory both diagrammatically and in terms of the "laws" of habit formation. The article continues,

This is the essence of the facts held together by and subsumed under the reflex-arc concept. Let us take, for our example, the familiar child-candle instance. (James, *Psychology,* I, 25). The ordinary interpretation would say the sensation of light is a stimulus to the grasping as a response, the burn resulting is a stimulus to withdrawing the hand as response and so on. There is, of course, no doubt that is a rough practical way of representing the process. But when we ask for its psychological adequacy, the case is quite different. Upon analysis, we find that we begin not with a sensory stimulus, but with a sensori-motor

[8] This paper is republished in its original form in Wayne Dennis (ed.), *Readings in the History of Psychology.* New York: Appleton-Century-Crofts, Inc., 1948, pp. 355–365. Reprinted by permission by Appleton-Century-Crofts. Dennis says that this article (which was written when Dewey was not yet 37 years of age) "may be considered a forerunner of Gestalt, and as a criticism, in advance, of behaviorism" (p. 355).

[9] *Ibid.,* p. 356. Italics ours.

[10] William James, *Talks to Teachers.* New York: Holt, Rinehart and Winston, 1900. See especially Chapters 6, 8, and 9.

coordination, the optical-ocular, and that in a certain sense it is the movement which is primary, and the sensation which is secondary, the movement of body, head and eye muscles determining the quality of what is experienced. In other words, the real beginning is with the act of seeing; it is looking, and not a sensation of light. The sensory quale gives the value of the act, just as the movement furnishes its mechanism and control, but both sensation and movement lie inside, not outside the act.

Now if this act, the seeing, stimulates another act, the reaching, it is because both of these acts fall within a larger coordination; because seeing and grasping have been so often bound together to reinforce each other, to help each other out, that each may be considered practically a subordinate member of a bigger coordination. More specifically, the ability of the hand to do its work will depend, either directly or indirectly, upon its control, as well as its stimulation, by the act of vision. If the sight did not inhibit as well as excite the reaching, the latter would be purely indeterminate, it would be for anything or nothing, not for the particular object seen. The reaching, in turn, must both stimulate and control the seeing. The eye must be kept upon the candle if the arm is to do its work; let it wander and the arm takes up another task. In other words, we now have an enlarged and transformed coordination; the act is seeing no less than before, but it is now seeing-for-reaching purposes. There is still a sensorimotor circuit, one with more content or value, not a substitution of a motor response for a sensory stimulus.[11]

Then, in an intermediate summary, Dewey says:

The discussion up to this point may be summarized by saying that the reflex arc idea, as commonly employed, is defective in that it assumes sensory stimulus and motor response as distinct psychical existences, while in reality they are always inside a coordination and have their significance purely from the part played in maintaining or reconstituting the coordination; and (secondly) in assuming that the quale of experience which precedes the "motor" phase and that which succeeds it are two different states, instead of the last being always the first reconstituted, the motor phase coming in only for the sake of such mediation.[12]

The entire article should be read with care by anyone who is inclined to think that the psychologies of James and Thorndike (to say nothing of Kilpatrick) are essentially or basically the same as that of Dewey. More than 40 years after publication of this article, in a discussion of "interaction," Dewey wrote as follows:

[11] Dennis, *op. cit.*, pp. 356–357.
[12] *Ibid.*, p. 357.

What has been said describes a difference between modes of environing-organical interactions to which the names excitation-reaction and stimulus-response may be applied. An animal at rest is moved to sniff, say, by a sensory excitation. If this special relation is isolated and complete in itself, or is taken to be such, there is simply excitation-reaction, as when a person jumps but does nothing else when he hears a sudden noise. The excitation is specific and so is the reaction. Now suppose an excitation comes from a remote object through a distance-receptor, as, the eye. There is also excitation-reaction. But if the animal is aroused to an act of pursuit the situation is quite different. The particular sensory excitation occurs, but it is coordinated with a larger number of other organic processes—those of its digestive and circulatory organs and its neuro-muscular system, autonomic, proprioceptor and central. This coordination, which is a state of the total organism, constitutes a *stimulus*. The difference between this condition (whatever name it be called by) and a specific sensory exitation, is enormous. The pursuit of prey is a response to the total state of the organism, not to a particular sensory excitation. Indeed, the distinction between what has been called stimulus and response is made only by analytic reflection. The so-called stimulus, being the total state of the organism, moves of itself, because of the tensions contained, into those activities of pursuit which are called the response. The stimulus is simply the earlier part of the total coordinated serial behavior and the response the later part.[13]

What exists in normal behavior-development is thus a *circuit* of which the earlier or "open" phase is the tension of various elements of organic energy, while the final and "closed" phase is the institution of integrated interaction of organism and environment.[14]

If what is designated by such terms as doubt, belief, idea, conception, is to have any objective meaning, to say nothing of public verifiability, it must be located and described as behavior in which organism and environment act together, or *inter*-act.[15]

. . . Unfortunately, however, a special philosophical interpretation may be unconsciously read [by others, including certain critics] into the common sense distinction. It will then be supposed that organism and environment are "given" as independent things and interaction is a third independent thing which finally intervenes. In fact, the distinction is a practical and temporal one, arising out of the state of tension in which the organism at a given time, in a given phase

[13] John Dewey, *Logic: The Theory of Inquiry*. New York: Holt, Rinehart and Winston, 1938, pp. 29–30. Italics in original.
[14] *Ibid.*, p. 31. Italics ours.
[15] *Ibid.*, p. 33. Italics in original.

of life-activity, is set over against the environment as it then and there exists. There is, of course, a natural world that exists independently of the organism, but this world is *environment* only as it enters directly and indirectly into life-functions. The organism is itself a part of the larger world and exists as organism only in active connections with its environment.

Integration is more fundamental than is the distinction designated by interaction of organism *and* environment. The latter is indicative of a partial disintegration of a prior integration, but one which is of such a dynamic nature that it moves (as long as life continues) toward redintegration.[16]

The reader might now refer back to our discussion on page 250, in which a water-pressure system is taken as an example. It is highly important to note that even a mechanical pressure-system of any kind is a function of the entire system, resulting from its various interrelated parts getting out of balance or equilibrium with one another and "seeking" to get back in; thus, "tension" or pressure is produced.

When one stops to think of it, it seems quite laughable that earlier reflex-arc theorists often used the analogy of an electric light to clinch their case. They said that human beings react as does an electric light—when the switch is snapped (stimulus) the light goes on (response). They seemingly never thought that, if an electrician worked on that theory, he could not possibly even repair a faulty system, let alone build a workable one. The "circuit" principle is a *sine qua non,* and disequilibrium within the circuit or system has to be maintained (by the dynamo at the power station) or there will be merely a surge of current to achieve equilibrium then no further flow. In fact, as a high-school-physics student knows, the difference between "static" and "current" electricity is simply that with the former there is no dynamo or generator to keep up the condition of disequilibrium after a given "discharge." To be accurate, reflex-arc theorists should have sought to *lift* mechanical theory toward the level of human or animate behavior rather than lower the latter to an erroneously conceived mechanical level.

But we must hasten to note that, to comprehend Dewey's principle of interaction, it must be taken as something more than mere push-and-pull among a coterie of forces. Dewey's thinking was in terms of *mental* processes; his was primarily *perceptual* or *cognitive* interaction, rather than the mere interplay of physical or physiological forces upon one another. Philosophically speaking, he was thinking in terms of epistemology; of truth-getting or of learning; in insightful or conceptual terms. Although he did often use the term to denote

16 *Ibid.,* pp. 33–34. Italics in original.

an interplay of forces of various and sundry kinds, his "contribution" was in connection with perceptual or cognitive interaction.

For example, what is the process of determining whether an object is hard or soft? One might say, merely observe it. But what *is* this observation process anyway? It is considerably more than merely a look-see. For clarity, let us personalize a bit. I (the viewer) approach a piece of iron pipe (the viewee) and, in effect, say, "What kind of thing, sir, are you?" "He" replies, "What kind of thing, sir, do you think I am?" I say, "I think you are soft." He says, "What, sir, do you mean by that?" I, "If I shove on you, you will 'give.' If I bat you over my head, you won't hurt." He, "OK, sir, try it." And the effect of the tryout is that he replies, "Brother, you can't do that to me; you can't consider me a softie."

The point of this example is that the truth-getting, or epistemological, process is not a case *merely* of making observations or getting sensations. It is basically *experimental;* a matter of trying out the logical (deducible) consequences of an idea or a hypothesis. The viewer *proposes,* but the viewee *disposes.* Both must be agreeable before the viewer can claim that his view is a *true* one. It is not a case of, "If I believe it strongly enough, it will indeed be true." Truth-getting is an *interactive* process: it is not active (self-active, or solipsistic) in the sense of what I say is true is indeed true; nor is it reactive in the Lockean-Newtonian (even Thorndikean) sense of passively letting the facts "speak for themselves." Agreement is registered on the part of viewee when experimentally-induced events turn out as anticipated or predicted—"anticipatory accuracy."

In this connection, a sophisticated reader who is willing to put forth the effort necessary to follow the thought line would do well to study the essay by Boyd H. Bode in the book, *Creative Intelligence.*[17] In this essay, Bode carried forward Dewey's original criticism of the reflex-arc concept and, though not naming it, gave further expression of the interactionist principle:

. . . In a reflex act we may suppose that the stimulus which evokes the first stage in the response is like the first in a row of upstanding bricks [he might have said dominoes] which in falling knocks down another. That is, the reflex arc is built up by agencies that are quite independent of the subsequent act. The arc is all set up and ready for use by the time the reflex act appears upon the scene.[18]

. . . In the case of conscious activity, on the other hand, we find a very different state of affairs. The arc is not first constructed and then used, but is

[17] John Dewey *et al., Creative Intelligence: Essays in the Pragmatic Attitude.* New York: Holt, Rinehart and Winston, 1917, pp. 228–281.
[18] *Ibid.,* p. 238.

constructed as the act proceeds; and this progressive organization is, in the end, what is meant by conscious behavior. If the course of a reflex act may be compared with traveling in a railroad train, the progress of a conscious act is more like that of a band of explorers, who hew their path and build their bridges as they go along.[19]

Later, he noted how behaviors that he thought of as "conscious activity"

. . . furnish a sort of diagram or sketch of further possible behavior, and the problem of consciousness is the problem of making the result or outcome of these incipient responses effective in the control of behavior. Future results or consequences must be converted into present stimuli; and the accomplishment of this conversion is the miracle of consciousness. To be conscious is to have a future possible result of present behavior embodied as a present existence functioning as a stimulus to further behavior. . . . A baseball player, for example, who is all "set" to field a ball as a preliminary to a further play, sees the ball, not simply as an approaching object, but as ball-to-be-caught-and-then-thrown-to-first-base.[20]

Excerpting falls far short of doing this essay justice; reading it in entirety is needful. But the above should be enough to show how, as early as 1917, Bode clearly saw what Dewey had stressed 20 years earlier and continued to stress during his lifetime—that a behaving person is not a reacting mechanism that *responds* to a "stimulus" that is outside of, and independent of, the mechanism itself. The very act of an infielder "seeing" the oncoming ball is itself a "response" (at least, an *act*); one of looking. He looks in order to see. Both are interactive aspects of a context or configuration that makes them something other than what they would be in some other context or configuration. In the mind of the umpire, for example, such an oncoming ball would be something-to-get-out-of-the-way-of. One's purposes or goals and one's insights (how one "sees" the thing) are highly influential in determining the kind of action one will take with reference to a given object or event. To deny or ignore this, whether intentionally or not, gives rise to the "difficulties" that caused Bode to say, "In the end these difficulties . . . may be traced back to the prejudice that experience or knowing is a process in which the objects concerned do not participate and have no share."[21]

In seemingly exact accord with the foregoing Dewey-Bode line of thought—cognitive interaction—Norbert Wiener and his collaborators have been working

19 *Ibid.*
20 *Ibid.*, pp. 240–241.
21 *Ibid.*, p. 254.

on the "feedback" principle as it relates to voluntary neural action, the development going under the name *Cybernetics*.[22] Originally working on self-directing mechanisms as used, for example, in self-guided missiles, Wiener and a colleague

. . . came to the conclusion that an extremely important factor in voluntary activity is what the control engineers term *feed-back*. . . . when we desire a motion to follow a given pattern, the difference between this pattern and the actually performed motion is used as a new input to cause the part regulated to move in such a way as to bring its motion closer to that given by the pattern. For example, one form of steering engine of a ship carries the reading of the wheel to an offset from the tiller which so regulates the valves of the steering engine as to move the tiller in such a way as to turn these valves off.[23]

In this way, the tendency of the ship's own momentum to swing it too far is self-corrected and the steersman is aided by the mechanism in bringing the ship to a desired position; hence the name, cybernetics, which means "steersmanship."
Wiener then continues,

Now, suppose that I pick up a lead-pencil. To do this I have to move certain muscles. However, for all of us but a few expert anatomists, we do not know what these muscles are; and even among the anatomists, there are few if any who can perform the act by a conscious willing in succession of the contraction of each muscle concerned. On the contrary, what we will is *to pick the pencil up*. Once we have determined on this, our motion proceeds in such a way that we may say roughly that the amount by which the pencil is not yet picked up is decreased at each stage. This part of the action is not in full consciousness.
To perform an action in such a manner, there must be a report to the nervous system, conscious or unconscious, of the amount by which we have failed to pick the pencil up at each instant. If we have our eye on the pencil, this report may be visual, at least in part, but it is more generally kinaesthetic, or to use a term now in vogue, proprioceptive.[24]

This "report to the nervous system" is what is known as *feedback*. Without it, once an action is launched there is no further control by the launcher; we have mechanical *re*action rather than cognitive *inter*action.
In terms of cognitive interaction and of Gestalt (or configurational) psychol-

22 Norbert Wiener, *Cybernetics: or Control and Communication in the Animal and the Machine*. New York: Wiley, 1948. Reprinted by permission of The M.I.T. Press, © 1961.
23 *Ibid.*, p. 13. Italics in original.
24 *Ibid.*, p. 14. Italics in original.

ogy, this feedback mechanism is known as *insight*. Insight, defined as "a sense of, or feeling for, pattern,"[25] is the way a person "sees" a developing situation and furnishes the "report to the nervous system," on the basis of which progressive adjustments are made during progression toward an end-in-view. The predictive principle, *the principle of least action,* is that an individual "will act in such a way as to achieve what he is after (goal) in the quickest and easiest way that he senses or comprehends (insight) under the circumstances (confronting situation)."[26]

The seemingly major shortcoming of consistent reflex-arc psychology was its theoretical omission or avoidance of feedback. Hence, the forward-backward, backward-forward communication among the functionally integrated parts of the self-nonself continuum, not being theoretically or officially recognized, had to be bootlegged. Thorndike's "laws" of readiness and effect and Skinner's principle of reinforcement are cases in point; neither make sense without inclusion of the concepts of insight and goal (or end-in-view).[27] Elsewhere,[28] one of the present writers has dealt with this aspect of Thorndike. As to "reinforcement," how can a later action possibly serve to reinforce an earlier one except through insight? Obviously, it sooner or later somehow "dawns" on Skinner's pigeons that, if they will stretch their necks enough, they will "get something good." Of course, pigeon insights are very short-spanned; hence, the "reward" must come quickly and persistently or the connection will not be noted. A device needs therefore to be employed that will neither get bored nor go to sleep, so that each and every requisite act of the bird will be rewarded. But to deny, for the benefit of one's theory, that pigeons have at least a modicum of common sense would seem at least to be highly ungenerous. Moreover, we may add that the concept of insight is indeed a scientific one because it demonstrates the quality of "anticipatory accuracy," which is what we ask of any scientific principle. Helping the bird "get the idea" is exactly what Skinner's reinforcement devices succeed in doing, or they do not succeed at all. Small wonder Wolfgang Koehler lamented the reluctance of psychologists to accord to insight the honor of formal acceptance; if the lady is being enjoyed, the seemingly decent thing to do is acknowledge and formalize the fact.

[25] See, for elaboration, Ernest E. Bayles, *Democratic Educational Theory.* New York: Harper & Row, 1960, pp. 40–43. For the insight theory of learning, see pp. 45–55.
[26] *Ibid.,* p. 38. All italicized in original.
[27] See Boyd H. Bode, *How We Learn.* Boston: Heath, 1940, Chaps. 11–13. Essentially the same treatment is in his earlier *Conflicting Psychologies of Learning.* Boston: Heath, 1929.
[28] Ernest E. Bayles, *The Theory and Practice of Teaching.* New York: Harper & Row, 1950, pp. 58–63.

Idea of "Continuous Reconstruction of Experience"

As may have become evident by now, the interactionist principle of Dewey is a relational one. Things have to be dealt with, not as Kantian "things in themselves" (*dinge an sich*) but as they relate to other things, including people. The way people *see* things—their insights—is an essential ingredient in determining how they will design their behavior with reference thereto. This is what the *principle of least action* expresses.

Mankind is an integral part of nature; not a "higher being" set apart. Hence, when man studies nature and scientifically formulates principles or laws that are expected to help him deal with nature, he has to take himself into account as well as what he is studying. Since, as we have noted, interactionistic investigation into the nature of something is essentially experimental, in the course of the investigation the investigator is manipulating what is being investigated and to a degree altering it. If the fact of such alteration is ignored, the investigation goes awry.

Strange as it may seem, prior to the work of Albert Einstein this aspect of what were presumably scientific investigations was not recognized, at least in terms of the *theory* of scientific investigation. Thus, Einstein the scientist bears the same relation to Dewey the philosopher that Newton the scientist bore to Locke the philosopher. And, since Thorndike's thought pattern was essentially that of Locke, it stands to reason that the thought patterns of Thorndike and of Dewey would be vitally, perhaps strikingly, different from one another.

Thinking relationally, as the Dewey-Einstein pattern requires, and doing so avowedly, intentionally, systematically, and consistently may well be called the touchstone of twentieth-century thought. However, in deference to the feelings of those who deem this too presumptuous a claim, we can at least say that it is the touchstone for John Dewey and Albert Einstein, who were outstanding pioneers in his kind of thinking. This is to say that Dewey's principle of cognitive interaction represents the idea of *relativity taken seriously*. Scientific principles or laws are not taken to be cosmic handouts, from some supernal or supernatural source, but as formulations by man—a part of nature—which have been subjected to experimental test and have, so far, demonstrated their dependability as instruments for prediction. Truth is not "discovered," it is "invented."

Furthermore, taken as inventions by beings as prone to error as are human ones, all extant "truths" must be deemed *relatively* true; not finally or absolutely so.

They are always subject to question; open to further investigation whenever occasion seems to demand it. But, while they are *assumed* to be true, they are taken as the bases for all lines of action to which they are pertinent. In other words, *assumptions* deemed to be *truthful* are merely human insights that have been experimentally tested and found to be dependable guides for designing whatever courses of action involve them. Since truths, then, are taken as, or assumed to be, *instruments* suitable for use as tools for aiding mankind in working out plans for doing the things he wants to do—hence, instrumental—Dewey made considerable use of the name *Instrumentalism* to designate this point of view.

The educational enterprise is one in which people have long been vitally interested and for which, since the dawn of history, they have been continually formulating plans of action. These action plans have, perforce, been based on assumptions as to what constitutes good education. We have studied the outworkings of the assumptions of education as discipline and for salvation, of education as habit formation and for use, of education as unfoldment and for perfection, and of various and sundry combinations of these. In each case, however, proponents have been prone to argue about "what education ought to be," rather than "what *they assume* education ought to be." In other words, the premises tended to be asserted rather than proposed. What with Dewey?

Since education deals with learning, assumptions regarding the nature of learners and of learning obviously have to be established and it would seem that a record should be made of them. We have already dealt at length with the neutral-interactive one. We have also noted the behavioral principle of least action, and that conscious, intentional, or designed human behavior is insightful in nature. Whatever may be the nature of involuntary action, voluntary action appears always to be guided by insight—the way a given individual "sees" or senses the nature of a situation that confronts him and with which he must deal.

Learning is likewise assumed to be an insightful process; a process of developing insight. Being insightful, learning is impeded if not blocked by recourse to the time-honored practice of repetitive "drill." It is not the number of times one repeats an act that counts; it is what one learns, what insights are gained, that enables practice to "make perfect." Hence, practice should always be essentially experimental—this is tried, that is tried, possible refinements are noted, confidence develops, and a way of handling the matter evolves, which is adopted until such time as a better one is found. This is why Dewey could say that "thinking is the method of an educative experience."[29] He was not meaning that all cases of

---

[29] John Dewey, *Democracy and Education*. New York: Macmillan, paperback ed., 1961, p. 163. Originally published in 1916 (p. 192).

learning are deeply reflective; merely that each is, in essence, a matter of getting an idea and using it as long as it appears to be satisfactory.

Habit-level behavior is, then, the kind that obtains when, as a course of action develops, each new aspect of the confronting situation is simultaneously sensed as requiring certain actions and these actions are taken. Such a sensing of pattern we have called insight; hence, we can say that, as long as the developing insight into the developing situation is accurate or true and the necessary action can be and is taken, the line of action progresses on the habit level. Thus, the essence of habit is *not* repetition. Rather, it is keeping track of the "feedback" (see ante, p. 257)—keeping one's eye on the ball—, snap-judging accurately what must come next, and doing what is necessary to make it come. The instant this condition fails to develop, habit-level behavior terminates and a new insight must be gained. This is why mental alertness (the cognitive) is necessary to keep any activity progressing on the habit level. This is why an automobile driver must continually keep his eyes on the road and, the moment he gets drowsy, relinquish the wheel. Habit-level behavior is the principle of least action at work.

For Dewey, instead of education being for salvation, for habit formation, or for unfoldment, it is for the "continuous reconstruction of experience."[30] By "experience," Dewey meant not merely going through the motions of doing something; he meant *doing and undergoing.* "When we experience something we act upon it, we do something with it; then we suffer or undergo the consequences."[31] "To 'learn from experience' is to make a backward and forward connection between what we do to things and what we enjoy or suffer from things in consequence."[32] "It is not experience when a child merely sticks his finger into a flame; it is experience *when the movement is connected* with the pain which he undergoes in consequence."[33]

In light of the foregoing, it seems obvious that, for Dewey, experience means *doing with insight;* insight into the relation between the doing and what comes of it. Without the insight, we learn nothing; as when, after reading a passage in a book, we suddenly realize that we haven't the slightest idea of what was in the passage. It might be added, too, that, if the insight is caught *without* the doing, the job is done. This is one implication of the idea of learning as development of insight.

Therefore, to think of education as "continuous reconstruction of experience" is to take it as continuous reconstruction of insight. To deem Dewey responsible for the expression, "We learn to do by doing," is to misread Dewey completely.

[30] *Ibid.,* p. 80.
[31] *Ibid.,* p. 139.
[32] *Ibid.,* p. 140.
[33] *Ibid.,* pp. 139–140. Italics ours.

This is connectionist (Thorndike's) psychology; learning as conditioning, a path-wearing, repetitional concept. For Dewey, it is not the doing but the undergoing that makes an experience educative. Our excerpt from Dewey's pronouncement of 1899 (Chapter 11, pp. 221–222) should make that clear. Dewey's criterion of the fruitfulness of any activity deemed to be educative hinged on the nature of the insights gained.

Education for Democracy—Reflective Teaching

Besides assumptions regarding the nature of learners and of learning, an educational program also has to be posited on assumptions regarding the *nature of the Society* that is responsible for the program.[34] To avoid inconsistencies galore, a democratically committed nation requires a democratic educational program, just as an autocratically committed nation requires an autocratic one. Although not always explicitly saying so, this was something Dewey never forgot and what no reader should forget when he reads Dewey.

The educational profession as a whole seems heartily to agree that education in the United States should carry out the democratic commitment of the nation. But there is great disagreement, both in theory and in practice, as to what this means; and this disagreement apparently stems from the almost universal failure to base thinking on a clear-cut, comprehensive, non-self-contradictory definition of the term democracy. And it is on this matter that the present authors feel that they must do some quarreling with Dewey. We have very few such quarrels, but this one we feel important; for, unless from the beginning we are clear and explicit on what we take democracy to be, we cannot thereafter be clear and explicit on the nature of democratic education.

One of the educational classics of the twentieth century—if not *the* one— is Dewey's *Democracy and Education,* and its seventh chapter, "The Democratic Conception in Education," is a classic on that topic. Therein, Dewey ostensibly proposes two criteria for judging what is democratic: (1) "interests consciously communicated and shared," (2) "varied and free points of contact with other modes of association."[35] In the "summary" of the chapter, page 99, he writes, "The two points selected by which to measure the worth of a form of social life are the extent in which the interests of a group are shared by all its members,

[34] The term Society is capitalized to indicate that it is the broad sense—the social order —that we have in mind.
[35] *Op. cit.*, p. 83.

and the fullness and freedom with which it interacts with other groups." Afterwards, Boyd H. Bode took up the idea of "interests mutually shared" as the touchstone, and in 1947 wrote:

What the Founding Fathers had in mind was the kind of government typified by the New England town meeting. In idealized form such government is genuinely democratic because it affords opportunity for all interests concerned to make themselves heard and, furthermore, because it aims to devise a plan or program of action which will be acceptable all around and thus truly represent "the consent of the governed." What is needed to make such a government work is not agreement on the eternal structure of the universe, but a spirit of cooperation and good will, and so, in such government, atheists and skeptics can participate as wholeheartedly and effectively as anyone else. The only antecedent commitment involved is to the ideal or purpose of promoting a common life which will provide maximum opportunity for all its members. By this test and no other, standards of right and wrong are determined; which is to say that in a democratic society morality is shifted from the level of theological doctrine to the level of social relationships.

Since men have to live together, there are always common affairs which can and must be handled co-operatively for the benefit or "happiness" of the whole group. Democracy universalizes this principle. It holds that as men of good will, despite their differences, continuously widen the area of common interests, they are on the road towards building themselves a kingdom of heaven on earth. Morality has its roots in loyalty to this common life; and democracy instead of being merely a political arrangement becomes a principle of living which applies to all phases of human activity. In academic language, democracy means that the continuous extension of common interests and purposes among men is the road to the good life.[36]

Earlier, in *Democracy as a Way of Life*,[37] Bode stressed the idea of "mutual sharing of interests" as the essence. In consequence, in 1932 as a student of Bode and long before the above was written, one of the present writers suggested a definition of democracy as "progressive elimination of barriers to the principle of interests mutually shared." But even at that time this idea was for him not entirely satisfactory; for one reason because it was negative, not positive. It took this writer the remainder of the thirties to arrive at what he thought was a better definition, the one published (as well as previously) in 1960.[38] What

[36] *Modern Education and Human Values*, Pitcairn-Crabbe Foundation Lecture Series, Vol. 1. Pittsburgh: University of Pittsburgh Press, 1947, pp. 7–8.
[37] Boyd H. Bode, *Democracy as a Way of Life*. New York: Macmillan, 1937, Chap. 4.
[38] Bayles, *Democratic Educational Theory*, Chap. 10, p. 157.

we seek is a basic, working definition, from which logical deductions can be made, deductions that will both include intended or desired qualities and exclude unintended or undesired ones. Our definition is that *democracy is a governmental form in which there is equality of opportunity for members to participate in the establishment of rules and regulations (or laws) deemed needful, and equality of obligation to abide by them until they are abolished or changed.*

In seeming opposition to the point embodied in this definition, in 1916 Dewey wrote in *Democracy and Education* (p. 87), "A democracy is more than a form of government; it is primarily a mode of associated living, of conjoint communicated experience." Then, 11 years later, he wrote:

We have had occasion to refer in passing to the distinction between democracy as a social idea and political democracy as a system of government. . . . The idea of democracy is a wider and fuller idea than can be exemplified in the state even at its best. To be realized it must affect all modes of human association, the family, the school, industry, religion. And even as far as political arrangements are concerned, governmental institutions are but a mechanism for securing to an idea channels of effective operation.[39]

In a lecture delivered in 1938 and published later, Dewey spoke as follows:

The meaning of democracy . . . was expressed by Abraham Lincoln when he said that no man was good enough or wise enough to govern others without their consent; that is, without some expression on their part of their own needs, their own desires and their own conception of how social affairs should go and social problems be handled.

. . .

That asking other people what they would like, what they need, what their ideas are, is an essential part of the democratic idea.

. . .

Dr. Felix Adler expressed very much the same idea, I am not quoting his words, but this was what he said, that "no matter how ignorant any person is there is one thing that he knows better than anybody else and that is where the shoes pinch on his own feet"; and because it is the individual that knows his own troubles, even if he is not literate or sophisticated in other respects, the idea of democracy as opposed to any conception of aristocracy is that every individual must be consulted in such a way, actively not passively, that he himself

[39] *The Public and its Problems.* New York: Holt, Rinehart and Winston, 1927. This quotation taken from the Gateway Books edition, 1946, p. 143.

becomes a part of the process of authority, of the process of social control; that his needs and wants have a chance to be registered in a way where they count in determining social policy. . . .

The ballot box and majority rule are external and very largely mechanical symbols and expressions of this. They are expedients, the best devices that at a certain time have been found, but beneath them there are the two ideas: first, the opportunity, the right and the duty of every individual to form some conviction and to express some conviction regarding his own place in the social order, and the relations of that social order to his own welfare; second, *the fact that each individual counts as one and one only on an equality with others,* so that the final social will comes about as the cooperative expression of the ideas of many people.[40]

What we wish to point out is that, in this series of pronouncements extending over a period of 30 years, Dewey did not say that democracy is *not* a form of government but a way of life. It seems clear that what he was saying was that democracy is not to be confined to government in its narrow sense—to "politics" alone—but that it is a governmental form that should permeate all walks of life; "it must affect all modes of human association, the family, the school, industry, religion." (See the quotation above from *The Public and its Problems.*) It is in this sense that it is more than government; it is a way of life. What we wish to make explicit, however, is that whenever the question of democracy or nondemocracy arises it is in connection with the question of how to determine the rules and regulations by which a given enterprise shall be conducted. *And this is government;* it is the "governmental form," which is what our definition specifies. Whenever two or more persons come together in a joint enterprise, the question arises as to whether it shall be governed democratically or otherwise; in this sense "democracy is a way of life."

Therefore, we seem to have no quarrel with Dewey on this point. We prefer our definition because it is more explicit and concise than Dewey's numerous characterizations, none of which perhaps was originally intended as an exact definition. Our objection is to statements such as the one we quote on p. 262, "The two points selected by which to measure the worth of a form of social life are the extent in which the interests of a group are shared by all its members, and the fullness and freedom with which it interacts with other groups." However, to be exact we should note that this statement does not refer to democracy, but to "the worth of a form of social life." This speaks of what is *desirable;* not

[40] *Problems of Men.* New York: Philosophical Library, 1946, pp. 34–36. Italics ours. This is a compendium of essays "reprinted from periodicals in which they originally appeared."

of what is democratic. It is the aspiration, not the definition, of democratic organization. But in the chapter title "The Democratic Conception of Education," and on pages 86–87 wherein he says, "The two elements in our criterion both point to democracy," and "these two traits are precisely what characterize the democratically constituted society," Dewey came so close to presenting these as the *definition* of democracy that he has ever since been widely taken as having done so.

What people find desirable or what they want is one thing; how they propose to get it is quite another. The democratic *aspiration* is indeed manifold: the general welfare, respect for individuality, no differential status because of race or creed, eradication of poverty, freedom, mutual sharing of interests, freedom in interaction with other groups, and much more. But "the democratic process" is indeed *process*; it is not product. It is the way we, as a people, have decided is the best way to get what we see as desirable. It is machinery, and should be so defined. Dewey said,

We have every reason to think that whatever changes may take place in existing democratic machinery, they will be of a sort to make the interest of the public a more supreme guide and criterion of governmental activity, and to enable the public to form and manifest its purposes still more authoritatively.[41]

To *define* democracy in terms of aspirations, either one or many, is to deny to a people any other aspiration, hence to deny it opportunity, "to form and manifest *its* purposes . . . authoritatively." This constitutes self-contradiction. If a people is to be sovereign, its own wants, wishes, and desires must stand, whether (in the minds of others) they be good, bad, or indifferent. It is hoped—and believed—that they will be good, but it is not definitional that they must be.

In light of these considerations, the present writers believe that the *definition* of democracy given on page 264 is thoroughly in keeping with the thinking of the two writers who, during the first half of the twentieth century, have done most toward making American education more cognizant of democratic requirements, John Dewey and Boyd H. Bode. We think the advantages of the definition are coverage, clarity, conciseness, and consistency. What, now, are its implications for education?

First and foremost, if not in the broad sense essentially encompassing the meaning of democracy for education, is the requirement of *reflective teaching*. If a people is sovereign so that its decisions stand regardless of their quality, it then is of prime importance that all possible steps be taken to heighten the

---

[41] *The Public and its Problems*, p. 146.

quality of those decisions. High quality requires both knowledge and disposition. A people who lacks knowledge and discernment is not likely to make consistently good judgments, no matter how much it desires or is disposed to do so. On the other hand, without the disposition to do its best on every decision it has to make, no people will make consistently good judgments no matter how knowledgeable or discerning it may be.

It would seem that the definition itself furnishes the incentive necessary for making the best decisions a people is capable of making, provided only that it realizes what is at stake. To use the time-honored expression, if one has to sleep in the bed one makes, then one will take pains to make it the best he can. The latter part of the definition—obligation to abide by established decisions—embodies this principle. However, without realization that this condition really does hold true, the principle will not actually function. One of the requisites of democratic education, therefore, is to help children and youth achieve a realizing sense of the urgency of this matter. Politics will be dirty and rotten if the dirty and rotten people are allowed to take over; politics will be clean if the clean people require it. To know this is vital, and to study this issue with care is seemingly a basic obligation of the schools.

The definition, however, does not supply or specify the capability needed to make democracy successful. Only education can do that and, although many agencies in a democratic society are to a degree educational in nature and function, it would seem that in such a society the public schools alone have that as a primary and major task. Education for democracy should promote (1) instruction and practice in the process or art of making high-quality decisions and (2) acquisition of as much knowledge of the world of which these citizens-in-the-making are (or will be) a part as is possible in the time available. Knowledge merely placed in storage is inert. It is only when it is needed and employed in reaching the decisions that its possessor must make that it comes alive, takes on vitality. Acquiring knowledge in the process of decision-making makes such knowledge immediately vital, and also places it in order—logicalizes it in such way as to supply the filing system that Jerome Bruner's investigations have shown as needful for ready and successful recall when occasion demands.[42]

All this points to reflective teaching as *the* method of democratic education.[43]

[42] J. Bruner, J. Goodnow, and G. Austin, *A Study of Thinking.* New York: Wiley, 1956.
[43] H. G. Hullfish and P. G. Smith, *Reflective Thinking: The Method of Education.* New York: Dodd, Mead, 1961. Boyd H. Bode, *Modern Educational Theories.* New York: Macmillan, 1927 (now available in paperback), Chap. 9. Bayles, *Democratic Educational Theory,* Chaps. 1, 12. Dewey, *Democracy and Education,* Chaps. 11, 12; also his *How We Think,* Boston: Heath, 1910, revised in 1932. Maurice P. Hunt and Lawrence E. Metcalf, *Teaching High School Social Studies,* New York: Harper & Row, 1956.

And reflective teaching is conducting classes in a manner that will promote reflective thinking: problem-solving, or the "complete act of thought," as originally
described by Dewey in *How We Think*. Reflective thinking is not a case of
applying or using what one knows. It is, instead, a case of *coming* to know; of
working out a principle or generalization, which could and would later be applied
or used when needed. The term "critical thinking" as currently used seldom
makes it clear whether the intended meaning is reflective thinking or is the
process of applying or using a predetermined principle or generalization. The
latter should be given a distinctive name, so that such confusion may be avoided.
We have chosen to call it understanding-level or understanding-type thinking,
because that is what understanding implies—ability to put an idea or concept
to work.

Democracy in the classroom means many things, but the one that especially
concerns us here is the impact of the first part of the definition, "equality of
opportunity to participate in arriving at decisions." The school children of
today will be the decision-makers—the problem-solvers—of tomorrow, and that
is why reflective teaching is required. Teaching on the understanding level—
teaching that trains in the ability to apply and use prefixed principles but does
not furnish practice in arriving at or deriving them—is indeed of greater value
than mere memory-level teaching, or learning by rote. But understanding level
is not reflection level; understanding-level teaching is not reflective teaching; it
trains in the application and use of only one principle, therefore fails to give
equal hearing to all pertinent or likely candidates for adoption and employment,
which is what reflection and democracy both require. Understanding-level
teaching easily lends itself to being authoritarian, dictatorial, indoctrinative; it
gives preferred status to whatever ideas or points of view a teacher, a school
system, or a community holds to be right and proper. This denies democracy
in classroom instruction; it also violates the principle of "academic freedom,"
so vital in democratic education as well as so essential in the pursuit of truth
wherever it may lead.

It is reflective, nonindoctrinative teaching that democracy requires. Once
education comes to be dominated by the "party in power," so that only the views
of that party are supported and all others are suppressed, educational democracy
does not exist. It makes no difference whether the preferred views are good, bad,
or indifferent; it is authoritarian and indoctrinative when*ever,* prior to and
during investigation, one view is given preferred status over others. It also
makes no difference whether such preferential treatment is intentional or unin-
tentional; or whether preferment is achieved by positive opposition to alternatives
or by merely ignoring them.

Even democracy itself is not to be given preferential treatment when it comes to study of whether it should be continued, even though the method of conducting such a study should be necessarily a democratic one. Any people may democratically decide to become undemocratic. This is no paradox, though it might be surprising to many if it should happen. But it did, in fact, happen when Hitler felt obliged to (and did) hold a plebiscite and in this way secure an expression of approval by the German people of his accession to power.

Moreover, to set up or describe curriculum content in terms of certain "competencies" to be developed or certain knowledges, skills, and attitudes to be achieved is to prescribe a setup for indoctrination. It does this because preferred status is *pre*scribed; the specified matters are the ones that are "taught," others receive no consideration. To be democratically nonindoctrinative, curriculum content should be specified in terms of *issues to be studied;* questions whose answers will be worked out as each study progresses. Thereby, "teaching" becomes not impartation but investigation; the teacher not the "giver" but the director of an investigational body which with the teacher's help determines answers or reaches conclusions. As Bode would repeatedly say, "my teaching must develop partisans, but it must be non-partisan in so doing." To this matter we shall return.

The Build-a-New-Social-Order Movement

At this point it seems pertinent to digress momentarily in recognition of the build-a-new-social-order movement of the thirties, for at the time it led to much discussion on the place, or lack of place, of indoctrination in American education. It might be noted that since then many have tried to sweep the problem under the rug and insist that it does not exist. But it does exist, now as much as ever, even though death has for some time stilled the warningly critical voices of Bode and Dewey.

In *Culture and Education in America,*[44] Harold Rugg might be said to have furnished the rationale for this movement. First, he followed up *The Child-Centered School* by noting that there are two sides of man—"man thinking" and "man feeling." He proposed the "Progressive" emphasis—of unprogrammed, creative self-expression—for the "man feeling" side, and proposed a *program* for the "man thinking" side. This program was to be based on a "Description of Society," which Rugg presented (pp. 262–267) as a series of "Fundamental

[44] New York: Harcourt, Brace & World, 1931, especially Chap. 14.

Theme-Concepts of our Changing Civilization." These "theme-concepts" were obtained through a "scientific" investigation conducted throughout the 10 years prior to publication of the book, an investigation which methodologically was essentially the same as a Bobbitt-type activity analysis. In fact, Rugg specifically acknowledged this fact when he wrote:

The attack that the research students of economic, political, and social life and the educational measures and tabulators have made on this problem has been in terms of the job analysis of mass activities. They have recorded and classified with considerable accuracy what people do—not their desires and fears, their attitudes and stereotypes, but their routine activities. As a result of their researches during the past twenty years much classified information concerning the mass activities of our people is available for the program-maker. To these data we have turned constantly in our efforts to build an adequate description of society.[45]

Then he went on to say:

But the nub of our description of society does not lie in the routines of life, no matter how voluminous they are nor how objectively they may be studied. It lies rather in the concepts and generalizations of the cultured mind, in the problems and issues of social life, and in human desires, fears, attitudes, and stereotypes.[46]

The more fundamental insights, problems, and principles, then, were to be found in a study of expert judgment, not in the tabulation of what people do.[47]

To make sure that our study of these materials was as objective as possible, we copied verbatim the *frontier thinkers'* uses of concepts, generalizations, trends, problems, and issues. Thus, a huge mass of material was collected which could be reduced to order only by systematic tabulation and classification. Frequency and rank-order distributions were made, and unanimities and divergences in judgment were discovered by objective comparison.[48]

And from these, the "basic lists of concepts, generalizations, problems, and issues were prepared."[49]

Thus, from a Bobbitt-type study of the writings of "frontier thinkers" was obtained a "description" of the society that would come, and this doubtless be-

[45] *Ibid.*, p. 276.
[46] *Ibid.*
[47] *Ibid.*, p. 277.
[48] *Ibid.*, p. 279. Italics ours.
[49] *Ibid.*, p. 280.

came a significant portion of the "evidence" shortly afterwards referred to in the famed and controversial *Report of the Social Studies Commission:* "Cumulative evidence supports the conclusion that, in the United States as in other countries, the age of individualism and *laissez faire* in economy and government is closing and that a new age of collectivism is emerging."[50]

This statement seems to express succinctly the concept that the Commission chose to call its "Frame of Reference," something which every educational proposal—radical or otherwise—obviously has, but which is openly placed upon the record in connection with very few. The Commission's "frame," however, though seemingly clear on the economic outlook, seemed not at all clear on what teachers were expected to do about it. As to "Materials of Instruction" (chapter 4), it summarized, "The Commission refuses to endorse any detailed scheme of organization as best calculated to accomplish the purposes above stated and as suited in one precise form to the schools of the entire country."[51] And as to "Method of Teaching," it wrote,

Method of teaching is *conditioned by the organization of the materials of instruction.* Indeed a decision concerning the general pattern of the organization of the course of study in the social sciences is at the same time a decision in method. The Commission, as already pointed out, places its stamp of approval on no particular plan of organization.[52]

However, in spite of these and other disclaimers, the whole pattern or tenor of the report seemed to be a call for teachers to become aware of the growth-trend of human institutions and to organize education so that it would take a leading role in *promoting* those trends. In other words, the schools were to help "build a new social order." As we are admitting, close reading reveals no paragraph or sentence in the report that unequivocally says so; this is about the closest:

The implications for education are clear and imperative: (a) the efficient functioning of the emerging economy and the full utilization of its potentialities *require profound changes in the attitudes and outlook* of the American people, especially the rising generation—a complete and frank recognition that the old order is passing, that the new order is emerging, and that knowledge of realities and capacity to co-operate are indispensable to the development and even the perdurance of American Society; . . .[53]

[50] *Report of the Social Studies Commission of the American Historical Association,* Vol. 16, *Conclusions and Recommendations of the Commission.* New York: Scribner, 1934, p. 16. Italics in original.

[51] *Ibid.,* p. 66.

[52] *Ibid.,* p. 74. Italics ours.

[53] *Ibid.,* pp. 34–35. Italics ours.

Whether clear or not, appearance of the report during the summer of 1934 touched off a flood of discussion, both oral and written, of the justifiability of indoctrination in American education. Though not indicated in the report, the participants in the discussion recognized the great influence of the ideas of George S. Counts and Jesse H. Newlon. Ernest Horn, a longtime specific-objectivist, refused to sign the report, as did Frank A. Ballou, Edmund E. Day, and Charles E. Merriam. Franklin Bobbitt and Melvin E. Haggerty wrote reviews finding it violently objectionable; for them it took up cudgels in behalf of the wrong things.[54] As we have seen, Bobbitt's proposals were such as to support (and indoctrinate for?) the *status quo*, whereas Counts and Newlon (and Rugg) would have the educational system get ahead of social trends and become a participant, perhaps even a major one, in *making* them.[55]

In 1927, Counts traveled widely throughout Soviet Russia and became highly impressed with the way Soviet schools were functioning to promote the new social order that was in the making. And, when in 1932 he asked of the United States, "Dare the School Build a New Social Order?" he was skeptical that it did dare but seemingly thought it should.[56] Moreover, since promotion means advocacy and advocacy means indoctrination, Counts was clearly favoring indoctrination. Around 1940 when in a class conducted by one of the present writers Counts was asked to state his position on indoctrination, he responded, in effect, "I am in favor of good indoctrination and opposed to bad."

In his book *Education for Democracy in Our Time,*[57] Jesse Newlon spoke repeatedly of the "loyalties" the schools must develop, saying (p. 87) that "a democracy must foster in its members loyalty to the principles of a free society" and "foster those values that the race has found good." He wrote further:

[54] See Bobbitt, Franklin, "Questionable Recommendations of the Commission on the Social Studies," *School and Society,* vol. 40, no. 1025, August 18, 1934, pp. 201–208.

[55] In his book *The Transformation of the School* (New York: Knopf, 1961) Dr. Lawrence A. Cremin discusses (pp. 215–239) Dewey, Bode, and Kilpatrick, and on pp. 258–270 deals with Counts' attempts to get the Progressive Education Association to help "build a new social order." Moreover, in *American Pragmatism and Education* (New York: Holt, Rinehart and Winston, 1956, pp. 203–211), John L. Childs makes Kilpatrick the outstanding opponent of indoctrination in education. We cannot agree that either is a genuinely discerning treatise. Cremin speaks with seeming approval of Counts' expression, "the bogeys of *imposition* and *indoctrination*" (p. 259, italics in original) and Childs says of Kilpatrick's position on indoctrination that "undoubtedly, it deserves to rank as the most significant effort thus far made to embody the principles of pragmatism in a concrete educational program" (p. 210). Educational indoctrination is, for the United States, no mere bogey, and Kilpatrick was not the one who was thoroughly clear on its avoidance or even took the lead in opposing it.

[56] See Cremin, *op. cit.,* p. 259, including footnote.

[57] Reproduced, with permission, from *Education for Democracy in Our Time* by Jesse Newlon. Copyright, 1939, by McGraw-Hill, Inc.

Indoctrination or, better, propaganda has come to mean distortion, withholding of information, evasion, imposing upon the individual; propaganda is often plain lying. Techniques such as these have no place in education for democracy. But deliberately and consciously to teach democracy is in no sense either propaganda or indoctrination. For intellectual freedom is an essential of democracy.[58]

As late as 1941, in discussing "the discipline of democracy," the Educational Policies Commission wrote:

The educational task is to achieve the degree of devotion to the general welfare that the totalitarian systems arouse toward the person of the dictator. This means that *democracy must be presented* to the young as a way of life and a social faith immeasurably superior to all others.[59]

To repeat what we said on page 269, since our definition specifies equal status for all participants in a decision, democracy itself must *not* receive preferential treatment when the study-question is whether to continue the democratic way. It is the *study* that should determine the conclusions, not predetermined convictions. In fact, any *genuine* believer in democracy will feel no need for preferential treatment. All he will ask is a fair field, governed by agreed-upon rules applied equally to all. If, under those circumstances, democracy cannot win, then seemingly our allegiance should be changed; for we want only the best. It is indeed true that the field is not always fair; vested interests of divergent kinds compete with one another to secure special advantages for their favorites. That is wherein the teacher must be astute, alert, and courageous, as well as honest; neutral in a sense, but deeply concerned. And, at the conclusion of a given study, he will announce the outcome clearly and unequivocally. "In light of our study, *this* appears to be the conclusion." This is not indoctrination; it does not require a participant to *believe* in the ultimate rightness of the outcome but only that the adopted criteria and the consequent study necessitate the stated conclusion, or show why he feels otherwise.

During 1938–1939 in the pages of the short-lived but challenging magazine *The Social Frontier,* a number of articles appeared dealing with the question of indoctrination. They were touched off by John L. Childs' review of Boyd H. Bode's *Progressive Education at the Crossroads*[60] and represented several ex-

---

[58] *Ibid.,* p. 103.
[59] Educational Policies Commission, *The Education of Free Men in American Democracy,* Washington, D.C., 1941, p. 79. (Italics ours.)
[60] New York and Chicago: Newson & Company, 1938.

changes between Bode and Childs, as well as articles by Dewey, Hullfish, and others. In this series, Childs took the Counts-Newlon line, which favored indoctrination for democracy as well as for other desirable concepts and views, insisting that Bode's position in resisting indoctrination was one of colorless neutrality, of which there had already been too much in American education. Bode's argument was essentially that of the previous paragraph, so it need not be repeated. With Childs lining up in this way, we had the Counts-Newlon-Rugg-Childs group, often known as the Columbia Group because all were members of the faculty of Teachers College (Columbia University), actively campaigning during the thirties in behalf of the build-a-new-social-order idea for American education.

The thought pattern was, briefly, thus; Progressive Education overemphasized the autonomy of the individual—a social concern is also needful; the social concern must be future-oriented, not content with either present or past; conventional education was not concerned with either, it was neither child-centered nor society-centered; we must prepare a "frame of reference" or a "description of society" that will represent the way of life that is to be—when present school children are adults—and "prepare" for that. It was on the nature of such *preparation* that controversy focused. Are the schools to enter politics? Or are they to prepare oncoming citizens to become able participants in politics?[61]

The efforts of the "Columbia Group" under Counts' leadership were on a wide front and were quite successful. Around 1935, The Educational Policies Commission was authorized and organized, The John Dewey Society was formed, a Committee on Academic Freedom and Tenure was organized in the National Education Association and was given a meager annual appropriation, and *The Social Frontier*—"A Journal of Educational Criticism and Reconstruction"—was launched, and for several years was maintained and very ably run. All these were essentially the brain children of the Columbia Group, especially perhaps of Counts, and were brought through birth and early childhood as a result of Group effort.

The Educational Policies Commission, of the National Education Association and the American Association of School Administrators, serves the primary purpose of deliberating upon the direction of growth of American education and issuing periodical reports as to its findings. The John Dewey Society, named in Dewey's honor but in no way bound to or connected with his thinking, is a voluntary organization of several hundred members of Education faculties and other professional-education personnel throughout the nation.

[61] Ernest E. Bayles, "The Teacher's Function in Democratic Instruction." *Educational Administration and Supervision*, March, 1948, pp. 150–154.

Its purpose is also to promote thought for the improvement of American education and to foster publications devoted to this end. The function of the N.E.A. Committee on Academic Freedom and Tenure is to keep under surveillance these aspects of American education, particularly on elementary and secondary levels and with other public-school personnel, and keep its parent organization informed regarding them. During its years of publication, *The Social Frontier* was a stimulating and high-quality publication, unique in its field, but had to be discontinued because income never caught up with expenses. In 1939, the Progressive Education Association assumed responsibility for it, changed the name to *Frontiers of Democracy*, but finally in 1943 gave up publication.[62]

A factor important in the life of the build-a-new-social-order movement was the publication of Harold Rugg's series of elementary and junior-high-school textbooks in the social studies,[63] a 14-volume series for grades three through nine, inclusive; a series that during the thirties touched the lives of perhaps a million or more pupils. The story of these books—their development, why they were written, their success, and finally the attacks made upon them—is admirably told by Rugg himself in a book that deserves wide reading.[64] Probably more than any other factor, the Rugg series influenced the transition from the school subjects of civics, geography, and history to what are now called the social studies.

To comment adversely on these books will seem to many to be highly ungrateful and to place the commentator in the category of what Rugg called the "Merchants of Conflict" (Chapter 5), and Mary Anne Raywid "The Ax-Grinders" (*op. cit.*). These "attackers"—of Rugg during the late thirties but of public education in general and of John Dewey as well during and beyond the fifties—represent conservative if not reactionary thinking in economics and politics as well as in education. They inveigh for a *return* to something—it is seldom clear what, but it seemingly comes close to pre-Pestalozzian, Puritanic "discipline." They violently opposed the Rugg textbooks, even resorting in one reported case to book burning,[65] on the grounds that the books were indoctrinative. But their ire was not against indoctrination per se; it was against indoctrination in behalf of "the wrong thing," for they were quite happy with texts that were indoctrinative—either by commission or by omission—for what *they* deemed right.

[62] An excellent account of the life of *The Social Frontier* is given by Cremin, *op. cit.*, pp. 231–234.

[63] Published from 1929 on, by Ginn and Company, Boston, New York, Chicago, etc.

[64] From *That Men May Understand* by Harold Rugg. Copyright 1941 by Harold Rugg. Reprinted by permission of Doubleday & Company, Inc.

[65] *Ibid.*, p. 3.

As to the socioeconomic-political point of view embraced by Rugg and his group, the present writers are as fully in agreement as independent, individual minds are likely to be. We are at least as much opposed to the point of view of the "attackers" as Rugg and Company are or were. But, as to Rugg's way of presenting the point of view in the schools, as his theoretical writings seemed to say and as we believe his series of social-studies textbooks clearly showed, we are opposed. Ours also was the opposition of Bode, to which we have already referred, and of Dewey, based on the principle that any indoctrinative study is undemocratic. As Dewey wrote in *The Educational Frontier,*

We believe profoundly that society requires planning; that planning is the alternative to chaos, disorder, and insecurity. But there is a difference between a society which is plann*ed* and a society which is continuously plann*ing*—namely, the difference between autocracy and democracy, between dogma and intelligence in operation, between suppression of individuality and that release and utilization of individuality which will bring it to full maturity.[66]

A plann*ing* society is continually re-evaluating itself; a plann*ed* society has the plans made for it, by one or a few persons not answerable to the rest. The sentence preceding the above excerpt explicitly stated, "Russia and Italy both present us with patterns of planned societies." (Remember that the Italy of 1933 was Mussolini's.)

To show Rugg's mode of writing in his social-studies series, we present the following, taken from a chapter—"Man and His Changing Society"—selected by Rugg himself as typical and presented *in toto* in his aforementioned book, which was for him defense and explanation.

Do you think these many changes in ways of living could take place without corresponding changes in the personal characteristics of the individual American—in the way he looks at life? Look back at the list of the characteristics we gave earlier (page 600). Some of them, of course, are the same today. Desire for success, for example, is still ingrained in the people. Many still feel independent, saying "I'm as good as you." But take the remaining items on that list—for example, resourcefulness, looking out for oneself. Do most of the people living in cities surrounded by stores, markets, doctors, hospitals, and the like,

[66] William H. Kilpatrick (ed.), *The Educational Frontier.* New York: Appleton-Century-Crofts, 1933, p. 72 (italics in original). This was a joint effort of seven writers, each assigned responsibility for a certain chapter but all in essential agreement on the basic point of view. Kilpatrick was chairman of the group and editor of the final manuscript, but his can hardly be said to have represented the dominant outlook. The chapter from which the above is taken was credited to Dewey and John L. Childs, but Dewey unquestionably dominated its writing.

have to do everything for themselves as the frontiersmen did? Take private ownership. Do most farmers own their farms? Do city-dwellers own their houses? Do shop and factory workers own the plants they work in? Is there free land to find and develop? Are there still good opportunities to invent a new machine and get it built and sold? How is the American character affected by changed conditions?

Consider the problem of producers. On the frontier all men could say, "We are producers; we make the things we use and consume." Do most people do that today? Indeed not. An enormous, complicated, world-wide scheme of buying and selling things has come in its place. Small farmers may have a truck garden, a few hens, a pig, and a cow or two, but, for the most part, they do not consume the things they raise. They produce things to sell.

Take the changes brought about by industry. In most cases the workers in factories do not even see the finished product on which they have worked. Each does only one step in the process of making it. They are denied the thrill of making a complete article. But, most important of all, the actual number of people needed to produce a manufactured thing has seriously declined, whereas the number who buy and sell things has greatly increased.

What about integrity of craftsmanship or workmanship? There is no doubt that the fine spirit of craftsmanship is disappearing. This is partly due to the increasing dependence upon machines to do man's work. In recent years, as power-machine factories have supplanted the hand craftsman, there has been much less demand for craft skill. Work has become more specialized—each person doing one separate special job over and over again. Also the spirit of "do it well enough to get by," not "do the best job you can," has unfortunately grown among the workers in many industries and businesses of the great cities.[67]

What we see in the foregoing is Rugg's robust but assertive style, in which he is "making a case," rather than guiding study. The questions are all leading ones, the answers almost put in the reader's mouth before he has a chance to react on his own. Sometimes they actually are: "Do most people do that today? Indeed not." The whole atmosphere, flavor, or context of the presentation is argumentative; not investigational. "Do you see now how the American spirit came to be *both individualistic and co-operative?*" (*Ibid.*, p. 67). We are aware that the distinction we are noting is a fine one and may not be immediately sensed by the reader, but we feel that it is a real one, as well as vital. Moreover, it is one that is quite readily sensed in a living classroom, hence one that the

[67] Rugg, *That Men May Understand*, pp. 68–69. The reprinted chapter is No. 24, of *Citizenship and Civic Affairs*, Vol. 5 of the junior-high-school series. Our excerpt is from pp. 603–604 of that textbook.

students in the classroom will grasp quickly and to which, if they are not completely docile, they are likely to react with closed lips but unconvinced minds.

However, whether the Rugg texts actually were indoctrinative need not be convincingly settled here. We have raised the issue, indicated somewhat of its nature, and noted its bearings on democratic education. We are fully confident that all members of the "Columbia Group," the sponsors of the build-a-new-social-order movement, were as desirous of promoting a thoroughly democratic educational program as anyone, including ourselves. The only question is whether the working pattern they chose or seemed to choose was itself genuinely democratic, and this we shall have to leave with the reader. It might be added that, as time has gone on, the living members of the group have seemingly come to see that Bode's contentions were more aggressive and not as neutralist as they at first thought. What is important for the future of American education is that, if there is any virtue in consistency, the means we adopt should be thoroughly in keeping with the ends we seek.

The advent of World War II was accompanied by somewhat of a cessation of the build-a-new-social-order movement, but the idea afterwards assumed a somewhat different form in the *Reconstructionism* of Theodore Brameld.[68] Brameld is distressed with what he lumps together as the pragmatic-progressivist view because he sees it as too aloof and noncommitted. He wants "commitment to agreed-upon, future-looking goals," hence "the question is ultimately whether public education should become the dedicated ally of certain social forces and aims or whether it should remain so far as possible neutral and impartial, true to the ideal of academic freedom at its liberal best."[69] But for the present writers there is high ambiguity—at least lack of clarity—in these two quotations themselves, as well as in the over-all effect of Brameld's contentions.

Does commitment to agreed-upon goals constitute neutrality and impartiality? We cannot see how, yet the above clearly favors both. Brameld immediately goes on to explain how, in his mind, the above is not ambiguous and, on the following page, says:

The preceding interpretation of philosophical and educational principles should already have provided the outlines of an answer to such a challenge. This answer, in essence, is unequivocal opposition to indoctrination and equally unequivocal support of academic freedom in the sense of impartial and thorough

[68] Brameld has written a number of books on the subject. We find the one most suitable for reference here is *Education for the Emerging Age*. New York: Harper & Row, 1961.
[69] *Ibid.*, p. 152.

study of all kinds of evidence and alternatives. At the same time, it insists that the vital utilization of these principles is entirely compatible with the development of clear social convictions and concerted action from them.

In short, this position supports that kind of "partiality" which is at the same moment "defensible." Here indeed is the ultimate test of whether learning is woven into the warp and woof of individual and group behavior—whether patterns of belief not only are professed but consistently and fully practiced.[70]

Thus, we see that Brameld is opposed to "indoctrination" but in favor of "defensible partiality." Seemingly, the latter represents, "commitment to agreed-upon . . . goals," but avoids indoctrination by ostensibly adopting Woodrow Wilson's principle of "open covenants, openly arrived at." However, who are to be the participants in the process of arriving at agreement or consensus? Are they to be representative members of a given community (be it large or small) getting together and (somehow or other) achieving consensus, then taking the consensus into the schools and, under the guise of "defensible partiality," securing further agreement to it there? If so, within the schoolroom this is still indoctrination, even though supposedly defensible because it represents the partiality of the community at large.

Thus, Brameld still leaves us in the build-a-new-social-order quandary of how to put the schools on the side of progress, yet maintain democracy in education. Therefore, let us now return to the Dewey-Bode pattern of thought regarding education.

Teacher "Guidance" Without Indoctrination

Bode's oft-repeated principle was that we should "study the tradition with a view to its progressive refinement." This obviously is in full accord with Dewey's "continuous reconstruction of experience." But it makes the school's job one of enlightenment, of promoting thoughtful evaluation; the *precursor* to commitment, but not commitment itself. Democratically, commitment is taken to be the domain of each individual member of a body politic; even though he commits himself "wrongly," it is his commitment that is to be registered in the final count. This is authentic democracy. Dangerous? Yes; but the heart of democratic respect for individuality and of personal freedom.

On the other hand, the teacher-student relationship is different from the

[70] *Ibid.,* p. 153.

person-to-person relationships among members of a body politic. In the latter, there is no obligation for one to set another aright. If one chooses to do it and the other is amenable, as in a political campaign, there is nothing amiss, even in the absence of obligation. But a teacher's obligation to superintend the education of a student does indeed mean attempting to "set the student aright," should he appear to need it. To do this without indoctrination, then, is a central task in democratic education, and *how* to do it is perhaps one of the least understood aspects.

But the solution to this problem, even though the problem has been a knotty one, is seemingly very simple, once it is clearly comprehended. It merely requires establishing a basis for making judgments regarding a matter under consideration, with all participants agreeing to be equally bound by it. Such a basis is known as a *criterion,* and its establishment makes possible the placement of all participants on equal terms; all proposals are to be equally heard, but *all* are equally obligated to stand judgment in accordance with the adopted criteria. Proposals are accepted or rejected on how well they satisfy the criteria; not on the relative prestige of those who proposed them. And, in a classroom, it is highly important to note that a teacher's or a textbook writer's or a community's proposals or ideas are to be included in this equal-status relationship. Obviously, a teacher's or a textbook writer's ideas will most often turn out to be recognized as best, but this will be because of demonstrated merit under the circumstances of the investigation, not because of who proposed them.[71]

How does the foregoing enable a teacher to "set a student aright"? When seemingly needful, the teacher points out wherein the student has appeared to violate the adopted criteria. But that is not the end; the student is then expected to respond with whatever comment he sees as merited, pointing out whatever flaw in the teacher's comment he may think he sees, and the matter is studied through in man-to-man give-and-take. Though such discussion (not argumentation) will usually demonstrate the superior merit of the teacher's contention, such merit is not taken as a foregone conclusion. In fact, if a teacher will sometimes intentionally undertake the defense of an untenable position, the educative value of the teaching will probably be enhanced because of the encouragement received when the student finds that he will not always be the loser. Thus, both teacher's and student's concepts are sharpened and improved; all participants are gainers.

Possibly, the present reader has the feeling that this proposal was made by neither Dewey nor Bode. Maybe it was not, as explicitly as this. But Dewey once

[71] For a somewhat different discussion of this whole issue, see Bayles, *Democratic Educational Theory,* pp. 177–185.

wrote that indoctrination is avoided if a teacher acquaints students not only with his conclusions but also with his reasons for arriving at them. And in class Bode would continually present, in turn, a variety of points of view, each one at first very sympathetically, afterwards with critical appraisal, all the while eliciting student reaction either in favor or in disfavor. In fact, Bode's *How We Learn* and Dewey's *Democracy and Education* employ essentially this strategy. What we may have done is to make explicit what with them was implicit. But we do feel we learned it from them.

A study conducted under these conditions is one that goes beyond the formulation of *possible* conclusions (or hypotheses), thereby leaving students to reach whatever conclusions they may choose. It is carried through, to conclusions. But the conclusions are those that the *study* appears to require and, since each study is conducted under the auspices of a given criterion or set of criteria, the conclusion is seen by the class to be the one required by the *criteria*. When the participants realize fully that such is the case, they become cognizant of what criteria accomplish, of the importance of being aware of what criteria are in use at any given time, and of what kind of conclusions given sets of criteria entail. On the basis of these insights, participants become able to judge what criteria are best suited to given investigations, and thereby arises additional competence in the art of independent thinking.

Should the reader feel the need for further explication of the concept of criteria, a few illustrations may help. In judging whether a given roadway is good, we need to know whether it is to be used for travel by automobile, by horseback, or by stagecoach. Whether a given art object be judged high quality or low requires a judge to know, among other things, what was the artist's intention. To render a competent decision as to the winner in a given section of a dog or cat show, the judge must take full and accurate account of all the points that are adopted as indicative of quality in that section. To determine accurately what is fair or foul in a basketball game, the referee must know the rules. To know what constitutes genuinely democratic educational procedure, one must first formulate a clear and acceptable definition of democracy. And so it goes. In the absence of prior agreements on criteria, there is little possibility or likelihood of agreements in judgment.

Reflective Teaching

Reflective teaching, as a methodology, has come slowly in the United States, though it seems to be gathering momentum. Dewey's *How We Think* was highly praised when it first appeared, in 1910. In 1916, he pursued the matter in chapters 11 and 12 of *Democracy and Education*. Bode ably carried forward during the twenties with three different books.[72] Both Dewey's and Bode's books were well received, but they had little effect on schoolroom practice. The first third of the twentieth century was a ripe time for Thorndikean theory, but not for that of Dewey.

The Bayles-Burnett[73] and Bayles-Mills[74] textbooks for high school were conscious attempts to write books that would promote reflective study, as the prefaces in both will show. Bayles' *Theory and Practice of Teaching* of 1950 (*op. cit.*) carried a chapter on the theory of reflective teaching, and five chapters that presented illustrative units in a wide variety of subjects from elementary school into college. His *Democratic Educational Theory* of 1960 carried it on. In 1956, the Hunt-Metcalf *Teaching High School Social Studies* (*op. cit.*) was published; it carried a highly enlightening discussion of reflective thinking and teaching and introduced the "closed areas" principle of curriculum construction. In 1961, the Hullfish-Smith text, *Reflective Thinking: the Method of Education* (*op. cit.*), was published. In 1956, the Bruner-Goodnow-Austin *A Study of Thinking* (*op. cit.*) appeared, and in 1960 Bruner's *The Process of Education*,[75] which hints at reflective teaching. Burton-Kimball-Wing brought out *Education for Effective Thinking*, in 1960,[76] in which their definition is, "Thinking results when there is persistent effort to examine the evidence which supports any belief, solution, or conclusion which is suggested for acceptance, together with the implications and further conclusions of the evidence" (p. v), which of course means problem-solving; but they do not keep this point clear throughout the book.

Finally, there are the recent books on *creativity*.[77] Those by Getzels-Jackson,

[72] Boyd H. Bode, *Fundamentals of Education*. New York: Macmillan, 1921, Chaps. 6, 7; also his *Modern Educational Theories*, Chap. 9; and *Conflicting Psychologies of Learning*, Chap. 16 (especially p. 274). *How We Learn*, 1940, is essentially a rewrite of *Conflicting Psychologies of Learning*; corresponding chapters are 14 and 15, especially pp. 248–251.

[73] *Biology for Better Living*. New York: Silver Burdett, 1941, 1942.

[74] *Basic Chemistry*. New York: Macmillan, 1947.

[75] Jerome S. Bruner, *The Process of Education*. Cambridge: Harvard University Press, 1960; in paperback, Vintage Books, 1963.

[76] New York: Appleton-Century-Crofts, 1960.

[77] John Dewey, *Art as Experience*. New York: Minton, 1934. Jacob W. Getzels and Philip W. Jackson, *Creativity and Intelligence*. Chicago: University of Chicago Press (also Wiley), 1962. J. P. Guilford, *Personality*. New York: McGraw-Hill, 1959. L. S. Kubie, *Neurotic Distortion of the Creative Process*. Lawrence: University of Kansas Press, 1958. V. Lowenfeld, *Creative and Mental Growth*, rev. ed. New York: Macmillan, 1957. Mary Lee Marksberry, *Foundations of Creativity*. New York: Harper & Row, 1963. E. P. Torrance, *Educational Achievement of the Highly Intelligent and the Highly Creative*, Research Memorandum BER-60-18, Bureau of Educational Research, The University of Minnesota, September, 1960. Max Wertheimer, *Productive Thinking*. New York: Harper & Row, 1954. Laura Zirbes, *Spurs to Creative Teaching*. New York: Putnam, 1959.

by Guilford, and by Torrance do not fully assure us that the authors have much recognition of their kinship or obligation to the foregoing, though it is specifically acknowledged by Marksberry. Also there is the posthumously published book by Harold Rugg, *Imagination*,[78] in which he quite pointedly carried on his denial that Dewey's "complete act of thought" had much to do with creativity or creative education.

When all this will begin really to take hold in the schools is at present a matter for conjecture. As the present writers come in contact with practicing teachers, from widely scattered parts of the nation, and with young persons in training for teaching, we find them continually reiterating the plea, "Why have we never been told of reflective teaching before?" Seemingly, School or Department of Education teachers of general methods, of special methods, and of curriculum pay it little or no attention.

An encouraging sign to those who hope for the coming of genuinely reflective teaching in the United States is to be found, however, in the work of the recently organized efforts of the curriculum-revision commissions, especially in the sciences and in mathematics, sponsored largely though not wholly by the National Science Foundation.[79] With eminent research minds playing active if not dominant roles on these commissions, the resulting curricula emphasize both concentration on basic, orientational principles in the various fields (instead of masses of detailed, informational or factual items) and essentially reflective-scientific study, by which young minds gain through personal experiences the "feel" for scholarly investigation. In this way the *method* of scholarly investigation can be caught as a functional, working whole; as contrasted with former

[78] New York: Harper & Row, 1963.

[79] The following textbooks for high school, output of the several commissions or study groups, are very impressive because of the imposing array of very important persons (VIP) who reportedly participated in the preparation of each volume. The large money grants that were available made possible an innovation in authorship, in each case making it an entire professional group rather than single persons or no more than three or four. To date, these are available, together with manuals, pamphlets, and other aids to teachers and students: School Mathematics Study Group (SMSG), *Geometry*, preliminary Ed. Boston: Ginn, 1961. The same Group's *Introduction to Matrix Algebra*. New Haven: Yale University Press, 1960. Also, Biological Sciences Curriculum Study (BSCS), *Biological Science: Molecules to Man*, Blue Version. Boston: Houghton Mifflin, 1963. BSCS, *High School Biology*, Green Version. Chicago: Rand McNally, 1963. Also their *Biological Science: An Inquiry into Life*, Yellow Version. New York: Harcourt, Brace & World, 1963. Chemical Bond Approach Project (CBA), *Chemical Systems*. St. Louis: Webster Division of McGraw-Hill, 1964. Chemical Educational Material Study (CHEM), *Chemistry: An Experimental Science*. San Francisco: Freeman, 1960–1963; Physical Science Study Committee (PSSC), *Physics*. Boston: Heath, 1960.

It may be noted that these texts vary in terms of reflective treatment, from the SMSG, the PSSC, and the Blue Version of BSCS as most so, to the CHEM and CBA as essentially explanatory rather than exploratory. All, however, are organized around basic, orientational principles, hence broadly cultural rather than narrowly eruditional.

practices (or attempted practices) of breaking up the process into "steps" or elements, supposedly learning these step by step or item by item (seriatim), then testing for these, item by item, and finally "adding up the score." Thus, there is beginning to be some promise of getting out from under the obstructive, atomistic pall of specific-objectivist theory.

In this way, Dewey's recasting of the dualistic, psychological-versus-logical opposition may be achieving incorporation in practice. In discussing "Science in the Course of Study," he wrote,

Science, in short, signifies a realization of the *logical* implications of any knowledge. Logical order is not a form imposed upon what is known; it is the proper form of knowledge as perfected. For it means that the statement of subject matter is of a nature to exhibit to one who understands it the premises from which it follows and the conclusions to which it points.[80]

He then spoke of the psychological as the *chronological*, and commented,

The chronological method which begins with the experience of the learner and develops from that the proper modes of scientific treatment is often called the "psychological" method in distinction from the logical method of the expert or specialist.[81]

Thus, it is not logical *versus* psychological, but a *psychological approach to logical organization,* wherein the psychological may be considered the logic of a growing mind and the logical the logic of a grown or matured mind.

"Study the Tradition with a View to its Progressive Refinement"

Finally, Bode's expression, "study the tradition with a view to its progressive refinement" (ante, p. 279), calls for elucidation of the term, progressive refinement. We are not merely to accept the tradition—the funded wisdom of a people, the culture—and pass it on; we are to promote study as to how it might possibly be improved. This is not to organize and carry on a crusade, but it is to prepare would-be crusaders so that they may be helped better to know what they are about; thus education is differentiated from politics.

[80] *Democracy and Education,* paperback ed., p. 219. Pp. 219–223 should be read, as well as pp. 188–191. Italics in original.
[81] *Ibid.,* p. 220.

But how become definite or tangible on refinement or improvement, without becoming indoctrinative? In light of our earlier discussion, we must formulate and adopt criteria on the basis of which proposals shall be judged. Moreover, such criteria must have an open-ended quality that makes for "progressive reconstruction." Furthermore, they must be thoroughly American; they must represent basic commitment of the American people.

Seemingly, the democratic-scientific pattern goes at least a long way toward satisfying the foregoing conditions. We have defined democracy, noting that it is a way by which a people formulates and carries forward its outlook as to how life shall be lived; a way of arriving at agreement—progressively, from time to time—as to what shall be taken as constituting "the good life." On the other hand, science is a way of getting truth; but it is a democratic way, because no proposals are to be taken as having pre-established sanction over any others. In other words, the scientific way of achieving knowledge is a thoroughly democratic one. And it is one to which, "when the chips are down," the American people seems overwhelmingly committed. Few of those who claim allegiance to "other ways of obtaining truth" are willing to settle for other than the scientific when a given matter under consideration can be so handled.

What is the scientific criterion for determining truth? Truth is to be based on observable and observed facts; it is in this sense empirical, or objective. But it is also personal or subjective in that, either as a designated or as a proposed truth, it is always a humanly formulated statement or proposition as to what will happen under specified conditions. If what does happen under such conditions is what the proposition logically anticipated or predicted, the proposition is taken to have been true. Hence, the test for truth is *predictive or anticipatory accuracy*. And, to be as widely usable as possible, the coverage of the proposition must be as wide as possible. Thus, breadth of coverage—*adequacy*—is one criterion for judging the truthfulness of a given proposition, and logicality or consistency—self-agreement or *harmony*—is a second. And the composite criterion for scentifically defining and judging truth is *adequacy and harmony of outlook or conclusion in light of obtainable data.*

Of course, there are many aspects of one's outlook on life that are not scientifically determinable. This means that such aspects are not subject to judgment on the basis of data, and are in this sense not empirical. But it would seem that "adequacy and harmony of outlook" is still a serviceable judgmental basis, even when applied to matters other than observed or observable data. So, if this be taken as a measure of the goodness of a given person's *outlook on the world or life of which he is a part*—on the universe of push and pull that affects one willy-nilly, whether he knows about it or not, hence one's "world of effect"—then

our criterion for judging the goodness of a view regarding "progressive refinement" of our tradition or culture is that *it should grow in the direction of a
more adequate and more harmonious outlook on the life of which its holder
is a part.*

Thus, we have a publicly stated criterion for judging "progressive refinement,"
and one that is both open-ended and thoroughly American because it is in keeping with both democracy and the method of science. For this criterion, there
is no claim, either expressed or implied, of ultimacy, finality, or infallibility.
The claim is only the one just made, and the basis for making it has been delineated. It gives promise of workability and serviceability, and can be tested
on the proving grounds of human experience. Moreover, as presented here, it
seems to be only a matter of making explicit what has been at least implicit in the
writings of both Dewey and Bode.[82]

By logical deduction, we can now obtain a statement of educational purpose,
and from that a statement of educational program. The statement of *purpose* is
*to develop more adequate and more harmonious student outlooks on the life of
which they are and are likely to be a part, and heightened capacity to reconstruct
outlooks independently.* For democracy requires independent reconstructional
capacity, and the scientific outlook furnishes the suggestion of adequacy and
harmony as necessary qualities of a way of looking at and dealing with life
that can be considered good. The consequent statement of *program* is *to conduct
reflective studies of problems that represent not only inadequacies but also dis-
harmonies in student outlooks on the life of which they are and will be a part.*
For, to achieve greater adequacy (or coverage) of outlook, we have to *start*
with areas of subject matter that represent inadequacies in coverage; to achieve
greater harmony in outlook, we have to *start* with cases of disharmony—many
of them representing the "closed areas" treated by Hunt and Metcalf[83]—and,
to promote "heightened capacity to reconstruct outlooks independently," we
have to "conduct reflective studies of problems." Thus, there are three separate
and distinct (but harmonious) aspects of educational program, each designed
to promote its corresponding aspect of educational purpose.

Suggested Readings

Bayles, Ernest E., *The Theory and Practice of Teaching.* New York: Harper & Row,
    1950.
Bayles, Ernest E., *Democratic Educational Theory.* New York: Harper & Row, 1960.

[82] See Bayles, *op. cit.,* Chap. 13.
[83] *Op. cit.,* Chaps. 11–16, incl.

Bode, Boyd H., "Consciousness and Psychology," in John Dewey *et al., Creative Intelligence: Essays in the Pragmatic Attitude.* New York: Holt, Rinehart and Winston, 1917, pp. 228–281.

Bode, Boyd H., *Modern Educational Theories.* New York: Macmillan, 1927.

Bode, Boyd H., *Conflicting Psychologies of Learning.* Boston: Heath, 1929.

Bode, Boyd H., *Democracy as a Way of Life.* New York: Macmillan, 1937.

Bode, Boyd H., *How We Learn.* Boston: Heath, 1940.

Bode, Boyd H., "Reorientation in Education," in *Modern Education and Human Values.* Pittsburgh: University of Pittsburgh Press, 1947. Pitcairn-Crabbe Foundation Lecture Series, Vol. 1.

Bruner, J., Goodnow, J., and Austin, G., *A Study of Thinking.* New York: Wiley, 1956.

Cremin, Lawrence A., *The Transformation of the School.* New York: Knopf, 1961.

Childs, John L., *American Pragmatism and Education.* New York: Holt, Rinehart and Winston, 1956.

Dewey, John, *Democracy and Education.* New York: Macmillan, 1916. Paperback ed., 1961.

Dewey, John, *The Public and its Problems.* New York: Holt, Rinehart and Winston, 1927.

Dewey, John, *The Quest for Certainty.* New York: Minton, 1929.

Dewey, John, *How We Think.* Boston: Heath, 1932.

Dewey, John, *Logic: The Theory of Inquiry.* New York: Holt, Rinehart and Winston, 1938.

Dewey, John, *Problems of Men.* New York: Philosophical Library, 1946.

Dewey, John, "The Reflex Arc Concept in Psychology," in Wayne Dennis (ed.), *Readings in the History of Psychology.* New York: Appleton-Century-Crofts, 1948, pp. 355–365.

Dewey, John, *Art as Experience.* New York: Minton, 1954.

Dewey, John, *Experience and Nature.* New York: Dover, 1958.

Dewey, John, and Bentley, Arthur, F., *Knowing and the Known.* Boston: Beacon, 1949; particularly Chaps. 4, 5.

Educational Policies Commission, *The Education of Free Men in American Democracy,* Washington, D.C., 1941.

Getzels, Jacob W., and Jackson, Philip W., *Creativity and Intelligence.* Chicago: University of Chicago Press (also New York: Wiley), 1962.

Good, H. G., *A History of American Education,* 2nd ed. New York: Macmillan, 1962, Chap. 12.

Guilford, J. F., *Personality.* New York: McGraw-Hill, 1959.

Hoffman, Banesh, *The Tyranny of Testing.* New York: Crowell-Collier, 1962.

Hullfish, H. G., and Smith, P. G., *Reflective Thinking: The Method of Education.* New York: Dodd, Mead, 1961.

Hunt, Maurice P., and Metcalf, Lawrence E., *Teaching High School Social Studies.* New York: Harper & Row, 1955.

James, William, *Talks to Teachers.* New York: Holt, Rinehart and Winston, 1900; particularly Chaps. 6, 8, 9.

Kubie, L. S., *Neurotic Distortion of the Creative Process*. Lawrence: University of Kansas Press, 1958.

Lowenfeld, V., *Creative and Mental Growth*, rev. ed., New York: Macmillan, 1957.

Marksberry, Mary Lee, *Foundations of Creativity*. New York: Harper & Row, 1963.

Newlon, Jesse, *Education for Democracy in Our Time*. New York: McGraw-Hill, 1939.

Raywid, Mary Anne, *The Ax-Grinders*. New York: Macmillan, 1962.

Rugg, Harold, *Culture and Education in America*. New York: Harcourt, Brace & World, 1931.

Rugg, Harold, *That Men May Understand*. New York: Doubleday, 1941.

Rugg, Harold, *Imagination*. New York: Harper & Row, 1963.

Social Studies Commission of the American Historical Association. Vol. 16, *Conclusions and Recommendations of the Commission*. New York: Scribner, 1934.

Torrance, E. F., *Educational Achievement of the Highly Intelligent and the Highly Creative, Research Memorandum BER-60–18*. Bureau of Educational Research, The University of Minnesota, September, 1960.

Wertheimer, Max, *Productive Thinking*. New York: Harper & Row, 1954.

Wiener, Norbert, *Cybernetics: or Control and Communications in the Animal and the Machine*. New York: Wiley, 1948.

Zirbes, Laura, *Spurs to Creative Teaching*. New York: Putnam, 1959.

Possibly, here is the Johnny Jones that Miss Benedict had in mind in the description referred to on the following page. He and his classmates are obviously finding school a challenging and enjoyable experience, making exceptional the "feet that, creeping slow to school, went storming out to playing." (Courtesy of the Seattle School District)

13 ᴈ❧ Retrospect and Prospect

So stands American educational thought and practice as we approach the two-thirds mark of the twentieth century. Looking back, we indeed see what Agnes Benedict so aptly expressed in the title of her instructive and interesting book, "Progress to Freedom."[1] Though perhaps it should be *toward* freedom rather than *to,* the direction is unmistakable, as shown by Miss Benedict's sketches of the growing-up of the little Puritan 7-year-old Jonathan Jones, whose school was a veritable prison; John Jones's school, which, several generations later, and even after the labors of Horace Mann and Henry Barnard, "was a far better prison for children than it used to be, but it was still a prison;"[2] and, finally, the experience of Johnny Jones of 1942, whose school was no longer a prison but a place of challenging and enjoyable business and he a young "business man going to work," eager to get there and so absorbed while there that recess or quitting time came before he realized it and before he was really ready to call it quits.[3]

Of course, Miss Benedict knew that her final picture was, even in 1942, essentially a dream, at least as far as the general run of American schools was con-

1 Agnes E. Benedict, *Progress to Freedom.* New York: Putnam, 1942.
2 *Ibid.,* p. 213.
3 *Ibid.,* p. 290–294.

cerned; hence, her final chapter, "Shall We Realize the Dream?" As she said, "Ghosts of Puritanism still walk our classrooms today."[4] And, writing at the time when the United States had become embroiled in World War II, she closed her book with this paragraph:

The years ahead are indeed a test. The outcome will measure our faith in our dream, our belief in it. I believe we shall meet the test. We must fight armies with armies, ideas with ideas. We shall fulfill our obligation to our children—who, in their time will make the country, will be the country. As John Dewey says, "The ideal may seem remote of execution, but the democratic ideal of education is a farcical yet tragical delusion, except as the ideal more and more dominates our public school system."[5]

This is as we have found it; our ideas and ideals have always been far ahead of our practices. Educationally speaking, protestant Puritanism was little different from Catholicism, except for the ideal of universal literacy. Our first schools, transplants from the Old World, were an arm of the church—education for salvation. But they fell far short of achieving the innovation of universal literacy. Not until two centuries after the Massachusetts Bay Colony law of 1642, making all parents or guardians responsible for seeing that their children should learn to read and write, were compulsory school-attendance laws actually enacted.

Locke's "Some Thoughts Concerning Education" (1692)—education as habit formation and for use—were proposed by Franklin in 1749 for incorporation in his Academy, which was established a few years later. But even in his own school the influential Mr. Franklin was disappointed at only partial achievement of his hope; in his old age approximately a century after Locke's proposals, he was lamenting that secondary education was still primarily for college rather than for life. And our first public high school of 1821 was designed as an innovation—preparation for life rather than for college. What else was the basic issue involved in "The Eight Year Study," promoted by the Progressive Education Association in 1932–1940? Moreover, only after 1950 have foreign-language teachers begun to do much toward inaugurating Locke's proposals for such instruction, as he had explicitly stated them in "Some Thoughts Concerning Education."

In this same vein was also the Lockean principle: sensations (that is, personal experiences) preceding and leading inductively into ideas, and ideas in turn requiring words; the principle championed a half-century before Locke by

---

[4] *Ibid.,* p. 298.
[5] *Ibid.,* p. 299.

Comenius and harking back to Aristotle himself. This indeed was the principle underlying the "practice" (*q.v.*) of Rousseau, Pestalozzi's "Art of Sense Impressionism," Herbart's "apperception" and his five-step teaching procedure, and Thorndike's "connectionism," though perhaps not as clear with Thorndike as with his predecessors. Seemingly, little if any more is envisioned in our twentieth-century idea of "experience curricula."

Yet, with the demise of the presumed last citadel of Puritanical *re-citationism* —the Lancasterian monitorial schools—and with the continued stress during the Mann-Barnard period on Pestalozzian developmental teaching, the majority of American classrooms continued to be conducted on essentially re-citational terms. Optimistic as our account of changes in American elementary education during our later national period (Chapter 7) may have seemed, it has to be admitted that decades after Mann and Barnard the dominant methodology in our schools was repetitional re-citation, though the memorized words may have been more meaningful to pupils than were the scriptural texts of the earlier days. In other words, the changes in curricular content that gradually came with the shift in theory from education for salvation to education for use were such as to make even re-citation more educational.

After Locke, the unfoldment theory of Rousseau also was long delayed as to incorporation in practice. Very soon after publication of *Emile* in 1762, the youthful Pestalozzi read it and was much impressed. However, more than four decades later when Pestalozzi really began to demonstrate his thoughts on teaching, what he said and wrote *about* teaching was essentially Lockean, even though, when he himself handled classes or otherwise dealt with school children, the spirit of Rousseau shone through with sufficient clarity that a few perceptive souls were able to carry on. Froebel was one of these, but his kindergarten did not come to the United States until after 1860 and did not take much hold until after 1900. Moreover, Froebel's own kindergarten practices were a far cry from unfoldment, and it remained for American Progressivism to do much toward popularizing even the idea—to say nothing of the practice—of "creative self-expression."

Finally, we come to Dewey's relativistic idea of "perceptual interaction," the one aspect of his theorizing that we have found to be uniquely innovational, albeit a key concept that is so crucial as to be genuinely revolutionary. However, we find little evidence even up to now of sufficient understanding or appreciation of the concept to have enabled it yet to effect the changes in educational practice that it can do, and that we are confident it sooner or later will do. What we are saying, in other words, is that American education, to say nothing of education elsewhere, has not yet caught up with Dewey.

The permissivism that so many recent and not-so-recent critics *think* they have been seeing in American education stems not from Dewey but from Roussellian "unfoldment"—negative education, never found acceptable by Dewey. His insistent and persistent emphasis on democracy in education should be sufficient evidence of that, for, since both place limitations on freedom, democracy is in that way closer to autocracy than to anarchy. Anarchy alone represents unlimited freedom, or permissivism.

As to the principle "We learn to do by doing," so often imputed to Dewey, that is not Dewey at all. For Dewey, it was "doing and undergoing," with the undergoing aspect as the one vital for learning. By undergoing, he meant the noting of consequences that grow out of actions taken; hence, insight. Thus, in Dewey's thinking, the more authentic expression is, "We learn to do by *seeing*," for, if an insight is gained without actually going through the indicated actions (and in life it is the case perhaps more often than not), then the doing is not necessary. It is Thorndike's connectionism that makes the "doing" necessary, for without it a bond does not become strengthened. For Dewey, the fruitfulness of a process, designed to be educational, is to be measured in terms of insights gained, not by actions taken. Dewey's theory of learning as perceptual interaction was a far cry from Thorndike's conditioning as well as from Herbart's apperception. Dewey indeed wanted a flexible schoolroom with a relatively informal atmosphere, including furniture that could be moved about as occasion required, but "activity schools" and "the activity movement" were not his concoction and for him did not represent what is critical in an educational program.

With the *bad-active* assumptions of Puritanism, effective discipline meant denying child nature; breaking the spirit of the child. A schoolmaster was remiss if he permitted the milk of human kindness to flow; he was doing his pupils a disservice. With the *neutral-reactive* assumptions of Locke, child nature was accepted and respected; but only as something to be moulded and shaped as an adult world would have it, as "clay in the hands of the potter." Although schools became more comfortable than before, they were still prisons.

With the *good-active* assumptions of Rousseau, child nature was enthroned; the child could do no wrong, as long as he remained his own, true, natural self. But this utopian dream was recognized, even by Rousseau himself, as in practice unattainable. Hence, educational theorists labored thenceforth to achieve proper recognition, on the one hand of the legitimate requirements or demands of child nature, and, on the other of the legitimate requirements or demands of the society or culture of which the children are a part. Those of the Locke-Herbart-Thorndike persuasion tended to ignore or play down the natural propensities of children, assuming that adult wisdom is sufficient to do justice to any and all of the demands of childhood. Those of the Rousseau-Froebel-

Kilpatrick persuasion usually found themselves (or at least were found) in the quandary of bridging the gap between the needs of children and the needs of society. In actuality, they came forward with no theoretical principle that would fuse these two ingredients into a harmonious whole wherein each would complement the other; not be mutually contradictory.

With Dewey's neutral-interactive assumptions, the fusion is seemingly accomplished. The self is neither good nor bad, in and of itself alone (*ab soli,* absolutely), but only as it relates to the nonself (the environment) in which it "lives, moves, and has its being." It is a relational, a relativistic, matter. Furthermore, the self is initiatory; it does not wait "with arms akimbo set," it moves out on its own. But it does so with the hope of full cognizance of what it is doing with reference to its surroundings, the nonself. The self proposes, the nonself disposes. This is not absolute free will on the one hand, nor absolute determinism on the other. It is interaction; relationalism; relativism. The over-all, self-nonself configuration or context is the unit to be taken into account; not the one *or* the other. It is *both-and,* not *either-or.* This represents the twentieth-century revolution; rejection of the Newton-Locke, scientific-philosophical orientation and adoption of that of Einstein and Dewey. When modern science recognized that its investigations must take into account the nature of the investigator as well as the nature of what is investigated, it became interactive, relational, relativistic. This is twentieth-century thinking, and Dewey's principle of perceptual interaction is part of its focal core. Should we not use this as a base point, from which to move toward new horizons?

∾ *Index*

NOTE: This index refers to manuscript proper; it does not include bibliographical items appearing in chapter-end reference lists.